Learning Ionic

Second Edition

Build hybrid mobile applications with HTML5, SCSS, and Angular

Arvind Ravulavaru

BIRMINGHAM - MUMBAI

Learning Ionic

Second Edition

Copyright © 2017 Packt Publishing

First published: July 2015
Second edition: April 2017

Production reference: 1260417

Published by Packt Publishing Ltd.
Livery Place
35 Livery Street
Birmingham
B3 2PB, UK.
ISBN 978-1-78646-605-1

www.packtpub.com

Credits

Author
Arvind Ravulavaru

Reviewer
Mike Hartington

Commissioning Editor
Amarabha Banerjee

Acquisition Editor
Reshma Raman

Content Development Editors
Divij Kotian
Johann Barretto

Technical Editor
Rashil Shah

Copy Editor
Safis Editing

Project Coordinator
Ritika Manoj

Proofreader
Safis Editing

Indexer
Tejal Daruwale Soni

Graphics
Jason Monteiro

Production Coordinator
Melwyn Dsa

About the Author

Arvind Ravulavaru is a full stack consultant having over 8 years of experience in software development. For the last 4 years, Arvind has been working extensively on JavaScript, both on the server- and the client-side. Before that, Arvind worked on big data analytics, cloud provisioning, and orchestration. Arvind has good exposure on various databases and has also developed and architected applications built using Node.js.

For the past 2 years, Arvind has been working on his own startup, named *The IoT Suitcase* h ttp://theiotsuitcase.com. With his experience in software development and his passion for building products, Arvind has architected and developed an end-to-end platform for rapidly building IoT products and solutions. The IoT Suitcase provides all the pieces needed to build an IoT solution, right from hardware to a mobile app with analytics and IFTTT as add-ons.

Apart from that, Arvind provides training, empowering companies with the latest and greatest technology in the market. He also conducts startup workshops, where he teaches rapid prototyping with today's amazing tooling stack and how to take ideas to the market in a very short time.

Arvind always looks for ways to contribute to the open source community in making this world a better place for developers. As an architect/consultant, he always tries to power amazing business ideas with awesome technology solutions (he is language agnostic), moving the human race up the technology evolution chain.

You can reach Arvind on his blog at http://thejackalofjavascript.com.

Arvind has written a book named *Learning Ionic*, which talks about building Mobile Hybrid applications using Ionic Framework v1. He has also signed the contract for his next book, named *Advanced IoT with JavaScript*, where he plans to show how to build IoT solutions using JavaScript.

Acknowledgements

First off, I would like to thank all the people who have purchased my *Learning Ionic* book. The support from you guys was tremendous; I really appreciate it. I would like to thank the Packt team for doing an amazing job in releasing the books on time.

Since the book was released, I have been busy building The IoT Suitcase. Thanks to Udaykanth Rapeti for spending a good year with me bringing this to the position it is now. I would like to take a moment to thank Surya Narayana Murthy for being part of this start up. He has given me tremendous support and invaluable advice in taking things to the next level. I would like to give special thanks to Murthy Prakki for everything he has done for the team and me.

Thanks to the awesome team at The IoT Suitcase, who would kept asking me about the status of the book frequently, and have been eagerly waiting for its release.

Last but not least, thanks to the entire team of Packt for supporting me. I sincerely thank my content editors Divij Kotian (and team), Sachin Karnani, and Merwyn D'souza. Thanks to Reshma Raman and the production team for taking the book to press.

Special thanks to my family for bearing me every day and going through all my shenanigans without complaining. Thank you.

About the Reviewer

Mike Hartington is a developer for the Ionic Framework with years of experience in mobile development with hybrid technologies. Within Ionic, Mike works with the framework team and the community members, helping to ensure that the code being shipped is well documented, tested, and easy to understand. Along with working on Ionic for his day to day, Mike is also a Google Developer Expert and an Egghead.io author, helping people learn new technologies with both.

www.PacktPub.com

For support files and downloads related to your book, please visit www.PacktPub.com.

Did you know that Packt offers eBook versions of every book published, with PDF and ePub files available? You can upgrade to the eBook version at www.PacktPub.com and as a print book customer, you are entitled to a discount on the eBook copy. Get in touch with us at service@packtpub.com for more details.

At www.PacktPub.com, you can also read a collection of free technical articles, sign up for a range of free newsletters and receive exclusive discounts and offers on Packt books and eBooks.

https://www.packtpub.com/mapt

Get the most in-demand software skills with Mapt. Mapt gives you full access to all Packt books and video courses, as well as industry-leading tools to help you plan your personal development and advance your career.

Why subscribe?

- Fully searchable across every book published by Packt
- Copy and paste, print, and bookmark content
- On demand and accessible via a web browser

Customer Feedback

Thanks for purchasing this Packt book. At Packt, quality is at the heart of our editorial process. To help us improve, please leave us an honest review on this book's Amazon page at https://www.amazon.com/dp/1786466058.

If you'd like to join our team of regular reviewers, you can e-mail us at customerreviews@packtpub.com. We award our regular reviewers with free eBooks and videos in exchange for their valuable feedback. Help us be relentless in improving our products!

Thanks to Mike Hartington for reviewing the book and providing valuable insights into the world of Ionic.

The only way out is through

Table of Contents

Preface

This book explains how to build Mobile Hybrid applications with ease using Ionic. Be it simple apps that integrate with REST APIs or complex apps that involves native features, Ionic provides a simple API to work with them.

With a basic knowledge of web development and TypeScript, and a decent knowledge of Angular, one can easily convert a million-dollar idea into an app with a few lines of code. In this book we will explore how you can do this.

What this book covers

Chapter 1, *Angular - A Primer*, introduces you to the power of all-new Angular. We will look at the basics of TypeScript and the concepts to understand Angular. We will be looking at Angular Modules, Components, and Services. We will conclude the chapter by building an app using Angular.

Chapter 2, *Welcome to Ionic*, talks about the Mobile Hybrid framework called Cordova. It shows how Ionic fits into the bigger picture of Mobile Hybrid application development. This chapter also walks through the software needed for application development using Ionic.

Chapter 3, *Ionic Components and Navigation*, walks you through the various components of Ionic, right from Header to a Navbar. We also take a look at navigation between pages using the Ionic Framework.

Chapter 4, *Ionic Decorators and Services*, explores the decorators that we use for initializing various ES6 classes. We will also be looking at the Platform Service, Config Service, and a couple more to get a better understanding of Ionic.

Chapter 5, *Ionic and SCSS*, talks about theming Ionic apps with the help of the built-in SCSS support.

Chapter 6, *Ionic Native*, shows how an Ionic app can interface with device features such as Camera, and the Battery using Ionic Native.

Chapter 7, *Building Riderr App*, shows how the book can be able to build an end-to-end application that interfaces with Device APIs as well as REST APIs using the knowledge gained so far in this book. The app we are going to build is going to be a frontend for the Uber API. Using this app, a user can book a Uber ride.

Chapter 8, *Ionic 2 Migration Guide*, shows how an Ionic app built using v1 of the Ionic Framework can be migrated to Ionic 2, and how the same approach can be used for Ionic 3 as well.

Chapter 9, *Testing an Ionic 2 App*, walks you through the various of testing an Ionic app. We are going to look at Unit Testing, end-to-end testing, monkey testing, and device testing using AWS Device Farm.

Chapter 10, *Releasing the Ionic App*, shows how you can generate installers for the apps that you have built with Cordova and Ionic using the Ionic CLI and PhoneGap Build as well. Chapter 11, *Ionic 3*, talks about the upgrades to Angular 4 and Ionic 3. We will look at a couple of new features of Ionic 3 as well.

Appendix, shows how you can efficiently use the Ionic CLI and Ionic cloud services to build, deploy, and manage your Ionic applications

What you need for this book

To start building Ionic apps, you need to have a basic knowledge of Web Technologies, TypeScript, and Angular. A good knowledge of mobile application development, device native features, and Cordova is optional.
You need Node.js, Cordova CLI, and Ionic CLI installed to work with Ionic framework. If you want to work with device features such as the Camera or Bluetooth you need have the mobile OS setup on your machines.
This book is intended for those who want to learn how to build Mobile Hybrid applications using Ionic. It is also ideal for people who want to work with theming Ionic apps, integrating with the REST API, and learning more about device features such as Camera, Bluetooth using Ionic Native.
Prior knowledge of Angular is essential to complete this book successfully.

Conventions

In this book, you will find a number of text styles that distinguish between different kinds of information. Here are some examples of these styles and an explanation of their meaning.

Code words in text, database table names, folder names, filenames, file extensions, pathnames, dummy URLs, user input, and Twitter handles are shown as follows: "A TypeScript file is saved with a .ts extension."

A block of code is set as follows:

```
x = 20;
// after a few meaningful minutes
x = 'nah! It's not a number any more';
```

Any command-line input or output is written as follows:

```
npm install -g @angular/cli
```

New terms and **important words** are shown in bold. Words that you see on the screen, for example, in menus or dialog boxes, appear in the text like this: "We will be writing three methods, one to get a random gif, one to get the latest trends, and one to search the **Gif API** with a keyword."

Warnings or important notes appear in a box like this.

Tips and tricks appear like this.

Reader feedback

Feedback from our readers is always welcome. Let us know what you think about this book-what you liked or disliked. Reader feedback is important for us as it helps us develop titles that you will really get the most out of.

To send us general feedback, simply e-mail feedback@packtpub.com, and mention the book's title in the subject of your message.

If there is a topic that you have expertise in and you are interested in either writing or contributing to a book, see our author guide at www.packtpub.com/authors.

Customer support

Now that you are the proud owner of a Packt book, we have a number of things to help you to get the most from your purchase.

Downloading the example code

You can download the example code files for this book from your account at `http://www.p acktpub.com`. If you purchased this book elsewhere, you can visit `http://www.packtpub.c om/support`and register to have the files e-mailed directly to you.

You can download the code files by following these steps:

1. Log in or register to our website using your e-mail address and password.
2. Hover the mouse pointer on the **SUPPORT** tab at the top.
3. Click on **Code Downloads & Errata**.
4. Enter the name of the book in the **Search** box.
5. Select the book for which you're looking to download the code files.
6. Choose from the drop-down menu where you purchased this book from.
7. Click on **Code Download**.

Once the file is downloaded, please make sure that you unzip or extract the folder using the latest version of:

- WinRAR / 7-Zip for Windows
- Zipeg / iZip / UnRarX for Mac
- 7-Zip / PeaZip for Linux

The code bundle for the book is also hosted on GitHub at `https://github.com/PacktPubl ishing/Learning-Ionic-Second-Edition`. We also have other code bundles from our rich catalog of books and videos available at `https://github.com/PacktPublishing/`. Check them out!

Errata

Although we have taken every care to ensure the accuracy of our content, mistakes do happen. If you find a mistake in one of our books-maybe a mistake in the text or the code-we would be grateful if you could report this to us. By doing so, you can save other readers from frustration and help us improve subsequent versions of this book. If you find any errata, please report them by visiting `http://www.packtpub.com/submit-errata`, selecting your book, clicking on the **Errata Submission Form** link, and entering the details of your errata. Once your errata are verified, your submission will be accepted and the errata will be uploaded to our website or added to any list of existing errata under the Errata section of that title.

To view the previously submitted errata, go to `https://www.packtpub.com/books/content/support`and enter the name of the book in the search field. The required information will appear under the **Errata** section.

Piracy

Piracy of copyrighted material on the Internet is an ongoing problem across all media. At Packt, we take the protection of our copyright and licenses very seriously. If you come across any illegal copies of our works in any form on the Internet, please provide us with the location address or website name immediately so that we can pursue a remedy.

Please contact us at `copyright@packtpub.com` with a link to the suspected pirated material.

We appreciate your help in protecting our authors and our ability to bring you valuable content.

Questions

If you have a problem with any aspect of this book, you can contact us at `questions@packtpub.com`, and we will do our best to address the problem.

1
Angular - A Primer

When Sir Timothy Berners-Lee invented the Internet, he never anticipated that the Internet would be used to publish selfies, share cat videos, or bomb web page with ads. His main intention (guessing) was to create a web of documents so a user on the Internet can access these hypertexts from anywhere and make use of it.

An interesting article published by Craig Buckler at Sitepoint titled, The Web Runs Out of Disk Space (`http://www.sitepoint.com/web-runs-disk-space/`), shows how the content on the Internet is spread out:

- 28.65% pictures of cats
- 16.80% vain selfies
- 14.82% pointless social media chatter
- 12.73% inane vlogger videos
- 9.76% advertising/clickbait pages
- 8.70% scams and cons
- 4.79% articles soliciting spurious statistics
- 3.79% new JavaScript tools/libraries
- 0.76% documents for the betterment of human knowledge

You can see, since the invention of the Internet to the present day, how we have evolved. *Better evolution needs better frameworks* to build and manage such apps that need to be scalable, maintainable, and testable. This is where Angular stepped in back in 2010 to fill the gap and it has been evolving quite well since then.

We are going to start our journey by understanding the new changes to Angular, the importance of TypeScript, and see how Ionic 2 has adapted itself with Angular to help build performance-efficient and modern Mobile Hybrid apps.

In this chapter, we will take a quick peek at new topics added as part of Angular with the help of an example. The main changes that have taken place in Angular (2) are primarily on the lines of performance and componentization, apart from the language update. We will be going through the following topics in this chapter:

- What is new in Angular?
- TypeScript and Angular
- Building a Giphy app

What is new in Angular?

Angular 2 is one of the most anticipated and dramatic version upgrades I have seen for any software. Angular 1 was a boon to web/mobile web/hybrid app developers, where managing a lot of things was made easy. Not only did Angular 1 help restructure client-side app development, but it also provided a platform to build applications; not websites, but applications. Though the first release suffered performance issues when dealing with large datasets, the Angular team bounced back quite well with the later releases of Angular 1, that is, Angular 1.4.x and above, and fixed these performance issues by releasing a more stable version in the form of Angular (2).

Some of the new changes that have accompanied with Angular (2) are:

- Speed and performance improvements.
- Component based (not the typical MV*).
- Angular CLI.
- Simple and expressive syntax.
- Progressive Web Apps (PWA).
- Cross-platform app development, which includes desktops, mobile, and web.
- Cordova-based Hybrid app development.
- Angular Universal provider for the server side for fast initial views.
- Upgrades to better animation, internationalization, and accessibility.
- Angular can be written on ES5, ES6, TypeScript, and Dart are based on the user's comfort with the JavaScript flavor.

With these new updates, developing apps has never been easier, be it on the desktop, mobile, or Mobile Hybrid environments.

Note: The latest version of Angular is going to be called just Angular, not Angular 2, or AngularJS 4, or NG4. So throughout this book, I will refer to Angular version 2 as Angular.

The current latest version of Angular is 4. Do checkout `Chapter 11`, *Ionic 3*, to know a bit more about Angular 4 and how it improves Ionic.

 You can find more information about Angular here: `https://angular.io`.

Note: If you are new to Angular, you can refer to these books:

`https://www.packtpub.com/web-development/learning-angular-2`

`https://www.packtpub.com/web-development/mastering-angular-2-components`

`https://www.packtpub.com/web-development/mastering-angular-2`

`https://www.packtpub.com/web-development/angular-2-example`

Or these videos:

`https://www.packtpub.com/web-development/angular-2-projects-video`

`https://www.packtpub.com/web-development/web-development-angular-2-and-bootstrap-video`

`https://www.packtpub.com/web-development/angular-2-web-development-TypeScript-video`

TypeScript primer

Angular uses TypeScript extensively for app development. Hence as part of the Angular primer, we will refresh the necessary TypeScript concepts as well.

If you are new to TypeScript, TypeScript is a typed superset of JavaScript that compiles to plain JavaScript. TypeScript provides static typing, classes, and interfaces and supports almost all features of ES6 and ES7 before they land in the browser.

A TypeScript file is saved with a `.ts` extension.

The main advantage of adding typings to an untyped language (JavaScript) is to make IDEs understand what we are trying to do and better assist us while coding; in other words, Intellisense.

Having said that, here is what we can do with TypeScript.

Variable typing

In vanilla JavaScript, we would do something like this:

```
x = 20;
// after a few meaningful minutes
x = 'nah! It's not a number any more';
```

But in TypeScript, we cannot do as shown in the preceding code snippet, the TypeScript compiler would complain as we are modifying the variable type at runtime.

Defining types

When we declare variables, we can optionally declare the types of variables. For instance:

```
name: string = 'Arvind';
age: number  = 99;
isAlive: boolean = true;
hobbies: string[];
anyType: any;
noType = 50;
noType = 'Random String';
```

This increases the predictability of what we are trying to do.

Classes

I am a guy who believes that JavaScript is an object-based programming language and not an object-oriented programming language, and I know quite a lot of people who disagree with me.

In vanilla JavaScript, we have functions, which act like a class and exhibit prototype-based inheritance. In TypeScript/ES6, we have the class construct:

```
class Person {
  name: string;

constructor(personName: string) {
this.name = personName;
}
```

```
getName {
    return "The Name: " + this.greeting;
}
}
// somewhere else
arvind:Person = new Person('Arvind');
```

In the preceding example, we have defined a class named Person and we are defining the class constructor, which accepts the name on initialization of the class.

To initialize the class, we will invoke the class with a new keyword and pass in the name to the constructor. The variable that stores the instance of the class -- the object, arvind in the preceding example, can also be typed to the class. This helps in better understanding the possibilities of the arvind object.

Note: The classes in ES6 still follow Prototypal-based Inheritance and not the classical Inheritance model.

Interface

As we start building complex apps, there will be a common need for a certain type of structure to be repeated throughout the app, which follows certain rules. This is where an interface comes into the picture. Interfaces provide *structural subtyping* or *duck typing* to check the type and *shape* of entities.

For instance, if we are working with an app that deals with cars, every car will have a certain common structure that needs to be adhered to when used within the app. Hence we create an interface named ICar. Any class working with cars will implement this interface as follows:

```
Interface ICar {
  engine : String;
  color: String;
  price : Number;
}

class CarInfo implements ICar{
  engine : String;
  color: String;
  price : Number;

  constructor(){ /* ... */}
}
```

Modules and imports

In vanilla JavaScript, you must have observed code blocks like this:

```
(function(){
  var x = 20;
  var y = x * 30;
})(); //IIFE
// x & y are both undefined here.
```

Modules are achieved in ES6/TS using the imports and exports syntax:

```
logic.ts
export function process(){
  x = 20;
  y = x * 30;
}

exec.ts
import { process } from './logic';
process();
```

These are the bare essentials that we would need to get started with TypeScript. We will look at more such concepts where needed.

With this we wrap up the key concepts needed to get started with TypeScript. Let us get started with Angular.

For more information on TypeScript, check out:
`https://www.TypeScriptlang.org/docs/tutorial.html`. Also check out the TypeScript introduction video:
`https://channel9.msdn.com/posts/Anders-Hejlsberg-Introducing-Typ eScript`.

Angular

Angular (2) has added a bunch of new features and updated existing features and removed a few over Angular 1.x. In this section, we will go through some of the essential features of Angular.

Components

Angular components are inspired by the Web Components specification. At a very high level, Web Components have four pieces:

- **Custom elements**: A user can create their own HTML element.
- **HTML imports**: Import one HTML document into another.
- **Templates**: HTML definitions of the custom elements.
- **Shadow DOM**: A specification to write encapsulated logic of custom elements.

The preceding four specifications explain how a frontend developer can develop their own standalone, isolated, and reusable components, similar to a HTML select box (`<select></select>`), or a text area (`<textarea></textarea>`), or an input (`<input />`).

You can read more about the Web Component specification here: `https://www.w3.org/standards/techs/components#w3c_all`.

 If you would like to dig deeper into the Web Component, check out: `http://webcomponents.org/`.

As mentioned, Angular is (loosely) built on Web Components, where the preceding four specifications are implemented in an Angular way.

In simple terms, our entire app is a tree of components. For example, if we look at the world's most viewed page, `https://www.google.com`, it would look something like this:

And if we had to build this page in Angular, we would first split the page into components.

A visual representation of all the components that go into the preceding page would look like this:

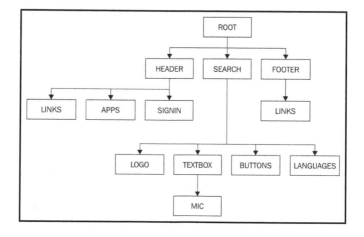

Note: Each black box is a (custom) component.

As we can see from the preceding figure, the entire page is a tree of custom components.

A (custom) component would typically consist of three pieces:

- `component.ts`: This represents the component logic
- `component.html`: This represents the component view (template)
- `component.css`: This represents the component specific styles

To build a custom component, we need to use a `Component` decorator on top of a class. In simple terms, a decorator lets us configure a class with specific metadata on them. This metadata will then be used by Angular to understand the behavior of that class. Decorators start with an @, followed by the name of the decorator.

The component decorator tells Angular that the class being processed needs to exhibit the behavior of an Angular component. A simple decorator would look as follows:

```
@Component({
  selector: 'app-root',
  templateUrl: './app.component.html',
  styleUrls: ['./app.component.css']
})
export class AppComponent {
  // This is where we write the component logic!
  title = 'Hello World!';
}
```

Some of the properties that go into a component decorator are:

- `selector`: CSS selector that identifies this component in a template
- `templateUrl`: URL to an external file containing a template for the view
- `styleUrls`: List of URLs to style sheets to be applied to this component's view
- `providers` : List of providers available to this component and its children

 To know more about the Component decorator, refer to the following link:
`https://angular.io/docs/ts/latest/api/core/index/Component-decorator.html`

Zones

Zones are one of the new concepts that have been introduced in Angular. The concept of Zones was migrated from Dart to JavaScript.

The main reason why a lot of developers were attracted towards Angular initially was by its *Auto-magic Data Binding* among other things. This was achieved using scopes in Angular 1.x. In Angular 2, we are using Zone.js (https://github.com/angular/zone.js) to achieve the same.

Whenever there is a change in the data, Angular updates the appropriate *stakeholders* (variables, interfaces, providers, and so on) with new data. Angular can track all synchronous activities quite easily. But for change detection in asynchronous code, such as event handling, AJAX calls, or Timers, Angular 2 uses Zone.js.

To know more about zones, how they work, and change detection in Angular, check out Zones in Angular: http://blog.thoughtram.io/angular/2016/02/01/zones-in-angular-2.html and Angular change detection explained: http://blog.thoughtram.io/angular/2016/02/22/angular-2-change-detection-explained.html.

Templates

Templates are used to bind the component logic to the HTML. Templates are also used as an interface between the user interaction of the user and app logic.

Templates have changed quite a bit when compared to version 1 of Angular. But there are a few things that still remain the same. For instance, the way we take a value from a component and display it in the user interface remains the same with the double curly brace notation (interpolation syntax).

The following is a sample app.component.ts:

```
@Component({
  selector: 'app-root',
  templateUrl: './app.component.html',
  styleUrls: ['./app.component.css']
})
export class AppComponent {
  // This is where we write the component logic!
  title = 'Hello World!';
}
```

The `app.component.html` would look something like this:

```
<h1>
{{title}} <!-- This value gets bound from app.component.ts -->
</h1>
```

Templates can also be made inline by passing in the template metadata to the decorator instead of `templateUrl`. This would look something like this:

```
@Component({
  selector: 'app-root',
  template: '<h1>{{title}}</h1>',
  styleUrls: ['./app.component.css']
})
export class AppComponent {
  // This is where we write the component logic!
  title = 'Hello World!';
}
```

The `template` metadata takes higher priority over `templateUrl`. For example, if we have defined both a `template` and `templateUrl` metadata, `template` is picked up and rendered. We can also write multiline templates using backtick(`) instead of quotes, in both ES6 as well as TypeScript. For more information, refer to Template Literals: https://developer.mozilla.org/en/docs/Web/JavaScript/Reference/Template_literals

In Angular 1.x, we have core/custom directives. But in Angular (2), we have various notations, using which we achieve the same behavior of a directive from Angular 1.

For instance, if we want to add a custom class to an element based on the truthiness of an expression, it would look this:

```
<div [class.highlight]="shouldHighlight">Hair!</div>
```

The preceding is a replacement for the famous `ng-class` Angular 1.x directive.

To handle events, we use the `( )` notation, as in:

```
<button (click)=pullHair($event)">Pull Hair</button>
```

And this `pullhair()` is defined inside the component class.

To keep the data bindings up to date, we use the `[ ( ) ]` notation, as in:

```
<input type="text" [(ngModel)]="name">
```

This keeps the name property in the component class in sync with the textbox.

An example of *ngFor, which is a replacement for ng-repeat, is shown here:

```
<ul>
  <li *ngFor="let todo in todos">{{todo.title}}</li>
</ul>
```

Note that let in front of todo indicates that it is a local variable in that zone.

These are some of the basic concepts that we need to get started with our hands-on example. I will talk about other Angular (2) concepts as and when they appear in our app.

Giphy app

Using the concepts we have learned so far, we are going to build a simple app using Angular and an Open JSON API provider named Giphy.

Giphy (http://giphy.com) is a simple Gif search engine. The guys at Giphy exposed an open REST API that we can consume and do a bunch of things with the data.

The app we are going to build is going to talk to the Giphy JSON API and return the results. Using Angular, we are going to build interfaces for three features in the app:

- Show a random Gif
- Show trending Gifs
- Search a Gif

We will be using Angular CLI (https://cli.angular.io/) and Twitter Bootstrap (http://getbootstrap.com/) with the Cosmos theme (https://bootswatch.com/cosmo/).

Before we start building the app, let's first understand the app structure.

Architecture

The first thing we are going to look at is the architecture of the app. On the client side, we will have a router, from which all things start flowing. The router will have four routes:

- Home route
- Browse route

- Search route
- Page Not Found route

We will have one service, with three methods that will interact with the Giphy REST API.

Apart from the previously mentioned items, we will have the following components:

- **Nav Component**: App Navbar
- **Home Component**: Home Page which shows a random gif
- **Trending Component**: Show trending gifs
- **Search Component**: Search a gif
- **Giphy Component**: Template for a gif
- **Page not found Component**: To show a page that tells the user that nothing is found

The component tree for this would look as follows:

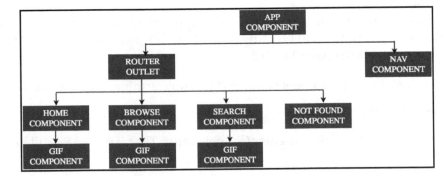

API

The Giphy API is quite easy to understand and use. You can find the official API documents here: `https://github.com/Giphy/GiphyAPI`.

The APIs that we are going to consume are:

- Random Gif: `http://api.giphy.com/v1/gifs/random?api_key=dc6zaTOxFJmzC`
- Trending Gifs:
  `http://api.giphy.com/v1/gifs/trending?api_key=dc6zaTOxFJmzC`
- Search Gifs:
  `http://api.giphy.com/v1/stickers/search?q=cat&api_key=dc6zaTOxFJmzC`

You can navigate to the preceding links to see the sample data.

 At the time of writing, Giphy exposed `dc6zaTOxFJmzC` as the API key to use.

Angular CLI

To develop our Giphy app, we are going to use Angular CLI. If you are new to the CLI and its features, I recommend checking out this video: Simple Angular 2 App With Angular CLI: `https://www.youtube.com/watch?v=QMQbAoTLJX8`.
This example is written with Angular CLI version 1.0.0-beta.18.

Installing software

For us to successfully develop the Angular-Giphy App, we need to have Node.js installed (`https://nodejs.org/en`). We will be using NPM (`https://www.npmjs.com`) to download the required modules via the Angular CLI.

Once Node.js is installed, open a new command prompt/terminal and run the following:

```
npm install -g @angular/cli
```

This will go ahead and install the Angular CLI generator. That is all we would need to start developing our app.

Note: I have used angular-cli version 1.0.0 to build this app.

Text editors

Regarding text editors, you can use any editor to work with Angular as well as Ionic. You can also try Sublime text (`http://www.sublimetext.com/3`) or Atom editor (`https://atom.io/`) or Visual Studio Code (`https://code.visualstudio.com/`) for working with the code.

If you are using Sublime text, you can take a look at:
`https://github.com/Microsoft/TypeScript-Sublime-Plugin` to add TypeScript intelligence to your editor. And for Atom, refer to the following link:
`https://atom.io/packages/atom-TypeScript`.

Scaffolding an Angular 2 app

The first thing we are going to do is scaffold an Angular app using the Angular CLI. Create a new folder named chapter1 and open a command prompt/terminal in that folder and run the following:

```
ng new giphy-app
```

Now Angular CLI generator will go ahead and create all the files and folders necessary to work with our Angular app.

 As mentioned earlier, you can check out Simple Angular 2 app with Angular CLI: https://www.youtube.com/watch?v=QMQbAoTLJX8, as well to go through Angular CLI docs: https://cli.angular.io/reference.pdf to know more about it.

The scaffolded project structure would look as follows:

```
.
├── .angular-cli.json
├── .editorconfig
├── README.md
├── e2e
│   ├── app.e2e-spec.ts
│   ├── app.po.ts
│   ├── tsconfig.e2e.json
├── karma.conf.js
├── node_modules
├── package.json
├── protractor.conf.js
├── src
│   ├── app
│   │   ├── app.component.css
│   │   ├── app.component.html
│   │   ├── app.component.spec.ts
│   │   ├── app.component.ts
│   │   ├── app.module.ts
│   ├── assets
│   │   ├── .gitkeep
│   ├── environments
│   │   ├── environment.prod.ts
│   │   ├── environment.ts
│   ├── favicon.ico
│   ├── index.html
│   ├── main.ts
│   ├── polyfills.ts
│   ├── styles.css
```

```
|       ├── test.ts
|       ├── tsconfig.app.json
|       ├── tsconfig.spec.json
|       ├── typings.d.ts
├── tsconfig.json
├── tslint.json
```

We will be spending most of our time inside the `src` folder. Once the project is completely scaffolded, `cd` into the `giphy-app` folder and run the following:

ng serve

This will start the built-in server. Once the build is completed, we can navigate to `http://localhost:4200` to view the page. The page should look something like this:

Building the Giphy app

Now that we have all the pieces to get started, we will start off by adding Twitter Bootstrap CSS to the app.

For this example, we will be using a Bootstrap theme from `https://bootswatch.com/` named Cosmos. We can find the Cosmos CSS theme on the theme page: `https://bootswatch.com/cosmo/`, by clicking on the Cosmos dropdown and selecting the `bootstrap.min.css` option. Or alternatively, we can find it here: `https://bootswatch.com/cosmo/bootstrap.min.css`.

 If you want, you can use any other theme or the vanilla Bootstrap CSS as well.

To add the theme file, navigate to `giphy-app/src/styles.css` and add the following line inside it:

```
@import "https://bootswatch.com/cosmo/bootstrap.min.css";
```

That is it, now our app is powered with Twitter Bootstrap CSS.

Next, we will start working on our app's main page. For that we will be leveraging an example template from Twitter Bootstrap named the Starter Template. The template can be found here: `http://getbootstrap.com/examples/starter-template/`.

The Starter template consists of a navigation bar and a body section where the content gets displayed.

For the Navbar section, we will be generating a new component named `nav-bar` and updating the relevant code in it.

To generate a new custom component using Angular CLI, navigate to the `giphy-app` folder and run the following:

```
ng generate component nav-bar
```

Note: You can either kill the current running command or spawn a new command prompt/terminal to run the preceding command.

And you should see something like this:

```
create src/app/nav-bar/nav-bar.component.css
create src/app/nav-bar/nav-bar.component.html
create src/app/nav-bar/nav-bar.component.spec.ts
create src/app/nav-bar/nav-bar.component.ts
update src/app/app.module.ts
```

Now open `giphy-app/src/app/nav-bar/nav-bar.component.html` and update it as follows:

```html
<nav class="navbar navbar-inverse navbar-fixed-top">
    <div class="container">
        <div class="navbar-header">
            <a class="navbar-brand" [routerLink]="['/']">Giphy App</a>
        </div>
        <div id="navbar" class="collapse navbar-collapse">
            <ul class="nav navbar-nav">
                <li [routerLinkActive]="['active']"><a [routerLink]="
                    ['/trending']">Trending</a></li>
                <li [routerLinkActive]="['active']"><a [routerLink]="
                    ['/search']">Search</a></li>
```

```
            </ul>
        </div>
    </div>
</nav>
```

All we are doing here is creating the header bar with two menu items and the app name, which acts as a link to the home page.

Next, we will update the `giphy app/src/app/app.component.html` to load the `nav-bar` component. Replace the contents of that file with the following:

```
<nav-bar></nav-bar>
```

Next, we will start adding routes to the app. As discussed earlier, we are going to have three routes.

To add routing support to the current app, we need to do three things:

1. Create the routes needed.
2. Configure `@NgModule`.
3. Tell Angular where to load the content of these routes.

At the time of writing, Angular CLI has disabled route generation. Hence we are going to create the same manually. Otherwise we could simply run `ng generate route home` to generate the home route.

So first, let's define all the routes. Create a new file named `app.routes.ts` inside the app folder. Update the file as follows:

```
import { HomeComponent } from './home/home.component';
import { TrendingComponent } from './trending/trending.component';
import { SearchComponent } from './search/search.component';
import { PageNotFoundComponent } from './page-not-found/page-not-
found.component';

export const ROUTES = [
  { path: '', component: HomeComponent },
  { path: 'trending', component: TrendingComponent },
  { path: 'search', component: SearchComponent },
  { path: '**', component: PageNotFoundComponent }
];
```

All we have done here is exported an array of routes. Do notice the path `'**'`. This is how we define the other section of the routes.

We will create the required components now. Run the following:

```
ng generate component home
ng generate component trending
ng generate component search
ng generate component pageNotFound
```

Next, we will configure the `@NgModule`. Open `giphy-app/src/app/app.module.ts` and add the following imports at the top:

```
import { RouterModule }   from '@angular/router';
import { ROUTES } from './app.routes';
```

Next, update the `imports` property of the `@NgModule` decorator as follows:

```
//.. snipp
imports: [
    BrowserModule,
    FormsModule,
    HttpModule,
    RouterModule.forRoot(ROUTES)
  ],
//.. snipp
```

The completed page would look as follows:

```
import { BrowserModule } from '@angular/platform-browser';
import { NgModule } from '@angular/core';
import { FormsModule } from '@angular/forms';
import { HttpModule } from '@angular/http';
import { RouterModule }   from '@angular/router';

import { AppComponent } from './app.component';
import { NavBarComponent } from './nav-bar/nav-bar.component';
import { HomeComponent } from './home/home.component';
import { TrendingComponent } from './trending/trending.component';
import { SearchComponent } from './search/search.component';
import { PageNotFoundComponent } from './page-not-found/page-not-found.component';

import { ROUTES } from './app.routes';

@NgModule({
  declarations: [
    AppComponent,
    NavBarComponent,
    HomeComponent,
    TrendingComponent,
```

```
    SearchComponent,
    PageNotFoundComponent
  ],
  imports: [
    BrowserModule,
    FormsModule,
    HttpModule,
    RouterModule.forRoot(ROUTES)
  ],
  providers: [],
  bootstrap: [AppComponent]
})
export class AppModule { }
```

Now we will update the app component to show the Navbar as well as the current route content.

Update the `giphy-app/src/app/app.component.html` as follows:

```html
<app-nav-bar></app-nav-bar>
<router-outlet></router-outlet>
```

Using the `router-outlet`, we tell the router to load the current route content at that location.

If you want to know more about routing in Angular, you can check out: Routing in Eleven Dimensions with Component Router by Brian Ford:
`https://www.youtube.com/watch?v=z1NB-HG0ZH4`.

Next, we will update the home component HTML and test the app so far.

Open `giphy-app/src/app/home/home.component.html` and update it as follows:

```html
<div class="container">
    <div class="starter-template">
        <h1>Giphy App</h1>
        <p class="lead">This app uses the JSON API provided by Giphy to
Browse and Search Gifs.
            <br> To know more checkout : <a
href="https://github.com/Giphy/GiphyAPI#trending-gifs-endpoint">Giphy
API</a> </p>
    </div>
</div>
```

Once this is done, save the file and run the following:

```
ng serve
```

And we should see the following page:

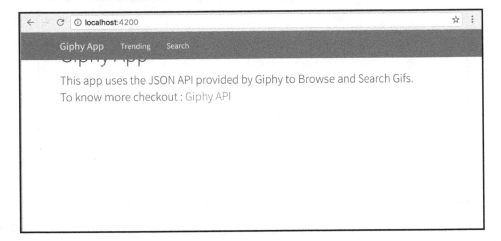

As we can see, the page looks broken. Let's fix this by adding a couple of styles. Open `giphy-app/src/styles.css` and add the following:

```
body {
  padding-top: 50px;
  padding-bottom: 20px;
}

.starter-template {
  padding: 40px 15px;
  text-align: center;
}
```

Now our page will look as expected:

Next, we will start by writing the service to talk to the **Giphy API**. We will be writing three methods, one to get a random gif, one to get the latest trends, and one to search the **Gif API** with a keyword.

To get started, we will generate a service. Run the following:

```
ng generate service giphy

WARNING Service is generated but not provided, it must be provided to be
used
```

As shown in the warning, the service that has been generated has not been marked as a provider. So we need to do that manually.

Open `giphy-app/src/app/app.module.ts` and import the `GiphyService`:

```
import { GiphyService } from './giphy.service';
```

Next, add the `GiphyService` as a provider in the `@NgModule` decorator, `providers` property:

```
//.. snipp
providers: [
    GiphyService
  ],
//..snipp
```

The complete `giphy-app/src/app/app.module.ts` would look as follows:

```
import { BrowserModule } from '@angular/platform-browser';
import { NgModule } from '@angular/core';
import { FormsModule } from '@angular/forms';
import { HttpModule } from '@angular/http';
import { RouterModule }  from '@angular/router';

import { AppComponent } from './app.component';
import { NavBarComponent } from './nav-bar/nav-bar.component';
import { HomeComponent } from './home/home.component';
import { TrendingComponent } from './trending/trending.component';
import { SearchComponent } from './search/search.component';
import { PageNotFoundComponent } from './page-not-found/page-not-
found.component';

import { ROUTES } from './app.routes';

import { GiphyService } from './giphy.service';

@NgModule({
  declarations: [
    AppComponent,
    NavBarComponent,
    HomeComponent,
    TrendingComponent,
    SearchComponent,
    PageNotFoundComponent
  ],
  imports: [
    BrowserModule,
    FormsModule,
    HttpModule,
    RouterModule.forRoot(ROUTES)
  ],
  providers: [
    GiphyService
  ],
  bootstrap: [AppComponent]
})
export class AppModule { }
```

Now we will update the `giphy-app/src/app/giphy.service.ts` with the three methods. Open `giphy-app/src/app/giphy.service.ts` and update it as follows:

```
import { Injectable } from '@angular/core';
import { Http, Response, Jsonp } from '@angular/http';
import { Observable } from 'rxjs/Rx';
```

```
import 'rxjs/Rx';

@Injectable()
export class GiphyService {
  private giphyAPIBase = 'http://api.giphy.com/v1/gifs';
  private APIKEY = 'dc6zaTOxFJmzC';

  constructor(private http: Http) { }

  getRandomGif(): Observable<Response> {
    return this.http.get(this.giphyAPIBase +
      '/random?api_key=' + this.APIKEY)
      .map((res) => res.json());
  }

  getTrendingGifs(offset, limit): Observable<Response> {
    return this.http.get(this.giphyAPIBase +
      '/trending?api_key=' + this.APIKEY + '&offset=' + offset +
      '&limit=' + limit)
      .map((res) => res.json());
  }

  searchGifs(offset, limit, text): Observable<Response> {
    return this.http.get(this.giphyAPIBase + '/search?api_key=' +
      this.APIKEY + '&offset=' + offset +
      '&limit=' + limit + '&q=' + text)
      .map((res) => res.json());
  }
}
```

All we are doing here is making an HTTP GET request to the corresponding Giphy API URLs and returning an Observable.

In RxJS (http://reactivex.io/rxjs/), an Observable is an entity, which can change over a period of time. This is the most basic building block of RxJS. An Observer subscribes to an Observable and reacts to its changes. This pattern is called a Reactive pattern.

Quoting from the documentation:

This pattern facilitates concurrent operations because it does not need to block while waiting for the Observable to emit objects, but instead it creates a sentry in the form of an observer that stands ready to react appropriately at whatever future time the Observable does so.

If you are new to Observables, you can start
here: `http://reactivex.io/documentation/observable.html` followed by: Taking
advantage of Observables in Angular:
`http://blog.thoughtram.io/angular/2016/01/06/taking-advantage-of-observables-in`
`-angular2.html` and Angular 2 HTTP requests with Observables:
`https://scotch.io/tutorials/angular-2-http-requests-with-observables`.

Now that the service is completed, we will update the `HomeComponent` to get a random gif
and display it on the home page.

Open `giphy-app/src/app/home/home.component.ts` and update it as follows:

```
import { Component, OnInit } from '@angular/core';
import { GiphyService } from '../giphy.service';

@Component({
  selector: 'app-home',
  templateUrl: './home.component.html',
  styleUrls: ['./home.component.css']
})
export class HomeComponent implements OnInit {
  public gif: string;
  public result: any;
  public isLoading: boolean = true;

  constructor(private giphyService: GiphyService) {
    this.getRandomGif();
  }

  ngOnInit() {
  }

  getRandomGif() {
    this.giphyService.getRandomGif().subscribe(
      (data) => {
        this.result = data;
        this.gif = this.result.data.image_url;
        this.isLoading = false;
      },
      (err) => console.log('Oops!', err),
      () => console.log('Response', this.result)
    )
  }
}
```

In the preceding code, first off, we have imported `GiphyService` and added it to the constructor. Next, we have written `getRandomGif()` and invoked `getRandomGif()` from the constructor. In `getRandomGif()`, we have invoked `getRandomGif()` on `giphyService` to get a random gif. We are then assigning the gif to a class variable named `gif`.

Just to see if everything is working fine, we will run the app by executing `ng serve` and opening developer tools. If everything goes well, we should see the response from the Giphy API:

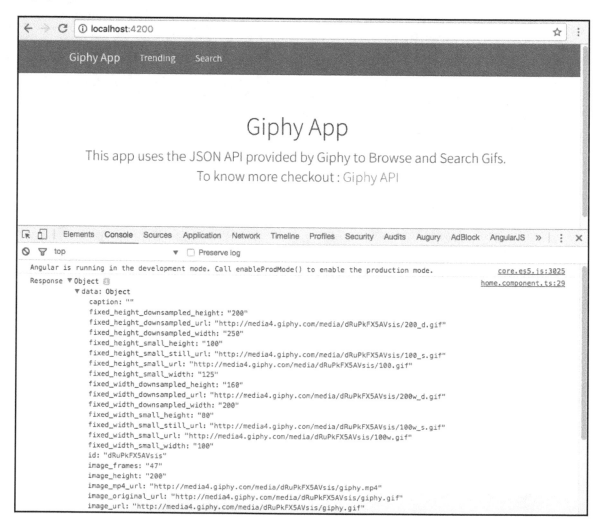

Now that we have the response, we want to build a component that will display the gif. We want to build a separate component for this because we will be using the same component on other pages as well to display a gif where needed.

Let's go ahead and scaffold the component. Run the following:

```
ng generate component gif-viewr
```

Next, open `giphy-app/src/app/gif-viewr/gif-viewr.component.html` and update it as follows:

```
<div class="item">
  <div class="well">
    <img src="{{imgUrl}}">
  </div>
</div>
```

Once this is done, we need to tell the component to expect the data from the parent component, as the home component will pass the `imgUrl` to the `gif-viewer` component.

Open `giphy-app/src/app/gif-viewr/gif-viewr.component.ts`. First, update the import statement by adding a reference to the Input decorator:

```
import { Component, OnInit, Input} from '@angular/core';
```

Next, add an Input decorator to the `imgUrl` variable:

```
@Input() imgUrl: string;
```

The updated `giphy-app/src/app/gif-viewr/gif-viewr.component.ts` would look as follows:

```
import { Component, OnInit, Input} from '@angular/core';

@Component({
  selector: 'app-gif-viewr',
  templateUrl: './gif-viewr.component.html',
  styleUrls: ['./gif-viewr.component.css']
})
export class GifViewrComponent implements OnInit {
  @Input() imgUrl: string;

  constructor() { }

  ngOnInit() {
  }
}
```

Note: To define an input for a component, we use the @Input decorator. To know more about the @Input decorator, refer to the Attribute Directives section in Angular docs: `https://angular.io/docs/ts/latest /guide/attribute-directives.html`.

Save the file and open `giphy-app/src/app/home/home.component.html`. We will add the `app-gif-viewr` component inside this page:

```
<app-gif-viewr class="home" [imgUrl]="gif"></app-gif-viewr>
```

The complete file would look as follows:

```
<div class="container">
    <div class="starter-template">
        <h1>Giphy App</h1>
        <p class="lead">This app uses the JSON API provided by Giphy to
          Browse and Search Gifs.
            <br> To know more checkout :
            <a href=
            "https://github.com/Giphy/GiphyAPI#trending-gifs-endpoint">
            Giphy API</a> </p>
    </div>

    <app-gif-viewr class="home" [imgUrl]="gif"></app-gif-viewr>
</div>
```

Next, we will update CSS to beautify the page. Open `giphy-app/src/styles.css` and add the following CSS to the existing styles:

```
.home .well{
   width: 70%;
    margin: 0 auto;
}

img{
  width: 100%;
}
```

If we go back to the browser and refresh, we should see the following:

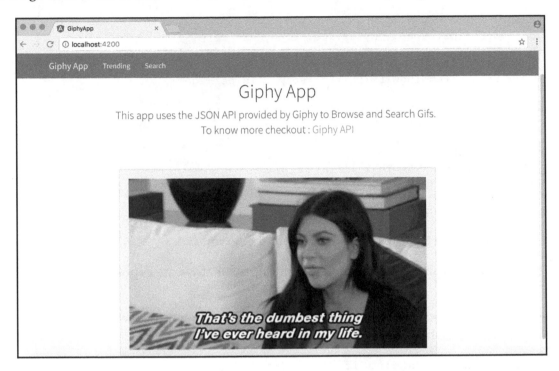

And every time we refresh a page, we will see a new gif come up.

Next, we are going to work on the Trending page. This page will show gifs that are trending using the Pintrest layout (or Masonry layout). The Trending REST API supports pagination. We will be making use of this to load 12 gifs at a time. And then provide a Load More button to fetch the next 12 gifs.

First, let's get the data from the Giphy API. Open `giphy-app/src/app/trending/trending.component.ts`. We will first import the `GiphyService`:

```
import { GiphyService } from '../giphy.service';
```

Now, we will add the same to the constructor and update the constructor to invoke `getTrendingGifs()`:

```
constructor(private giphyService: GiphyService) { }
In ngOnInit(), we will call the getTrendingGifs() API:
  ngOnInit() {
    this.getTrendingGifs(this.offset, this.perPage);
  }
Next, we will add the required class variables:
private offset = 0;
private perPage = 12;
public results: any;
public gifs: Array<any> = [];
public isLoading: boolean = true;
```

`offset` and `perPage` will be used to manage pagination.

`results` will be used to store the response from the server.

`gifs` is the array consisting of an array of trending gifs that we are exposing to the template.

`isLoading` is a `boolean` variable to keep track if a request is in progress or not. Using `isLoading`, we will show/hide the **Load More** button.

Next, we will add `getTrendingGifs()`:

```
getTrendingGifs(offset, limit) {
    this.giphyService.getTrendingGifs(offset, limit).subscribe(
      (data) => {
        this.results = data;
        this.gifs = this.gifs.concat(this.results.data);
        this.isLoading = false;
      },
      (err) => console.log('Oops!', err),
      () => console.log('Response', this.results)
    )
  }
And finally getMore(), which will be invoked by the Load More button:
  getMore() {
    this.isLoading = true;
    this.offset = this.offset + this.perPage;
    this.getTrendingGifs(this.offset, this.perPage);
  }
```

To display the gifs retrieved, we will update the trending component template. Open `giphy-app/src/app/trending/trending.component.html` and update it as follows:

```html
<div class="container">
    <h1 class="text-center">Trending Gifs</h1>
    <div class="wrapper">
        <app-gif-viewr [imgUrl]="gif.images.original.url" *ngFor="let gif
of gifs"></app-gif-viewr>
    </div>
    <input type="button" value="Load More" class="btn btn-primary btn-
block" *ngIf="!isLoading" (click)="getMore()">
</div>
```

All we are doing here is setting up `app-gif-viewr` to take the gif URL by applying an `*ngFor` directive on it. And at the bottom, a Load More button, so a user can load more gifs.

And finally to achieve the Pintrest/Masonry layout, we will add a couple of CSS rules. Open `giphy-app/src/styles.css` and add the following styles:

```css
*, *:before, *:after {
  box-sizing: border-box !important;
}

.wrapper {
  column-width: 18em;
  column-gap: 1em;
}

.item {
  display: inline-block;
  padding: .25rem;
  width: 100%;
}

.well {
  position: relative;
  display: block;
}
```

Save all the files and head back to the browser. If we click on the trending menu item in the Navbar, we should see the following:

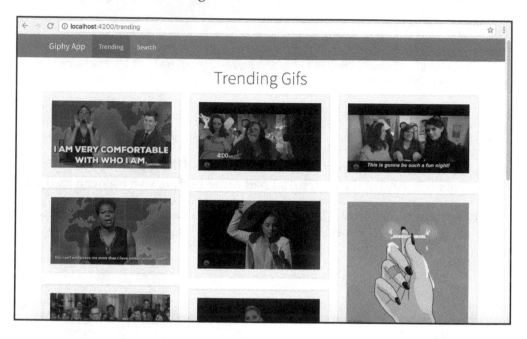

And if we scroll down completely, we should see a Load More button:

Clicking on the Load More button will load the next set of gifs:

I wasted about 15 minutes clicking Load More and watching the gifs. I think this is why APIs should have a rate limit.

Finally, we will implement searching gif. Open giphy-app/src/app/search/search.component.ts and import GiphyService:

```
import { GiphyService } from '../giphy.service';
```

Add giphyService as a class variable in the constructor:

```
constructor(private giphyService: GiphyService) { }
```

Next, we will add variables to manage pagination as well as the response:

```
private offset = 0;
private perPage = 12;
public results: any;
public query: string;
public gifs: Array<any> = [];
public isLoading: boolean = true;
```

Now we will invoke `searchGifs`, which makes a REST call to get the searched gifs, by passing in the query string:

```
searchGifs(offset, limit, query) {
    this.giphyService.searchGifs(offset, limit, query).subscribe(
      (data) => {
        this.results = data;
        this.gifs = this.gifs.concat(this.results.data);
        this.isLoading = false;
      },
      (err) => console.log('Oops!', err),
      () => console.log('Response', this.results)
    )
  }
```

The following is a method to manage the search form submit button:

```
search(query) {
  this.query = query;
  this.isLoading = true;
  this.searchGifs(this.offset, this.perPage, this.query);
}
```

And finally, `getMore()` to load more pages of the same query:

```
getMore() {
    this.isLoading = true;
    this.offset = this.offset + this.perPage;
    this.searchGifs(this.offset, this.perPage, this.query);
}
```

The updated `giphy-app/src/app/search/search.component.ts` would look as follows:

```
import { Component, OnInit } from '@angular/core';
import { GiphyService } from '../giphy.service';

@Component({
  selector: 'app-search',
  templateUrl: './search.component.html',
  styleUrls: ['./search.component.css']
})
export class SearchComponent implements OnInit {
  private offset = 0;
  private perPage = 12;
  public results: any;
  public query: string;
  public gifs: Array<any> = [];
```

```
public isLoading: boolean = true;

constructor(private giphyService: GiphyService) { }

ngOnInit() {
}

searchGifs(offset, limit, query) {
  this.giphyService.searchGifs(offset, limit, query).subscribe(
    (data) => {
      this.results = data;
      this.gifs = this.gifs.concat(this.results.data);
      this.isLoading = false;
    },
    (err) => console.log('Oops!', err),
    () => console.log('Response', this.results)
  )
}

search(query) {
  this.query = query;
  this.isLoading = true;
  this.searchGifs(this.offset, this.perPage, this.query);
}

getMore() {
  this.isLoading = true;
  this.offset = this.offset + this.perPage;
  this.searchGifs(this.offset, this.perPage, this.query);
}
}
```

Now we will update the `giphy-app/src/app/search/search.component.html`. Open `giphy-app/src/app/search/search.component.html` and update it as follows:

```
<div class="container">
    <h1 class="text-center">Search Giphy</h1>
    <div class="row">
        <input class="form-control" type="text" placeholder="Search
            something.. Like.. LOL or Space or Wow" #searchText
            (keyup.enter)="search(searchText.value)">
    </div>
    <br>
    <div class="wrapper">
        <app-gif-viewr [imgUrl]="gif.images.original.url" *ngFor="let
            gif of gifs"></app-gif-viewr>
    </div>
    <input type="button" value="Load More" class="btn btn-primary btn-
```

```
block" *ngIf="!isLoading" (click)="getMore()">
</div>
```

This view is the same as the Trending component, except there is a search textbox, which will allow the user to search by entering a string.

If we save all the files, go back to the browser, and navigate to the Search page, we should see an empty page with a search textbox. At this point, the load more button will not be shown. If we enter text and hit the return key, we should see results, as shown in the following screenshot:

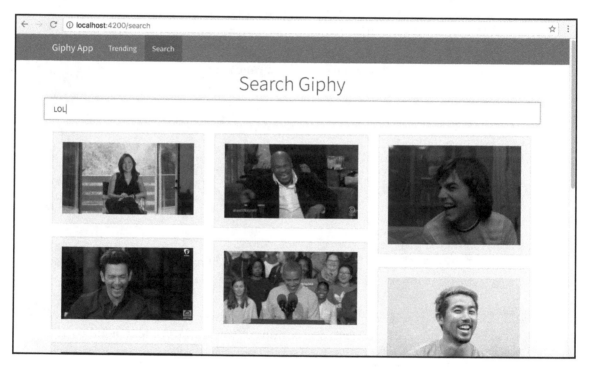

With this we have completed the implementation of a Giphy API with an Angular app.

To bring this example to a closure, we will update `giphy-app/src/app/page-not-found/page-not-found.component.html` as follows:

```
<div class="container">
    <div class="starter-template">
        <h1>404 Not Found</h1>
        <p class="lead">Looks Like We Were Not Able To Find What You Are
Looking For.
            <br>Back to : <a [routerLink]="['/']">Home</a>? </p>
```

```
      </div>
  </div>
```

And when we navigate to `http://localhost:4200/nopage`, we should see the following page:

Summary

In this chapter, we have gone through a high level overview of TypeScript and why we use TypeScript. Next we got acquainted with Angular's new syntax and the component structure. Using this knowledge, we have built an app named Giphy, which interfaces with the Giphy REST API to get gifs.

You can read more about Angular here: `https://angular.io`.

Also, check out `Chapter 11`, *Ionic 3*, to know more about the changes to Angular 4.

In the next chapter -- Welcome to Ionic, we will get started with Mobile Hybrid development using Cordova and we will look at how Ionic fits into the bigger scheme of things.

2
Welcome to Ionic

In the previous chapter, we went through Angular 2 with the help of an example. In this chapter, we will look at the big picture of Mobile Hybrid apps, set up the required software to develop Ionic apps, and finally scaffold a few apps and explore them.

The topics covered in this chapter are as follows:

- Mobile Hybrid architecture
- What is Apache Cordova?
- What is Ionic?
- Setting up the tools needed to develop and run Ionic apps
- Working with Ionic templates

Mobile Hybrid architecture

Before we start working with Ionic, we need to understand the bigger picture of Mobile Hybrid development.

The concept is pretty simple. Almost every mobile operating system (also called platform, when working with Cordova) has an API to develop apps. This API consists of a component named WebView. A WebView is typically a browser that runs inside the scope of a mobile application. This browser runs the HTML, CSS, and JS code. This means that we can build a web page using the preceding technologies and then execute it inside our app.

We can use the same knowledge of web development to build native-hybrid mobile apps (here, native refers to installing the platform-specific format file on the device after it has been packaged along with the assets), for instance:

- Android uses Android Application Package (.apk)
- iOS uses iPhone Application Archive (.ipa)
- Windows Phone uses Application Package (.xap)

The package/installer consists of a piece of native code that initializes the web page and a bunch of assets needed to show the web page content.

This setup of showing a web page inside the mobile app container that consists of our application business logic is called a Hybrid App.

What is Apache Cordova?

In simple terms, Cordova is the piece of software that stitches the web application and the native application together. The Apache Cordova website states that:

> *"Apache Cordova is a platform for building native mobile apps using HTML, CSS and JavaScript."*

Apache Cordova does not just stitch the web app with the native app--but it also provides a set of APIs written in JavaScript to interact with the native features of the device. Yes, we can use JavaScript to access our camera, take a picture, and send it in an e-mail. Sounds exciting, right?

To get a better understanding of what is happening, let's take a look at the following screenshot:

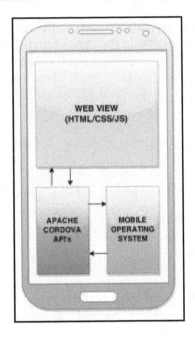

As we can see, we have a WebView where the HTML/CSS/JS code gets executed. This code can be a simple standalone piece of user interface; at best we are making an AJAX request to get some data from a remote server. Or, this code can do much more, such as talk to the Bluetooth of the device and get the list of devices in the vicinity.

In the latter case, Cordova has a bunch of APIs that interface with the WebView using JavaScript and then talk to the device in its native language (for example, Java for Android), thus providing a bridge between Java and JavaScript in this scenario. For instance, if we would like to know more about the device, which is running our app, all we need to do is write the following code inside the JS file and launch the app:

```
var platform = device.platform;
```

After installing the device plugin, we can also access the UUID, model, OS version, and the Cordova version of the device from inside the WebView using JavaScript as follows:

```
var uuid = device.uuid;
var model = device.model;
var version = device.version;
var Cordova = device.Cordova;
```

We will deal more with Cordova plugins in Chapter 6, *Ionic Native*.

The preceding explanation was to give you an idea of how Mobile Hybrid apps are structured and how we can use device features from the WebView using JavaScript.

 Cordova does not convert the HTML, CSS, and JS code to an OS-specific binary code. All it does is wrap the HTML, CSS, and JS code and execute it inside a WebView.

So you must have guessed by now that Ionic is the framework with which we build the HTML/CSS/JS code that runs in the WebView and talks with Cordova to access device-specific APIs.

What is Ionic 2?

Ionic 2 is a beautiful, open source, frontend SDK for developing Hybrid Mobile apps with HTML5. Ionic provides mobile-optimized HTML, CSS, and JS components, as well as gestures and tools for building highly interactive apps.

Ionic 2 is performance efficient with its minimal DOM manipulation and hardware-accelerated transitions as compared to other frameworks in this league. Ionic uses Angular 2 as its JavaScript framework.

With the power of Angular inside a framework like Ionic 2, the possibilities are unlimited (we can use any Angular component inside Ionic as long as it makes sense in a mobile app). Ionic 2 has a very good integration with Cordova's device API. This means that we can access device APIs using Ionic Native and integrate it with the beautiful user interface components of Ionic.

Ionic has its own command-line interface (CLI) to scaffold, develop, and deploy Ionic apps. Before we start working with the Ionic CLI, we need to set up a few pieces of software.

Ionic 3

The latest version of Ionic at the time of this book's release is 3. I have put together another chapter named Ionic 3 (Chapter 11), to which you can refer to know more about Ionic 3 and its changes.

Also, please note that the examples in this book are still valid when working with Ionic 3 as well. There may be few syntactic and structural changes, but the overall gist should ideally remain the same.

Software setup

Now we are going to set up all the required software needed to develop and run an Ionic app smoothly.

Installing Node.js

Since Ionic uses Node.js for its CLI as well as for the build tasks, we will first install it as follows:

1. Navigate to `https://nodejs.org/`.

   Click on the Install button on the homepage and an installer for our OS will automatically be downloaded. We can also navigate to `https://nodejs.org/download/` and download a specific copy.

2. Install Node.js by executing the downloaded installer.

   To verify that Node.js has been successfully installed, open a new Terminal (`*nix` systems) or Command Prompt (Windows systems) and run the following command:

   ```
   node -v
   > v6.10.1
   ```

3. Now execute the following command:

   ```
   npm -v
   > 3.10.10
   ```

npm is a **Node Package Manager** that we will be using to download various dependencies for our Ionic project.

 We need Node.js only during the development. The version specified is only for illustration. You may have the same version or the latest version of the software.

Installing Git

Git is a free and open source distributed version control system designed to handle everything from small to very large projects with speed and efficiency. In our case, we will be using a package manager named Bower, which uses Git to download the required libraries. Also, the Ionic CLI uses Git to download the project templates.

To install Git, navigate to `http://git-scm.com/downloads` and download the installer for your platform. Once you have successfully installed it, we can navigate to the command prompt/terminal and run the following command:

```
git --version
```

We should see the following output:

```
> git version 2.11.0 (Apple Git-81)
```

Text editors

This is a totally optional installation. Everyone has their own preferred text editor. After running around many text editors, I fell in love with Sublime Text, purely for its simplicity and the number of Plug and Play packages.

 If you would like to give this editor a try, you can navigate to `http://www.sublimetext.com/3` to download Sublime Text 3.

Since we will be writing our JavaScript code in TypeScript, Microsoft's Visual Studio Code is another good option.

If you would like to give this editor a try, you can navigate to
https://code.visualstudio.com/.

You can also check out Atom as another alternative.

 If you would like to give this editor a try, you can navigate to https://at
om.io/.

Installing TypeScript

Next, we will be installing the TypeScript compiler. As mentioned in Chapter 1, *Angular - A Primer*, we will be using TypeScript to write the JavaScript code. To install the TypeScript compiler, run the following:

```
npm install typescript -g
```

Once TypeScript is successfully installed, we can verify it by running this command:

```
tsc -v
> message TS6029: Version 1.7.5
```

The latest version of TypeScript at the time of release of Ionic 3 is 2.2.2. You may need to update the version of TSC to 2.2.2 or higher when working with Ionic 3.

Installing Cordova and Ionic CLI

Finally, to complete the Ionic 2 setup, we will install the Ionic and Cordova CLI. Ionic CLI is a wrapper around the Cordova CLI with some additional features.

 All the code examples in this book use Cordova version 6.4.0, Ionic CLI version 2.1.14, and Ionic version 2.1.17. But the same should work with latest version of Ionic as well.

To install the Ionic CLI, run the following command:

```
npm install -g ionic cordova
```

To verify the install, run the following command:

```
cordova -v
> 6.4.0
```

You can also run this command:

```
ionic -v
> 2.1.14
```

You can run the following command to get the complete information regarding the Ionic setup:

```
ionic info

Your system information:
Cordova CLI: 6.4.0
Ionic CLI Version: 2.1.14
Ionic App Lib Version: 2.1.7
ios-deploy version: 1.8.4
ios-sim version: 5.0.6
OS: macOS Sierra
Node Version: v6.10.1
Xcode version: Xcode 8.3 Build version 8E162
```

 If you see an Ionic CLI version greater than or equal to 2.2.2, you have an Ionic CLI that can work with Ionic 3 apps. Nonetheless, the commands and examples in this book will work the same way.

To get a feel of what Ionic CLI is packed with, run the following:

```
ionic
```

We should see a list of tasks, as seen in the following screenshot:

```
[→ ~ ionic

 (_)           (_)

 _| |/_\| '_\| |/_|
| |(_)| | | | | |(_
|_|\_/|_| |_|_|\_|  CLI v2.1.14

Usage: ionic task args


=======================
Available tasks:
(use --help or -h for more info)

   start   .........  Starts a new Ionic project in the specified PATH
   serve   .........  Start a local development server for app dev/testing
   setup   .........  Configure the project with a build tool (beta)
   generate .......   Generate pages and components
   platform .......   Add platform target for building an Ionic app
   run     ..........  Run an Ionic project on a connected device
   emulate ........  Emulate an Ionic project on a simulator or emulator
   build   .........  Build (prepare + compile) an Ionic project for a given platform.

   plugin  .........  Add a Cordova plugin
   resources ......   Automatically create icon and splash screen resources (beta)
                      Put your images in the ./resources directory, named splash or icon.
                      Accepted file types are .png, .ai, and .psd.
                      Icons should be 192x192 px without rounded corners.
                      Splashscreens should be 2208x2208 px, with the image centered in the middle.

   upload  .........  Upload an app to your Ionic account
   share   .........  Share an app with a client, co-worker, friend, or customer
   lib     ..........  Gets Ionic library version or updates the Ionic library
   login   .........  Login to your Ionic account
   io      ..........  Integrate your app with Ionic Cloud services
   security .......   Store your app's credentials for the Ionic Cloud
   push    ..........  Upload APNS and GCM credentials to Ionic Push
   package ........  Use Ionic Package to build your app
   config  .........  Set configuration variables for your ionic app
   service ........  Add an Ionic service package and install any required plugins
   add     ..........  Add an Ion, bower component, or addon to the project
   remove  ........  Remove an Ion, bower component, or addon from the project
   list    ..........  List Ions, bower components, or addons in the project
```

 There are a few more tasks apart from the ones seen in the preceding screenshot.

We can read through the tasks and explanations to get an idea about what they do. Also, note that some of the tasks are still in beta, as of today.

With this, we have completed the installation of all the software needed to develop apps using Ionic.

The platform guide

By the end of this book, we will be building apps that are ready to be deployed on the device. Since Cordova takes HTML, CSS, and JS code as input and generates a platform-specific installer, we need to have the build environments available on our machine.

Android users can follow the instructions in the Android Platform Guide at `http://cordova.apache.org/docs/en/edge/guide_platforms_android_index.md.html#Android%20Platform%20Guide` to set up SDK on your local machine.
iOS users can follow the instructions in the iOS Platform Guide at `http://cordova.apache.org/docs/en/edge/guide_platforms_ios_index.md.html#iOS%20Platform%20Guide` to set up SDK on your local machine. You would need an macOS environment to develop iOS apps.

As of today, Ionic supports only Android 4.0+ (although it works on 2.3 as well) and iOS 6+ mobile platforms. But Cordova supports a few more.

You can check out the other supported platforms at: `http://cordova.apache.org/docs/en/edge/guide_platforms_index.md.html#Platform%20Guides`.

Hello Ionic

Now that we are done with the software setup, we will scaffold a few Ionic apps.

Ionic has three main/go-to templates, using which we can quickly start developing apps:

- Blank: This is a blank Ionic project with one page
- Tabs: This is a sample app that is built using Ionic tabs
- Side menu: This is a sample app that is built to consume side menu driven navigation

To understand the basics of scaffolding, we will start with the blank template.

To keep our learning process clean, we will create a folder structure to work with Ionic projects. Create a folder named `chapter2`.

Next, open a new command prompt/terminal and change the directory (`cd`) to the `chapter2` folder. Now run the following command:

```
ionic start -a "Example 1" -i app.example.one example1 blank --v2
```

The preceding command has the following features:

- `-a "Example 1"`: This is the human-readable name of the app.
- `-i app.example.one`: This is the app ID/reverse domain name.
- `example1`: This is the name of the folder.
- `blank`: This is the name of the template.
- `--v2`: This flag indicates that the project will be scaffolded with the latest version of Ionic. This may be removed in the future.

Refer to the `Appendix`, Additional Topics, and Tips, to know more about the Ionic start task.

Ionic CLI is very verbose when it comes to performing tasks. As we can see from the command prompt/terminal, while the project is being created, a lot of information is printed.

To start off, `ionic2-app-base` is downloaded from the `ionic2-app-base` GitHub repository, `https://github.com/driftyco/ionic2-app-base`. After that, `ionic2-starter-blank` is downloaded from the `ionic-starter-blank` GitHub repository at `https://github.com/driftyco/ionic2-starter-blank`. Then all the required dependencies are installed.

Once the project has been successfully created, we will see a bunch of instructions on how to proceed further. Our output should look something like the following:

```
♫ ♫ ♫ ♫  Your Ionic app is ready to go! ♫ ♫ ♫ ♫

Some helpful tips:

Run your app in the browser (great for initial development):
  ionic serve

Run on a device or simulator:
  ionic run ios[android,browser]

Test and share your app on device with Ionic View:
  http://view.ionic.io

Build better Enterprise apps with expert Ionic support:
  http://ionic.io/enterprise

New! Add push notifications, live app updates, and more with Ionic Cloud!
  https://apps.ionic.io/signup


New to Ionic? Get started here: http://ionicframework.com/docs/v2/getting-started
```

To proceed further, we will use the `cd` command to navigate to the `example1` folder. We will not follow the instructions provided in the command prompt/terminal, as we are yet to understand the project setup. Once we have a fair idea of Ionic, we can start using the commands from the command prompt/terminal output after we have scaffold, a new Ionic app.

Once we have changed the directory to the `example1` folder, we will serve the app by giving the following command:

```
ionic serve
```

This will start a new `dev` server on port `8100`, and will then launch the app in our default browser. I highly recommend setting Google Chrome or Mozilla Firefox as your default browser while working with Ionic.

When the browser launches, we should see the blank template's home page.

If we run `ionic serve` and port `8100` is already taken, Ionic will launch the app on `8101`.

We can also serve the Ionic app on any other port using the following command:

```
ionic serve -p 8200
```

Once the application is successfully launched and we have seen the output in the browser, we will navigate back to the command prompt/terminal and we should see something like the following screenshot:

```
→  example1 ionic serve

> ionic-hello-world@ ionic:serve /Users/arvindravulavaru/Arvind/Books/IonicFW2/red
o/final-drafts/chapter2/code/example1
> ionic-app-scripts serve

[11:04:40]  ionic-app-scripts 1.1.4
[11:04:40]  watch started ...
[11:04:40]  build dev started ...
[11:04:40]  clean started ...
[11:04:40]  clean finished in 1 ms
[11:04:40]  copy started ...
[11:04:40]  transpile started ...
[11:04:42]  transpile finished in 2.53 s
[11:04:42]  preprocess started ...
[11:04:42]  preprocess finished in less than 1 ms
[11:04:42]  webpack started ...
[11:04:42]  copy finished in 2.69 s
[11:04:50]  webpack finished in 8.36 s
[11:04:50]  sass started ...
[11:04:51]  sass finished in 957 ms
[11:04:51]  postprocess started ...
[11:04:51]  postprocess finished in 1 ms
[11:04:51]  lint started ...
[11:04:51]  build dev finished in 11.88 s
[11:04:52]  watch ready in 11.94 s
[11:04:52]  dev server running: http://localhost:8100/

[11:04:54]  lint finished in 3.01 s
```

The browser developer tools setup

Before we proceed further, I would recommend setting up the developer tools in your browser in the following format.

Google Chrome

Once the Ionic app is launched, open the developer tools by pressing *Command + Option + I* on Mac and *Ctrl + Shift + I* on Windows/Linux. Then click on the last but one icon in the top row, next to the close button, as seen in the following screenshot:

This will dock developer tools to the side of the current page. Drag the demarcation line between the browser and the developer tools until the view starts to resemble that of a mobile.

If you click on the Elements tab in the developer tools, you can easily inspect the page and see the output in one go, as shown in the following screenshot:

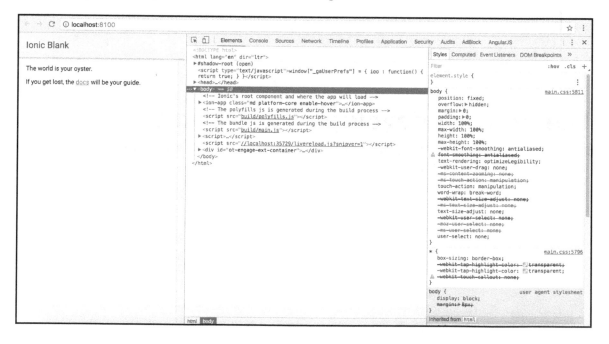

This view is very helpful for fixing errors and debugging issues.

Mozilla Firefox

If you are a Mozilla Firefox fan, we can achieve the preceding result using Firefox as well. Once the Ionic app is launched, open developer tools (not Firebug, Firefox's native development tools) by pressing *Command + Option + I* on Mac and *Ctrl + Shift + I* on Windows/Linux. Then click on the dock to the side of the browser window icon, as shown in the following screenshot:

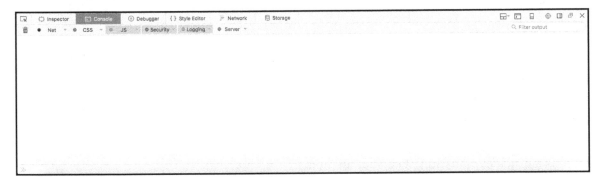

Now we can drag the demarcation line to achieve the same result as that we saw in Chrome:

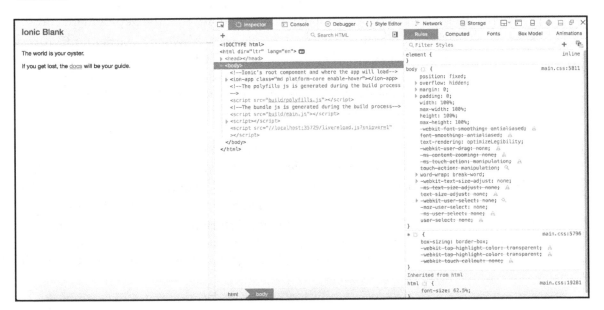

The Ionic project structure

So far, we have scaffolded a blank Ionic app and launched it in a browser. Now, we will walk through the scaffolded project structure.

If we open the `chapter2 example1` folder in our text editor, we should see the following folder structure at the root of the project:

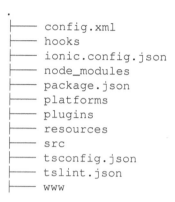

```
.
├── config.xml
├── hooks
├── ionic.config.json
├── node_modules
├── package.json
├── platforms
├── plugins
├── resources
├── src
├── tsconfig.json
├── tslint.json
├── www
```

Here is a quick explanation of each of the items:

- `src`: This is the folder where all the development happens. The app source code will be placed here. If you are coming from Ionic 1 to Ionic 2, this is the first change you would notice. For me, this is a very good upgrade to the folder structure, as it keeps the development code separate from the deployment code.
- `hooks`: This folder consists of scripts that get executed when a particular Cordova task is performed. A Cordova task can be any of the following: `after_platform_add` (after a new platform is added), `after_plugin_add` (after a new plugin is added), `before_emulate` (before emulation begins), `after_run` (before the app is run), and so on. Each task is placed inside a folder named after the Cordova task.
- `resources`: This folder consists of the various versions of the application icon and splash screen based on the mobile operating system.
- `www`: This folder consists of the build Ionic code, written inside the `src` folder. All the code present inside this folder is intended to land inside the WebView.
- `config.xml`: This file consists of all the meta information needed by Cordova while converting our Ionic app to a platform-specific installer. If you open `config.xml`, you will see a bunch of XML tags that describe our project. We will take a look at this file in detail again.

- `ionic.config.js`: This file consists of the configuration that is needed for the build task.
- `package.json`: This file consists of the project-level node dependencies.
- `tsconfig.json`: This file consists of the TypeScript configuration.
- `tslint.json`: This file consists of TS lint rules. To know more about these rules, refer to: `https://palantir.github.io/tslint/rules/`.

The config.xml file

The `config.xml` file is a platform-agnostic configuration file. As mentioned earlier, this file consists of all the information needed by Cordova to convert the code in the `www` folder to the platform-specific installer.

The setting up of the `config.xml` file is based on W3C's packaged web apps (widgets) specification (`http://www.w3.org/TR/widgets/`), and it is extended to specify core Cordova API features, plugins, and platform-specific settings. There are two types of configurations that we can add to this file. One is global, that is, common to all devices, and the other is specific to the platform.

If we open `config.xml`, the first tag we encounter is the XML root tag. Next, we can see the widget tag:

```
<widget id="app.example.one" version="0.0.1"
xmlns="http://www.w3.org/ns/widgets"
xmlns:cdv="http://cordova.apache.org/ns/1.0">
```

The `id` specified previously is the reverse domain name of our app, which we provided while scaffolding. Other specifications are defined inside the widget tag as its children. The children tags include the app name (which gets displayed below the app icon when installed on the device), app description, and author details.

It also consists of the configuration that needs to be adhered to while converting code in the `src` folder to a native installer.

The content tag defines the starting page of the application.

The access tag defines the URLs that are allowed to load in the app. By default, it loads all the URLs.

The preference tag sets the various options as name value pairs. For instance, `DisallowOverscroll` describes weather there should be any visual feedback when the user scrolls past the beginning or end of the document.

You can read more about platform-specific configurations at the following links:

- Android:
  ```
  http://docs.phonegap.com/en/edge/guide_platforms_android_config.md.htm
  l#Android%20Configuration
  ```
- iOS: `http://docs.phonegap.com/en/edge/guide_platforms_ios_config.md.h`
  `tml#iOS%20Configuration`

 The importance of platform-specific configurations and global configurations is the same. You can read more about global configuration at `http://docs.phonegap.com/en/edge/config_ref_index.md.html#The%20` `config.xml%20File`.

The src folder

As mentioned earlier, this folder consists of our Ionic app, the HTML, CSS, and JS codes. If we open the `src` folder, we will find the following file structure:

```
. .
├──── app
│     ├──── app.component.ts
│     ├──── app.html
│     ├──── app.module.ts
│     ├──── app.scss
│     ├──── main.ts
├──── assets
│     ├──── icon
├──── declarations.d.ts
├──── index.html
├──── manifest.json
├──── pages
│     ├──── home
├──── service-worker.js
├──── theme
├──── variables.scss
```

Let's look at each of these in detail:

- `app folder`: The app folder consists of the environment specific initializing files. This folder consists of `app.module.ts` where the `@NgModule` module is defined. `app.component.ts` consists of the root component.
- `assets folder`: This folder consists of all the static assets.

- `pages folder`: This folder consists of the pages that we are going to create. In this example, we already have a sample page named `home`. Each page is a component, which consist of the business logic - `home.ts`, the markup - `home.html` and the component related styles - `home.scss`.
- `theme folder`: This folder consists of `variables.scss`, overriding which will change the look and feel of the Ionic components.
- `index.html`: This is where everything starts from.

This completes our tour of the blank template. Before we scaffold the next template, let us take a quick peek at the `src/app/app.component.ts` file.

As you can see, we are creating a new app/root component. The `@Component` decorator needs a `template` or `templateUrl` property to correctly load the Ionic 2 application. As part of the template, we add the `ion-nav` component.

Inside the class definition, we have declared a `rootPage` and assigned it to the home page, and inside the constructor, we have the platform ready callback, which will be called when the platform is ready.

This is a very simple and basic Ionic app. So far you must have worked on Angular code related to the web. But when you are dealing with Ionic, you would be working with scripts related to device features as well. Ionic provides us services to make these things happen in a more organized fashion.

Scaffolding the tabs template

To get a good feel for the Ionic CLI and the project structure, we will scaffold the other two starter templates as well. First we will scaffold the tabs template.

Using the `cd` command, go back to the `chapter2` folder and run the following command:

```
ionic start -a "Example 2" -i app.example.two example2 tabs --v2
```

The tabs project is scaffolded inside the `example2` folder. Using the `cd` command, go to the `example2` folder and execute the following command:

```
ionic serve
```

We should see the tabbed interface app built using Ionic, as seen in the following screenshot:

The tabs are located at the bottom of the page. We will talk more about customizations in `Chapter 3`, *Ionic Components and Navigation*, and `Chapter 4`, *Ionic Decorators and Services*.

If you go back to the `example2` folder and analyze the project structure, everything would be the same except for the contents of the `src/pages` folder.

This time, you will see four folders in the pages folder. The tabs folder consists of the tabs definition and the about, contact, and home folders consist of the definition for each of the tabs.

Now you can get a good idea of how Ionic is integrated with Angular, and how all the components go hand-in-hand. When we deal with a few more pieces of Ionic, this structure will make a lot more sense.

Scaffolding the side menu template

Now we will scaffold the final template. Using the cd command, go back to the chapter2 folder and run the following command:

```
ionic start -a "Example 3" -i app.example.three example3 sidemenu --v2
```

To execute the scaffolded project, using the cd command, go to the example3 folder and give the following command:

```
ionic serve
```

The output should be similar to the following screenshot:

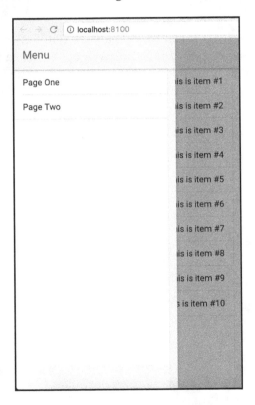

You can analyze the project structure yourself and see the difference.

> You can run ionic start -l or ionic templates to view the list of available templates. You can also use the ionic start task with the template name from the list to scaffold the app.

Summary

In this chapter, we gained some knowledge on Mobile Hybrid architecture. We have also learned how a hybrid app works. We saw how Cordova stitches the HTML, CSS, and JS code to be executed inside the WebView of a native app. Then we installed the required software to develop Ionic apps locally. We scaffolded a blank template using the Ionic CLI and analyzed the project structure. Later on, we scaffolded the other two templates and observed the difference.

 You can also refer to Ionic slides at `http://ionicframework.com/present-ionic/slides` for some more information.

In the next chapter, *Ionic Components and Navigation*, we will look at Ionic components and how to build a simple two page application and navigate between them. This will help us in building interesting user interfaces and multipage apps using the Ionic API.

3
Ionic Components and Navigation

So far we have seen what Ionic is and where it fits in the big picture of Mobile Hybrid application development. We have also seen how to scaffold an Ionic app.

In this chapter, we will work with Ionic components, the Ionic Grid system, and navigation in Ionic. We will look at the various components of Ionic, using which we can build apps that provide a great user experience out of the box

We will be covering the following topics in this chapter:

- Ionic Grid system
- Ionic components
- Ionic navigation

Core components

Ionic is a combination of a powerful mobile CSS framework and Angular. With Ionic, the time taken to market any idea is quite minimal. The Ionic CSS framework consists of most of the components you need to build an app.

To test drive the available components, we will scaffold a blank starter template and then add the visual components of Ionic.

Before we start scaffolding, we will create a new folder named chapter3, and scaffold all the examples from this chapter in that folder.

To scaffold a blank app, run the following code:

```
ionic start -a "Example 4" -i app.example.four example4 blank --v2
```

The Ionic Grid system

To get fine-grained control of your layout, in terms of positioning the components on the page or aligning elements next to each other with consistency, you need a grid system and Ionic provides one.

The beauty of the Ionic Grid system is that it is FlexBox-based. FlexBox--or the CSS Flexible Box Layout Module--provides a box model for an optimized user interface design.

 You can read more about FlexBox at:
http://www.w3.org/TR/css3-flexBox/
You can find an amazing tutorial about FlexBox at:
https://css-tricks.com/snippets/css/a-guide-to-flexbox/

The advantage of a FlexBox-based grid system is that you need not have a fixed-column grid. You can define as many columns as you want inside a row and they will be automatically assigned with equal width. This way, unlike any other CSS-based grid systems, you need not worry about the sum of class names adding up to the total number of columns in the grid system.

To get a feel for the grid system, open the home.html file that is present inside the example4/src/pages/home folder. Delete all the content inside the ion-content directive and add the following code:

```
<ion-row>
        <ion-col>col-20%-auto</ion-col>
        <ion-col>col-20%-auto</ion-col>
        <ion-col>col-20%-auto</ion-col>
        <ion-col>col-20%-auto</ion-col>
        <ion-col>col-20%-auto</ion-col>
</ion-row>
```

And, to visually see the difference, we add the following style in the home.scss present inside the src/pages/home folder:

```
ion-col {
    border: 1px solid red;
}
```

The preceding style is not needed to use the grid system; it is merely to show the visual demarcation of each column in the layout.

Save the `home.html` and `home.scss` files, and, using the `cd` command, go to the `example4` folder and run this:

```
ionic serve
```

Then you should see the following:

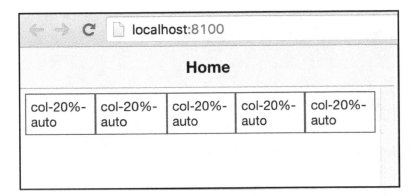

To check whether the width varies automatically, we reduce the number of child divs to three, as shown here:

```
<ion-row>
        <ion-col>col-33%-auto</ion-col>
        <ion-col>col-33%-auto</ion-col>
        <ion-col>col-33%-auto</ion-col>
</ion-row>
```

Then you should see the following:

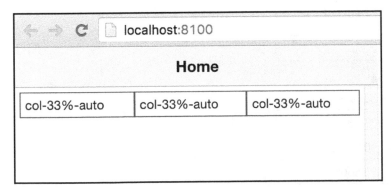

No hassle, no counting; all you need to do is add the ion-col that you want to use, and they are automatically allocated with equal width.

But this does mean that you cannot apply custom widths. You can do that easily with the width attribute provided by Ionic.

For instance, let's say that, in the preceding three columns scenario, you want the first column to span 50 percent and the remaining two columns to take the remaining width; all you need to do is add an attribute named `width-50` to the first `ion-col`, as shown here:

```
<ion-row>
    <ion-col width-50>col-50%-set</ion-col>
    <ion-col>col-25%-auto</ion-col>
    <ion-col>col-25%-auto</ion-col>
</ion-row>
```

Then you should see the following:

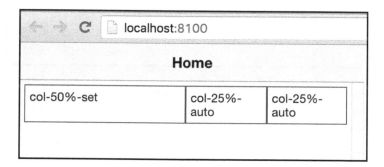

You can refer to the following table for a list of predefined width attributes and their implied widths:

Attribute Name	Percentage Width
width-10	10%
width-20	20%
width-25	25%
width-33	33.333%
width-34	33.333%
width-50	50%
width-66	66.666%

width-67	66.666%
width-75	75%
width-80	80%
width-90	90%

You can also offset a column by a certain percentage. For instance, append the following markup to our current example:

```
<ion-row>
        <ion-col offset-33>col-33%-offset</ion-col>
        <ion-col>col-33%-auto</ion-col>
</ion-row>
```

Then you should see the following:

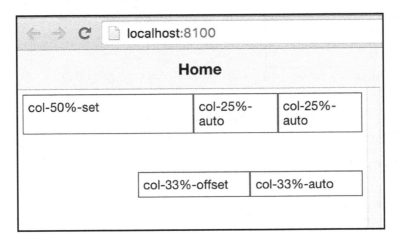

The first div is offset by 33 percent, and the remaining 66 percent will be split between the two divs. All the offset attribute does is add a margin of the specified percentage to the left of the div.

You can refer to the following table for a list of predefined classes and their implied offset width:

Attribute Name	Percentage Width
offset-10	10%
offset -20	20%
offset -25	25%
offset -33	33.333%
offset -34	33.333%
offset -50	50%
offset -66	66.666%
offset -67	66.666%
offset -75	75%
offset -80	80%
offset -90	90%

You can also align the columns in the grid vertically. This is another advantage of using FlexBox for a grid system.

Add the following code:

```
<h4 text-center>Align Cols to <i>top</i></h4>
    <ion-row top>
        <ion-col>
            <div>col</div>
        </ion-col>
        <ion-col>
            <div>col</div>
        </ion-col>
        <ion-col>
            <div>col</div>
        </ion-col>
        <ion-col>
            <div>
                This
                <br>is a tall
                <br> column
            </div>
        </ion-col>
```

```
</ion-row>
<h4 text-center>Align Cols to <i>center</i></h4>
<br>
<ion-row center>
    <ion-col>
        <div>col</div>
    </ion-col>
    <ion-col>
        <div>col</div>
    </ion-col>
    <ion-col>
        <div>col</div>
    </ion-col>
    <ion-col>
        <div>
            This
            <br>is a tall
            <br> column
        </div>
    </ion-col>
</ion-row>
<h4 text-center>Align Cols to <i>bottom</i></h4>
<ion-row bottom>
    <ion-col>
        <div>col</div>
    </ion-col>
    <ion-col>
        <div>col</div>
    </ion-col>
    <ion-col>
        <div>col</div>
    </ion-col>
    <ion-col>
        <div>
            This
            <br>is a tall
            <br> column
        </div>
    </ion-col>
</ion-row>
```

Then you should see the following:

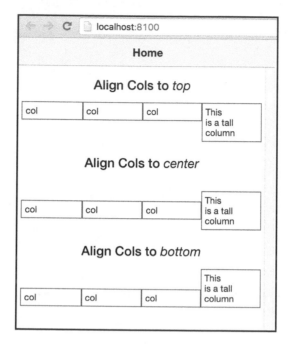

If one of the columns is tall, you can either add top, center, or bottom attributes on the `ion-row` tag, and things will fall into place, as shown in the preceding figure.

With such a simple and powerful grid system, the layout possibilities are unlimited.

 To know more about the Ionic Grid system, you can refer to the following link: `http://ionicframework.com/docs/components/#grid`

Ionic components

In this section, we are going to go over a few of the Ionic components. These components include buttons, lists, cards, and forms. Ionic components automatically adapt to the iOS theme, or Material Design for Android or Windows theme based on the device they are running on. When we are working with Ionic components, we will see the output in all three platforms.

To proceed further, we create a new project for working with buttons. You can `cd` into the `chapter3` folder and run the following command:

```
ionic start -a "Example 5" -i app.example.five example5 blank --v2
```

Next, we serve the app in lab mode. Use, `cd` command to navigate into the `example5` folder and run the following:

```
ionic serve --lab
```

This will serve the Ionic app in lab mode, which would look something like this:

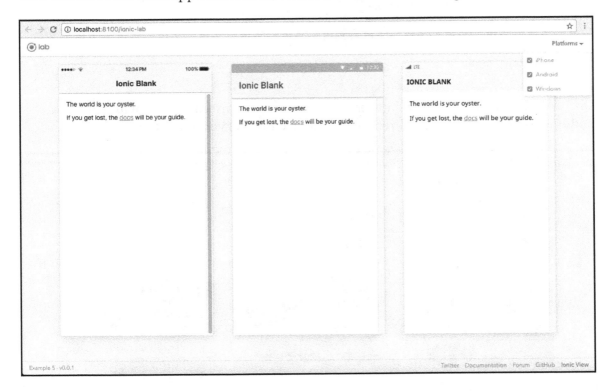

With this view, we can see the output of all our components in all three platforms.

Buttons

Ionic provides different variations on the buttons, by size and style.

Update the `ion-content` directive inside `src/pages/home/home.html` with the
following code and we should see different button variations:

```
<ion-content class="home" padding>
    <button ion-button>Button</button>
    <button ion-button color="light" outline>Light Outline</button>
    <button ion-button color="secondary" clear>Secondary Clear</button>
    <button ion-button color="danger" round>Danger Round</button>
    <button ion-button block>Block Button</button>
    <button ion-button color="secondary" full>Full Button</button>
    <button ion-button color="danger" large>Large Danger</button>
    <button ion-button dark>
        Home
        <ion-icon name="home"></ion-icon>
    </button>
</ion-content>
```

Do you notice the padding attribute on the `ion-content` directive? This will add `16px`
padding to the `ion-content` directive. If you save the file, you should see this:

The preceding screenshot covers your entire button needs based on the default Ionic color swatch.

Also, do you notice how the look and feel of the button varies between iOS, Android, and Windows? We will talk more about customizing these components in Chapter 5, *Ionic and SCSS*.

 For more information about the buttons components, refer to: http://ion icframework.com/docs/api/components/button/Button

Lists

The most essential component for any app that involves displaying a list of items is a list component. List structure is pretty simple. In Ionic, if you have a parent element named ion-list and any number of children inside it named ion-item, the items align themselves in the form of an Ionic-styled list. For instance, replace the preceding buttons snippet with the following lists snippet in the ion-content section:

```
<ion-list>
        <ion-item>
            Light
        </ion-item>
        <ion-item>
            Primary
        </ion-item>
        <ion-item>
            Secondary
        </ion-item>
        <ion-item>
            Danger
        </ion-item>
        <ion-item>
            Dark
        </ion-item>
    </ion-list>
```

You should see the following:

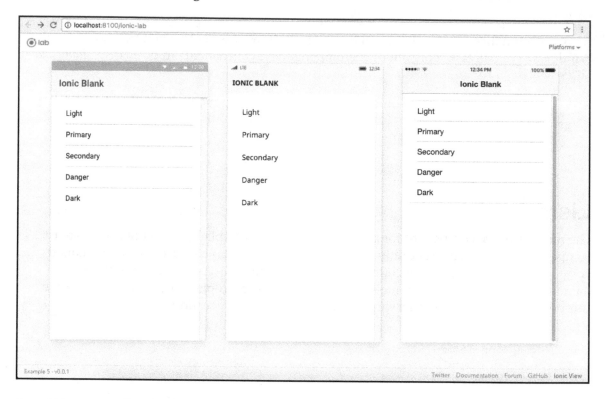

By adding an attribute called `no-lines` to the `ion-list` directive, the line will disappear. If you update the preceding snippet to the following:

```
<ion-list no-lines>
        <ion-item>
            Light
        </ion-item>
        <ion-item>
            Primary
        </ion-item>
        <ion-item>
            Secondary
        </ion-item>
        <ion-item>
            Danger
        </ion-item>
        <ion-item>
            Dark
        </ion-item>
```

```
</ion-list>
```

You should be able to see the following screen:

You can also group the list items together using the `ion-item-group`. The code for this is as follows:

```
<ion-list>
    <ion-item-group>
        <ion-item-divider light>A</ion-item-divider>
        <ion-item>Apple</ion-item>
        <ion-item>Apricots</ion-item>
        <ion-item>Avocado</ion-item>
        <ion-item-divider light>B</ion-item-divider>
        <ion-item>Bananas</ion-item>
        <ion-item>Blueberries</ion-item>
        <ion-item>Blackberries</ion-item>
    </ion-item-group>
</ion-list>
```

For this, `ion-list` will be replaced with `ion-item-group`, as shown in the preceding snippet. You should see the following screen:

A new addition to the Ionic Lists is the sliding List. In this type of list, each item can be swiped to the left to reveal new options.

The code snippet for this looks as follows:

```
<ion-list>
      <ion-item-sliding>
          <ion-item>
              <ion-avatar item-left>
                  <img src="https://placeholdit.imgix.net/~text?
                  txtsize=23&txt=80%C3%9780&w=80&h=80">
              </ion-avatar>
              <h2>Indiana Jones</h2>
              <p>Played by Harrison Ford in Raiders of the Lost Ark
              </p>
          </ion-item>
          <ion-item-options>
              <button ion-button color="light">
```

```
            <ion-icon name="ios-more"></ion-icon>
            More
        </button>
        <button ion-button color="primary">
            <ion-icon name="text"></ion-icon>
            Text
        </button>
        <button ion-button color="secondary">
            <ion-icon name="call"></ion-icon>
            Call
        </button>
    </ion-item-options>
  </ion-item-sliding>
  <ion-item-sliding>
    <ion-item>
        <ion-avatar item-left>
            <img src="https://placeholdit.imgix.net/~text?
             txtsize=23&txt=80%C3%9780&w=80&h=80">
        </ion-avatar>
        <h2>James Bond</h2>
        <p>Played by Sean Connery in Dr. No</p>
    </ion-item>
    <ion-item-options>
        <button ion-button color="light">
            <ion-icon name="ios-more"></ion-icon>
            More
        </button>
        <button ion-button color="primary">
            <ion-icon name="text"></ion-icon>
            Text
        </button>
        <button ion-button color="secondary">
            <ion-icon name="call"></ion-icon>
            Call
        </button>
    </ion-item-options>
  </ion-item-sliding>
</ion-list>
```

The output of the preceding code looks as follows:

 For more information about the list component, you can refer to the following link: `http://ionicframework.com/docs/components/#lists`

Cards

Cards are one of the best design patterns for showcasing content on a mobile device. For any page or app that displays a user's personalized content, cards are the way to go. The world is moving towards cards to display content on mobiles, and, in some cases, on desktops too. Examples include Twitter (`https://dev.twitter.com/cards/overview`) and Google Now.

So, you can simply port that design pattern to your app as well. All you need to do is design the personalized content that fits into a card and place it inside an `ion-card` component:

```
<ion-card>
 <ion-card-header>
     Card Header
 </ion-card-header>
<ion-card-content>
        Lorem ipsum dolor sit amet, consectetur adipisicing elit.
Dignissimos magni itaque numquam distinctio pariatur voluptas sint, id
inventore nulla vitae. Veritatis animi eos cupiditate. Labore, amet debitis
maxime velit assumenda.
</ion-card-content>
</ion-card>
```

As shown in the preceding snippet, you can add a header to the card using an `ion-card-header` directive and the output would look as follows:

You can get creative with cards by adding images to the cards as follows:

```
<ion-card>
    <img src="https://placeholdit.imgix.net/~text?
    txtsize=72&txt=600%C3%97390&w=600&h=390" />
    <ion-card-content>
        <h2 class="card-title">
    quas quae sunt
</h2>
        <p>
            Lorem ipsum dolor sit amet,
            consectetur adipisicing elit. Magni nihil
            hic vel fugit dignissimos ad natus eaque!
            Perspiciatis beatae quis doloremque soluta
            enim ratione laboriosam. Dolore illum,
            quas quae sunt.
        </p>
    </ion-card-content>
    <ion-row no-padding>
        <ion-col width-33>
            <button ion-button clear small color="danger">
                <ion-icon name='star'></ion-icon>
                Dolore
            </button>
        </ion-col>
        <ion-col width-33>
            <button ion-button clear small color="danger">
                <ion-icon name='musical-notes'></ion-icon>
                Perspi
            </button>
        </ion-col>
        <ion-col width-33>
            <button ion-button clear small color="danger">
                <ion-icon name='share-alt'></ion-icon>
                Magni
            </button>
        </ion-col>
    </ion-row>
</ion-card>
```

This would look as follows:

You can also use cards to display maps:

```
<ion-card>
    <div style="position: relative">
        <img src="http://maps.googleapis.com/maps/api/staticmap?
         center=Malaysia&size=640x400&style=element:
         labels|visibility:off&style=
         element:geometry.stroke|visibility:off&style=
         feature:landscape|element:
         geometry|saturation:-100&style=feature:
         water|saturation:-100|invert_lig
         htness:true&key=
         AIzaSyA4rAT0fdTZLNkJ5o0uaAwZ89vVPQpr_Kc">
        <ion-fab bottom right edge>
            <button ion-fab mini>
                <ion-icon name='pin'></ion-icon>
            </button>
        </ion-fab>
    </div>
    <ion-item>
```

```
            <ion-icon subtle large item-left name='map'></ion-icon>
            <h2>Malaysia</h2>
            <p>Truely Asia!!</p>
        </ion-item>
    </ion-card>
```

And you should be able to see the following screen:

With the power of `ion-card`, you can take your application to a new level!

Ionic icons

Ionic has its own set of 700+ font icons. The simplest way to add an icon is as follows:

```
<ion-icon name="heart"></ion-icon>
```

You can find the name of the icon from here: `http://ionicons.com`.

You can mark an icon as active or inactive using the `is-active` attribute. Active icons are typically full and thick, whereas inactive icons are outlined and thin:

```
<ion-icon name="beer" isActive="true"></ion-icon>
<ion-icon name="beer" isActive="false"></ion-icon>
```

Icons can also be made platform specific; the following snippet shows how:

```
<ion-icon ios="logo-apple" md="logo-android"></ion-icon>
```

You can also set the icon name programmatically, too, by first creating an attribute assigned to a variable and then populating that variable in the constructor. The HTML snippet would look as follows:

```
<ion-icon [name]="myIcon"></ion-icon>
```

The TypeScript code (in `home.ts`) would look as follows:

```
import { Component } from '@angular/core';

@Component({
  selector: 'page-home',
  templateUrl: 'home.html'
})
export class HomePage {

  myIcon: String;
  iconNames: Array<String> = ['home', 'map', 'pin', 'heart', 'star'];

  constructor(public navCtrl: NavController) {
    this.myIcon = this.iconNames[Math.floor(Math.random() *
    this.iconNames.length)];
  }
}
```

The consolidated output for the preceding snippets would look as follows:

Modals

In this section, we will take a look at modals in Ionic and how to implement them. To work with this example, we scaffold a new project:

```
ionic start -a "Example 6" -i app.example.six example6 blank --v2
```

`cd` into `example6` folder and run `ionic serve --lab`, and you should see the homepage of blank template.

To work with modals, we need to first create a component that we want to display as a modal.

From inside the `example6` folder, run the following:

```
ionic generate component helloModal
```

Note: We will look at sub-generators at a later point in this chapter.

Note: If you are using the latest Ionic CLI, you will see a file named `hello-modal.module.ts` generated along with the `hello-modal.html`, `hello-modal.scss`, and `hello-modal.ts`. To know more about `hello-modal.module.ts`, refer to Chapter 11, *Ionic 3*.

Once the component is generated, we need to add it to the `@NgModule`. Open `src/app/app.module.ts` and add the `import` statement:

```
import { HelloModalComponent }
from '../components/hello-modal/hello-modal';
```

Note: The scaffolded component may have a class name of `HelloModal` and not `HelloModalComponent`. If that is the case, please update accordingly.

Next, add `HelloModalComponent` to the declarations and `entryComponents` as follows:

```
@NgModule({
  declarations: [
    MyApp,
    HomePage,
    HelloModalComponent
  ],
  imports: [
    IonicModule.forRoot(MyApp)
  ],
  bootstrap: [IonicApp],
  entryComponents: [
    MyApp,
    HomePage,
    HelloModalComponent
  ],
  providers: [
    StatusBar,
    SplashScreen,
    {provide: ErrorHandler, useClass: IonicErrorHandler}
  ]
})
```

Now that it is done, we start configuring the component. Open `src/pages/home/home.ts` and update it as follows:

```
import { Component } from '@angular/core';
import { ModalController } from 'ionic-angular';
import { HelloModalComponent } from '../../components/hello-modal/hello-modal';

@Component({
```

```
    selector: 'page-home',
    templateUrl: 'home.html'
})
export class HomePage {

    constructor(public modalCtrl: ModalController) { }

    show() {
        let modal = this.modalCtrl.create(HelloModalComponent);
        modal.present();
        modal.onDidDismiss((data) => {
            console.log(data);
        });
    }
}
```

As you can see, for working with the `modal` component, we have a `ModalController`. Using `create()` of the `ModalController` instance, we can register a modal. Then, using `present()`, we display the modal.

Update `src/pages/home/home.html` to show a button. Clicking on which will present the modal:

```
<ion-header>
  <ion-navbar>
    <ion-title>
      My Modal App
    </ion-title>
  </ion-navbar>
</ion-header>

<ion-content padding>
  <button ion-button color="primary" (click)="show()">Show Modal</button>
</ion-content>
```

Next, we update the `HelloModalComponent`. Open `src/components/hello-modal/hello-modal.ts` and update it as follows:

```
import { Component } from '@angular/core';
import { ViewController } from 'ionic-angular';

@Component({
  selector: 'hello-modal',
  templateUrl: 'hello-modal.html'
})
export class HelloModalComponent {
```

```
constructor(public viewCtrl: ViewController) { }

close() {
  this.viewCtrl.dismiss({'random' : 'data'});
}
}
```

Here, we are using the instance of `ViewController` to manage the popup. Finally, for the popup content, open `src/components/hello-modal/hello-modal.html` and update it as follows:

```
<ion-content padding>
    <h2>I'm a modal!</h2>
    <button ion-button color="danger" (click)="close()">Close</button>
</ion-content>
```

With this, we have added all the code needed. Save all the files and run `ionic serve -lab` to see the output.

The output should look as follows:

Segment

Segment is another new introduction to Ionic. This component is used to control radio selections. We will be scaffolding another application to work with this example. From inside the `chapter3` folder, run the following:

```
ionic start -a "Example 7" -i app.example.seven example7 blank --v2
```

`cd` into `example7` folder and run `ionic serve --lab`, and you should see the home page of the blank template.

Now, to work with segment, we add the following code snippet inside the `ion-content` directive in the `src/pages/home/home.html` file:

```html
<ion-segment [(ngModel)]="food" color="primary">
    <ion-segment-button value="pizza">
        Pizza
    </ion-segment-button>
    <ion-segment-button value="burger">
        Burger
    </ion-segment-button>
</ion-segment>
<div [ngSwitch]="food">
    <ion-list *ngSwitchCase="'pizza'">
        <ion-item>
            <ion-thumbnail item-left>
                <img src="https://placeholdit.imgix.net/~text?
                txtsize=23&txt=80%C3%9780&w=80&h=80">
            </ion-thumbnail>
            <h2>Pizza 1</h2>
        </ion-item>
        <ion-item>
            <ion-thumbnail item-left>
                <img src="https://placeholdit.imgix.net/~text?
                txtsize=23&txt=80%C3%9780&w=80&h=80">
            </ion-thumbnail>
            <h2>Pizza 2</h2>
        </ion-item>
    </ion-list>
    <ion-list *ngSwitchCase="'burger'">
        <ion-item>
            <ion-thumbnail item-left>
                <img src="https://placeholdit.imgix.net/~text?
                txtsize=23&txt=80%C3%9780&w=80&h=80">
            </ion-thumbnail>
            <h2>Burger 1</h2>
        </ion-item>
```

```
        <ion-item>
            <ion-thumbnail item-left>
                <img src="https://placeholdit.imgix.net/~text?
                txtsize=23&txt=80%C3%9780&w=80&h=80">
            </ion-thumbnail>
            <h2>Burger 2</h2>
        </ion-item>
    </ion-list>
</div>
```

We initialize the food property as `pizza` in the `src/pages/home/home.ts` file as follows:

```
import { Component } from '@angular/core';
import { NavController } from 'ionic-angular';

@Component({
    selector: 'page-home',
    templateUrl: 'home.html'
})
export class HomePage {
    food: string;

    constructor(public navCtrl: NavController) {
        this.food = 'pizza';
    }
}
```

The output should look as follows:

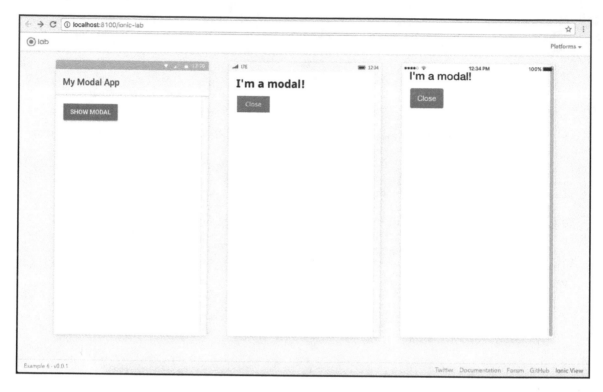

Ionic navigation

In this section, we are going to take a look at Ionic navigation. We are going to scaffold a blank template, and then add more pages and see how to navigate between them.

Ionic 3 has introduced the `@IonicPage` decorator for simplified and improved navigation, centered around native mobile experience. Do check out `Chapter 11`, *Ionic 3* for this.

Basic navigation

To get started, we scaffold a new project. Run the following:

```
ionic start -a "Example 8" -i app.example.eight example8 blank --v2
```

Run the Ionic app using the `ionic serve` command and you should see the home page of the blank template.

Navigation in Ionic does not require URLs; instead, pages are pushed and popped from the navigation controller's page stack. This approach is very much in line with how one would achieve navigation in a native mobile app, when compared to browser-based navigation. You can, however, deeplink pages with URLs, but that does not define the navigation.

To understand basic navigation, we open the `src/app/app.html` file and we should find the template as follows:

```
<ion-nav [root]="rootPage"></ion-nav>
```

`ion-nav` is the subclass of `NavController`, whose purpose is to work with the navigation page stack. For the `ion-nav` to work properly, we must set the root page to be loaded initially, where the root page is any `@component`.

So if we look at `app.component.ts`, it is pointing to a local variable named rootPage and that is set to HomePage .

Now, in `src/pages/home/home.html`, we will see a section at the very top, which looks as follows:

```
<ion-navbar>
  <ion-title>
    Ionic Blank
  </ion-title>
</ion-navbar>
```

This is the dynamic nav bar.

Inside the `src/pages/home/home.ts`, we can access the `NavController` as follows:

```
import { Component } from '@angular/core';
import { NavController } from 'ionic-angular';

@Component({
  selector: 'page-home',
  templateUrl: 'home.html'
})
export class HomePage {
  constructor(public navCtrl: NavController) {

  }
}
```

Now we can access the nav properties.

Ionic CLI Sub-Generator

The all-new Ionic CLI for v2 is now power packed with sub-generators, which can be helpful for scaffolding pages, components, providers, and so on. To view the list of available sub-generators, you can run the following:

```
ionic generate --list
```

You will see the following:

```
[→  example8 ionic generate --list
Available generators:
 * component
 * directive
 * page
 * pipe
 * provider
 * tabs
```

Now we are going to use the preceding sub generator and generate a couple of pages inside the `example8` project. Run the following:

```
ionic generate page about
```

Also run the following:

```
ionic generate page contact
```

Inside the `app/pages` folder, you should see two new folders, the about and contact folders, which have their own `html`, `ts`, and `scss` files, along with the `module.ts` files.

Class name of `About` and not `AboutPage`. If that is the case, please update the preceding accordingly.

Before we proceed further, we need to add `AboutPage` and `ContactPage` to the `src/app/app.module.ts` as follows:

```
import { NgModule, ErrorHandler } from '@angular/core';
import { IonicApp, IonicModule, IonicErrorHandler } from 'ionic-angular';
import { MyApp } from './app.component';
```

```
import { HomePage } from '../pages/home/home';
import { AboutPage } from '../pages/about/about';
import { ContactPage } from '../pages/contact/contact';

import { StatusBar } from '@ionic-native/status-bar';
import { SplashScreen } from '@ionic-native/splash-screen';

@NgModule({
  declarations: [
    MyApp,
    HomePage,
    AboutPage,
    ContactPage
  ],
  imports: [
    IonicModule.forRoot(MyApp)
  ],
  bootstrap: [IonicApp],
  entryComponents: [
    MyApp,
    HomePage,
    AboutPage,
    ContactPage
  ],
  providers: [
    StatusBar,
    SplashScreen,
    { provide: ErrorHandler, useClass: IonicErrorHandler }
  ]
})
export class AppModule { }
```

Multi page navigation

Now that we have three pages, we will see how to implement the navigation between them.
The idea is that from the Home page, a user should be able to go to the About and Contact
pages, and from the About page to Contact and Home, and, finally, from the Contact page
to Home and About.

First we update home.html as follows:

```
<ion-header>
    <ion-navbar>
        <ion-title>
            Home Page
        </ion-title>
```

```
        </ion-navbar>
    </ion-header>
    <ion-content padding>
        <ion-card>
            <ion-card-header>
                Home Page
            </ion-card-header>
            <ion-card-content>
                <button ion-button (click)="goTo('about')">About</button>
                <button ion-button color="danger"
                  (click)="goTo('contact')">Contact</button>
                <button ion-button color="light"
                  (click)="back()">Back</button>
            </ion-card-content>
        </ion-card>
    </ion-content>
```

Next, we update home.ts as follows:

```
import { Component } from '@angular/core';
import { NavController } from 'ionic-angular';

import { AboutPage } from '../about/about';
import { ContactPage } from '../contact/contact';

@Component({
    selector: 'page-home',
    templateUrl: 'home.html'
})
export class HomePage {
    constructor(private navCtrl: NavController) { }

    goTo(page) {
        if (page === 'about') {
            this.navCtrl.push(AboutPage);
        } else if (page === 'contact') {
            this.navCtrl.push(ContactPage);
        }
    }

    back() {
        if (this.navCtrl.length() >= 2) {
            this.navCtrl.pop();
        }
    }
}
```

Do you notice the `goTo` and `back` functions? This is how we navigate from one page to another.

Next, we will update the `about.html` as follows:

```html
<ion-header>
    <ion-navbar>
        <ion-title>
            About Page
        </ion-title>
    </ion-navbar>
</ion-header>
<ion-content padding>
    <ion-card>
        <ion-card-header>
            About Page
        </ion-card-header>
        <ion-card-content>
            <button ion-button (click)="goTo('home')">Home</button>
            <button ion-button color="danger"
              (click)="goTo('contact')">Contact</button>
            <button ion-button color="light"
              (click)="back()">Back</button>
        </ion-card-content>
    </ion-card>
</ion-content>
```

And `about.ts` as follows:

```typescript
import { Component } from '@angular/core';
import { NavController } from 'ionic-angular';

import { HomePage } from '../home/home';
import { ContactPage } from '../contact/contact';

@Component({
    selector: 'page-home',
    templateUrl: 'home.html'
})
export class AboutPage {
    constructor(private navCtrl: NavController) { }

    goTo(page) {
        if (page === 'home') {
            this.navCtrl.push(HomePage);
        } else if (page === 'contact') {
            this.navCtrl.push(ContactPage);
        }
```

```
        }

    back() {
        if (this.navCtrl.length() >= 2) {
            this.navCtrl.pop();
        }
    }
}
```

And finally, `contact.html`:

```html
<ion-header>
    <ion-navbar>
        <ion-title>
            Contact Page
        </ion-title>
    </ion-navbar>
</ion-header>
<ion-content padding>
    <ion-card>
        <ion-card-header>
            Contact Page
        </ion-card-header>
        <ion-card-content>
            <button ion-button (click)="goTo('home')">Home</button>
            <button ion-button color="danger"
             (click)="goTo('about')">About</button>
            <button ion-button color="light"
             (click)="back()">Back</button>
        </ion-card-content>
    </ion-card>
</ion-content>
```

And `contact.ts` as follows:

```typescript
import { Component } from '@angular/core';
import { NavController } from 'ionic-angular';

import { HomePage } from '../home/home';
import { AboutPage } from '../about/about';

@Component({
    selector: 'page-home',
    templateUrl: 'home.html'
})
export class ContactPage {
    constructor(private navCtrl: NavController) { }
```

```
    goTo(page) {
        if (page === 'home') {
            this.navCtrl.push(HomePage);
        } else if (page === 'about') {
            this.navCtrl.push(AboutPage);
        }
    }

    back() {
        if (this.navCtrl.length() >= 2) {
            this.navCtrl.pop();
        }
    }
}
```

If we save all the files and go back to the browser, we should see the following:

When we click on **About** button, we should see the following screen:

As we can see, the **Back** button is automatically added to the navigation bar. Now, when we click on the back button, we will go back to the Home page. If you did notice the back function, we added a condition to check if there is more than one view in the stack to pop the view. If there is only one view, it will be removed and the user will see a black screen, as follows:

To avoid the **Black Screen of Death** in an app, we have added this condition.

Now that we are aware of Navigation in an Ionic app, you can go back to the Tabs template and the Side menu template and take a look at the `src` folder to get started.

Also, do check out `Chapter 11`, *Ionic 3*, to find out more about `@IonicPage` decorator and to know more about deeplinking.

Summary

In this chapter, we have gone through the Ionic Grid system and a few of the main Ionic components, and have seen how to work with them. We went through buttons, lists, cards, icons, and segments. Next, we saw how to work with the Navigation component and how to navigate between pages.

In the next chapter, we will work with Ionic decorators and Services, and we will look at the decorators and services offered by Ionic.

4
Ionic Decorators and Services

In the last chapter, we went through a few Ionic components, using which one could easily build classy Mobile Hybrid apps. In this chapter, we will be working with Ionic 2 decorators and services. The entire Ionic 2 ecosystem is divided into two parts: the Components and the Service APIs. Components include buttons, cards, and lists, as we saw in the last chapter, and Service APIs include platform, `config`, `NavController`, `Storage`, and so on.

In this chapter, we are going to take a look at the following topics:

- Ionic module
- Component decorator
- Config service
- Platform service
- Storage API

Decorators

Before we start working with Ionic built-in decorators, we will quickly get an understanding of what decorators are and how they can make our life easy.

In simple words, a decorator is a function that takes a class and extend its behavior without actually modifying it.

For instance, if we had a person class and we want to add more information about the person to the class, such as age and gender, we can do so quite easily.

The following is an example of how we can write our own decorator in TypeScript:

```
@MoreInfo({
    age: 5,
    gender: 'male'
})
class Person {
    constructor(private firstName, private lastName) {}
}
```

And the `MoreInfo` decorator would look something like this:

```
function MoreInfo(config) {
    return function (target) {
        Object.defineProperty(target.prototype, 'age', {value: () =>
config.age});
        Object.defineProperty(target.prototype, 'gender', {value: () =>
config.gender});
    }
}
```

In the same way, Ionic also provides two decorators:

- Ionic Module or `NgModule` decorator
- Component decorator

Ionic module

The Ionic module or `NgModule` decorator bootstraps the Ionic app. If we open up any of the existing Ionic projects and look up `src/app/app.module.ts` file, we will see the following:

```
import { NgModule, ErrorHandler } from '@angular/core';
import { IonicApp, IonicModule, IonicErrorHandler } from 'ionic-angular';
import { MyApp } from './app.component';
import { HomePage } from '../pages/home/home';
import { AboutPage } from '../pages/about/about';
import { ContactPage } from '../pages/contact/contact';

@NgModule({
  declarations: [
    MyApp,
    HomePage,
    AboutPage,
    ContactPage
```

```
    ],
    imports: [
      IonicModule.forRoot(MyApp)
    ],
    bootstrap: [IonicApp],
    entryComponents: [
      MyApp,
      HomePage,
      AboutPage,
      ContactPage
    ],
    providers: [{ provide: ErrorHandler, useClass: IonicErrorHandler }]
})
export class AppModule { }
```

This is the place where we bootstrap the Ionic app. This app can also be configured by using `forRoot` on the `IonicModule`. `forRoot` takes care of providing and configuring services at the same time.

An example implementation of `forRoot` on `IonicModule` would look like the following:

```
import { IonicApp, IonicModule } from 'ionic-angular';
import { MyApp } from './app.component';

@NgModule({
    declarations: [MyApp],
    imports: [
        IonicModule.forRoot(MyApp, {
            backButtonText: 'Go Back',
            iconMode: 'ios',
            modalEnter: 'modal-slide-in',
            modalLeave: 'modal-slide-out',
            tabsPlacement: 'bottom',
            pageTransition: 'ios'
        }, {})
    ],
    bootstrap: [IonicApp],
    entryComponents: [MyApp],
    providers: []
})
```

Platform-specific configuration can also be passed, as shown here:

```
import { IonicApp, IonicModule } from 'ionic-angular';
import { MyApp } from './app.component';

@NgModule({
    declarations: [MyApp],
```

```
    imports: [
        IonicModule.forRoot(MyApp, {
            backButtonText: 'Go Back',
            platforms: {
                ios: {
                    iconMode: 'ios',
                    modalEnter: 'modal-slide-in',
                    modalLeave: 'modal-slide-out',
                    tabbarPlacement: 'bottom',
                    pageTransition: 'ios-transition',
                },
                android: {
                    iconMode: 'md',
                    modalEnter: 'modal-md-slide-in',
                    modalLeave: 'modal-md-slide-out',
                    tabbarPlacement: 'top',
                    pageTransition: 'md-transition',
                }
            }

        }, {})
    ],
    bootstrap: [IonicApp],
    entryComponents: [MyApp],
    providers: []
})
```

You can read more about the Ionic Module at
https://ionicframework.com/docs/v2/api/IonicModule/, about config
at: https://ionicframework.com/docs/v2/api/config/Config/, and
about NgModule
at https://angular.io/docs/ts/latest/guide/ngmodule.html.

Component decorator

The Component decorator marks a class as an Angular component and collects component
configuration metadata. A simple component decorator would look like this:

```
import { Component } from '@angular/core';
import { Platform } from 'ionic-angular';
import { StatusBar, Splashscreen } from 'ionic-native';

import { HomePage } from '../pages/home/home';
```

```
@Component({
  templateUrl: 'app.html'
})
export class MyApp {
  rootPage = HomePage;

  constructor(platform: Platform) {
    platform.ready().then(() => {
    StatusBar.styleDefault();
      Splashscreen.hide();
    });
  }
}
```

Components have all the Ionic and Angular core components and directives included, so we need not explicitly declare the directive property. Only the dependent properties on the child/parent component need to be explicitly specified.

To know more about the `Component` decorator, refer to
https://angular.io/docs/ts/latest/api/core/index/Component-decorator.html.

Navigation

In the previous chapter, we saw a basic implementation of navigation between two pages. In this section, we will dig deeper into the same.

To start off, we will scaffold a blank Ionic app. Create a new folder named `chapter4` and, inside that folder, open a new command prompt/terminal and run the following:

```
ionic start -a "Example 9" -i app.example.nine example9 blank --v2
```

Once the app has been scaffolded, `cd` into the `example9` folder. If we navigate to `example9/src/app/app.component.ts`, we should see the App component defined by a class named `MyApp`. And if we navigate to the corresponding template `example9/src/app/app.html`, we should see the `ion-nav` component.

The `ion-nav` component takes in an input property named root. The root property indicates which component will act as the root component/root page. In this example, we have indicated Home Page as the `root` from our `MyApp` class (`example9/src/app/app.component.ts`).

Now we are going to generate one new page named about, using the Ionic CLI's generate command. Run the following:

```
ionic generate page about
```

This command will create a new component inside the `src/pages` folder.

If we look at the `example9/src/pages/home/` and `example9/src/pages/about/` contents, we should see two standalone components.

Before we start stitching these two pages together, we will first need to register the about page with the `@NgModule`. Open `example9/src/app/app.module.ts` and update it as shown follows:

```
import { NgModule, ErrorHandler } from '@angular/core';
import { IonicApp, IonicModule, IonicErrorHandler } from 'ionic-angular';
import { MyApp } from './app.component';
import { HomePage } from '../pages/home/home';
import { AboutPage } from '../pages/about/about';

@NgModule({
  declarations: [
    MyApp,
    HomePage,
    AboutPage
  ],
  imports: [
    IonicModule.forRoot(MyApp)
  ],
  bootstrap: [IonicApp],
  entryComponents: [
    MyApp,
    HomePage,
    AboutPage
  ],
  providers: [{provide: ErrorHandler, useClass: IonicErrorHandler}]
})
export class AppModule {}
```

Next, we will add a button on the **Home Page** and when we click on it, we will show the **about** page. Update `example9/src/pages/home/home.html` as shown here:

```
<ion-header>
  <ion-navbar>
    <ion-title>
      Home Page
    </ion-title>
```

```
    </ion-navbar>
  </ion-header>

  <ion-content padding>
      <button ion-button color="secondary" (click)="openAbout()">Go To
  About</button>
  </ion-content>
```

Next, we will add the logic to navigate between pages.
Update `example9/src/pages/home/home.ts` as follows:

```
import { Component } from '@angular/core';
import { NavController } from 'ionic-angular';
import { AboutPage } from '../about/about';

@Component({
  selector: 'page-home',
  templateUrl: 'home.html'
})
export class HomePage {

  constructor(public navCtrl: NavController) {}

  openAbout(){
    this.navCtrl.push(AboutPage);
  }
}
```

Using `this.navCtrl.push(AboutPage);`, we move from the **Home Page** to the a**bout** page.

If we save the files and execute `ionic serve`, we should see the home page with the button. And when we click on the button, we should see the a**bout** page:

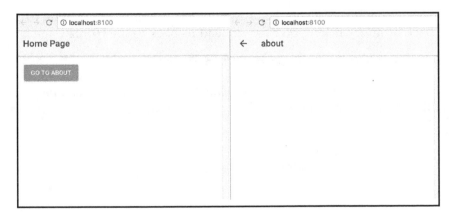

Now, if we want to navigate back, we can use the auto-generated back button or we can create a button on the **About** page to go back. To do that, update `example9/src/pages/about/about.html` as shown here:

```
<ion-header>
  <ion-navbar>
    <ion-title>About Page</ion title>
  </ion-navbar>
</ion-header>

<ion-content padding>
    <button ion-button color="light" (click)="goBack()">Back</button>
</ion-content>
```

And update `example9/src/pages/about/about.ts` as follows:

```
import { Component } from '@angular/core';
import { NavController } from 'ionic-angular';

@Component({
  selector: 'page-about',
  templateUrl: 'about.html'
})
export class AboutPage {

  constructor(public navCtrl: NavController) {}

  goBack(){
    this.navCtrl.pop();
  }
}
```

Do note `this.navCtrl.pop();` --that is how we pop a page from the view.

If we save all the files and go back to the browser, then navigate from **Home** to **About**, we should see a Back button. Clicking on this will lead us back to the **Home** page.

This is a simple example of how we can stitch two pages together.

Along with this, we have page events that indicate the various stages of a page. To understand this better, we will update `example9/src/pages/about/about.ts` as shown here:

```
import { Component } from '@angular/core';
import { NavController } from 'ionic-angular';

@Component({
```

```
  selector: 'page-about',
  templateUrl: 'about.html'
})
export class AboutPage {

  constructor(public navCtrl: NavController) { }

  goBack() {
    this.navCtrl.pop();
  }

  ionViewDidLoad() {
    console.log("About page: ionViewDidLoad Fired");
  }

  ionViewWillEnter() {
    console.log("About page: ionViewWillEnter Fired");
  }

  ionViewDidEnter() {
    console.log("About page: ionViewDidEnter Fired");
  }

  ionViewWillLeave() {
    console.log("About page: ionViewWillLeave Fired");
  }

  ionViewDidLeave() {
    console.log("About page: ionViewDidLeave Fired");
  }

  ionViewWillUnload() {
    console.log("About page: ionViewWillUnload Fired");
  }

  ionViewDidUnload() {
    console.log("About page: ionViewDidUnload Fired");
  }
}
```

Save all the files, navigate to the browser, and navigate from Home to About and back, and we should see the following:

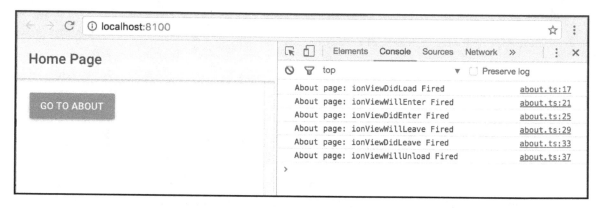

Based on this, we can hook onto various events and act accordingly if needed.

Passing data between pages

So far, we have seen how we can move from one page to another. Now, using `NavParams`, we will be passing data from one page to another.

In the same `example9` project, we will be adding on this functionality. On the home page, we will present a textbox for the user to enter data. Once the user enters the data and clicks on **Go to About**, we will take the value of the `textbox` and pass it on to the **About** page and print the text that we have captured on the **Home** page in the **About** page.

To get started, we will update `example9/src/pages/home/home.html` as shown here:

```html
<ion-header>
    <ion-navbar>
        <ion-title>
            Home Page
        </ion-title>
    </ion-navbar>
</ion-header>
<ion-content padding>
    <ion-list>
        <ion-item>
            <ion-label color="primary">Enter</ion-label>
            <ion-input placeholder="Something..." #text></ion-input>
        </ion-item>
    </ion-list>
```

```
    <button ion-button color="secondary" (click)="openAbout(text.value)">Go
To About</button>
</ion-content>
```

Do note that we have updated the `openAbout` method to take the text value. Next, we will update `example9/src/pages/home/home.ts`:

```
import { Component } from '@angular/core';
import { NavController } from 'ionic-angular';
import { AboutPage } from '../about/about';

@Component({
  selector: 'page-home',
  templateUrl: 'home.html'
})
export class HomePage {

  constructor(public navCtrl: NavController) {}

  openAbout(text){
    text = text || 'Nothing was entered';

    this.navCtrl.push(AboutPage, {
      data : text
    });
  }
}
```

Do notice the second argument that we are passing to the push method of the `navCtrl`. This is how we pass the data from the **Home page**. Now we will update `example9/src/pages/about/about.ts` to catch the data:

```
import { Component } from '@angular/core';
import { NavController, NavParams } from 'ionic-angular';

@Component({
  selector: 'page-about',
  templateUrl: 'about.html'
})
export class AboutPage {
  text: string;

  constructor(public navCtrl: NavController, public navParams: NavParams) {
    this.text = navParams.get('data');
  }

  goBack() {
    this.navCtrl.pop();
```

```
    }

    /// SNIPP :: Page events...
}
```

To catch the data, we need to import `NavParams` from `ionic-angular`. And using `navParams.get(data);`, we fetch the data that is passed from the Home Page inside the constructor.

And finally, to display the data in the About page, update `example9/src/pages/about/about.html` as shown here:

```html
<ion-header>
    <ion-navbar>
        <ion-title>About Page</ion-title>
    </ion-navbar>
</ion-header>
<ion-content padding>
    <label>Text Entered : {{text}}</label>
    <br>
    <button ion-button color="light" (click)="goBack()">Back</button>
</ion-content>
```

Save all the files and head back to the browser and we should be able to see the following:

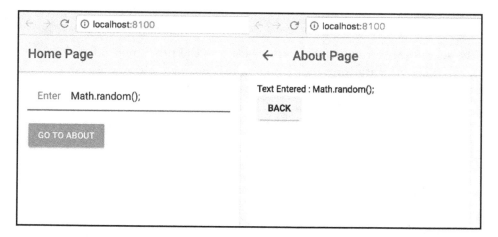

Now we know how to stitch two pages together and pass data between them.

We can implement navigation and lazy loading using the `@IonicPage` decorator. You can find more information about the same in Chapter 11, *Ionic 3*.

Config service

This service lets you configure and set up app-specific preferences.

To customize the look and feel of the app across platforms or within the same platform for various components, we use the config service.

To understand this service better, we will scaffold a new app and work with it. Run the following:

```
ionic start -a "Example 10" -i app.example.ten example10 tabs --v2
```

And then run `ionic serve --lab`.

This will run the tabs app in the lab view, where we can see the Android iOS and Windows apps side by side.

We can view the Ionic app in any of the three platform views by using the following URLs as well:

iOS: `http://localhost:8100/?ionicplatform=ios`
Android: `http://localhost:8100/?ionicplatform=android`
Windows: `http://localhost:8100/?ionicplatform=windows`

And we should see something like this:

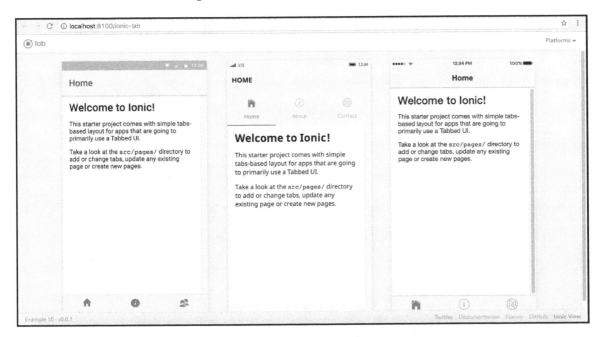

Config is set up on the `@NgModule`. If we open `example10/src/app/app.module.ts`, we should find the `NgModule` decorator, inside which we can find `IonicModule.forRoot(MyApp)`.

A simple config would look like the following:

```
//... snipp
imports: [
    IonicModule.forRoot(MyApp, {
        mode: 'md'
    })
],
//.. snipp
```

This will make the look and feel default to the material design irrespective of the platform. We should be able to see the following:

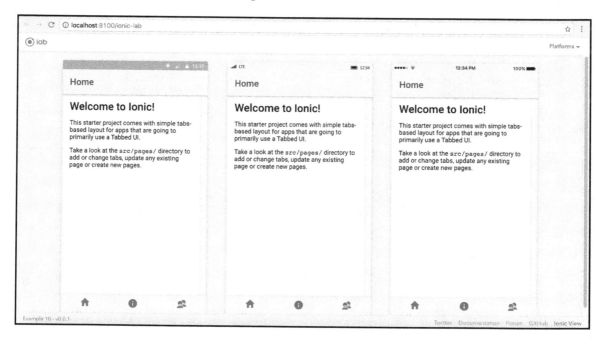

You can also set other config values like this:

```
//.. snipp
imports: [
    IonicModule.forRoot(MyApp, {
      backButtonText: 'Go Back',
      iconMode: 'ios',
      modalEnter: 'modal-slide-in',
      modalLeave: 'modal-slide-out',
      tabsPlacement: 'bottom',
      pageTransition: 'ios',
    })
  ],
//... snipp
```

The preceding values are quite self-explanatory.

The properties in the config can be overwritten at the app level, platform level, and component level.

For instance, you can overwrite the `tabberPlacement` property at the app level as well as the platform level, as follows:

```
//..snipp
imports: [
    IonicModule.forRoot(MyApp, {
      tabsPlacement: 'bottom', // bottom for all platforms
      platforms: {
        ios: {
          tabsPlacement: 'top', // top only for iOS
        }
      }
    })
  ],
//...snipp
```

And we will see the following:

And we can also overwrite at the component level as well. Update
`example10/src/pages/tabs/tabs.html` as follows:

```
<ion-tabs tabsPlacement="top">
  <ion-tab [root]="tab1Root" tabTitle="Home" tabIcon="home"></ion-tab>
  <ion-tab [root]="tab2Root" tabTitle="About" tabIcon="information-
circle"></ion-tab>
  <ion-tab [root]="tab3Root" tabTitle="Contact" tabIcon="contacts"></ion-
tab>
</ion-tabs>
```

And we should see the following:

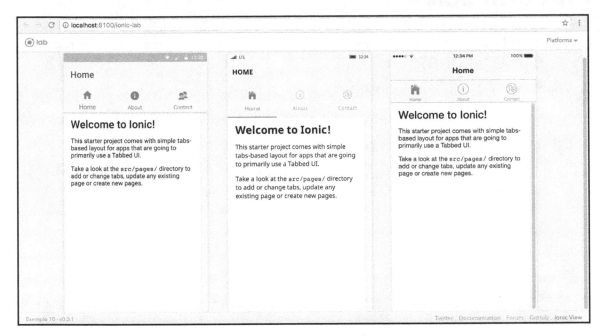

 For quick testing, we can also set the config property in the URL, without any overrides defined. For instance, to test how tabs would look when placed on top, we can navigate to this URL: `http://localhost:8100/?ionicTabsPlacement=top`

We can also set custom properties to the config and extract them later on. For instance, we can set the following properties:

```
config.set('ios', 'themePref', 'dark');
```

And then we can get the value using the following:

```
config.get('themePref');
```

 We can import `config` from `ionic-angular`, for example `import {Config} from 'ionic-angular';` and then initialize `config` in the constructor: `constructor(private config : Config) { //**// }`

Platform service

The platform service returns the available information about the current platform. The new and improved platform service of Ionic has more information that helps us to customize the app based on the device type.

To understand the platform service better, we will scaffold a blank app. Run the following:

```
ionic start -a "Example 11" -i app.example.eleven example11 blank --v2
```

And then run `ionic serve` to launch the blank app.

Now we are going to add a reference to the Platform class in `example11/src/pages/home/home.ts`. Update `home.ts` as follows:

```
import { Component } from '@angular/core';
import { Platform } from 'ionic-angular';

@Component({
  selector: 'page-home',
  templateUrl: 'home.html'
})
export class HomePage {
  constructor(public platform: Platform) {}
}
```

And now we will start working with various features of the `Platform` class.

The first one we are going to look at is the `userAgent` string. To access the `userAgent`, we can execute `userAgent()` on the platform.

Update the `example11/src/pages/home/home.html` content section as follows:

```
<ion-header>
    <ion-navbar>
        <ion-title>
            Ionic Blank
        </ion-title>
    </ion-navbar>
</ion-header>
<ion-content padding>
    <ion-card>
        <ion-card-header>
            Platform : User Agent
        </ion-card-header>
        <ion-card-content>
            {{platform.userAgent()}}
```

```
        </ion-card-content>
      </ion-card>
  </ion-content>
```

We should see the following:

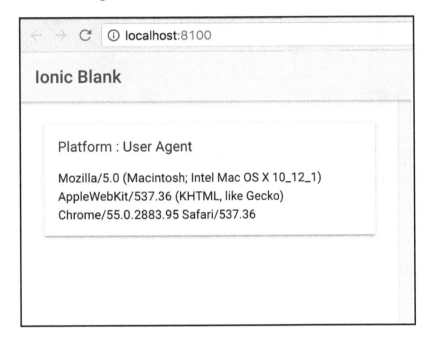

Next, we will find out the platform on which the app is running; for that, we update the `ion-content` contents in `home.html` as follows:

```
<ion-card>
    <ion-card-header>
      Platform : platformName
    </ion-card-header>
    <ion-card-content>
      <ion-list>
        <ion-item>
          android : {{platform.is('android')}}
        </ion-item>
        <ion-item>
          cordova : {{platform.is('cordova')}}
        </ion-item>
        <ion-item>
          core : {{platform.is('core')}}
        </ion-item>
        <ion-item>
```

```
      ios : {{platform.is('ios')}}
    </ion-item>
    <ion-item>
      ipad : {{platform.is('ipad')}}
    </ion-item>
    <ion-item>
      iphone : {{platform.is('iphone')}}
    </ion-item>
    <ion-item>
      mobile : {{platform.is('mobile')}}
    </ion-item>
    <ion-item>
      mobileweb : {{platform.is('mobileweb')}}
    </ion-item>
    <ion-item>
      phablet : {{platform.is('phablet')}}
    </ion-item>
    <ion-item>
      tablet : {{platform.is('tablet')}}
    </ion-item>
    <ion-item>
      windows : {{platform.is('windows')}}
    </ion-item>
  </ion-list>
 </ion-card-content>
</ion-card>
```

And when the browser refreshes, we should see the following:

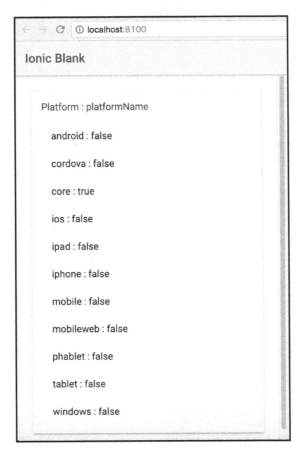

As we can see from the screenshot, when run in the browser, the preceding platform names are the values.

Now, let us add the browser platform and see if anything changes. Run the following:

```
ionic platform add browser
```

And then run:

```
ionic run browser
```

You should be able to see the Ionic app launch in the browser with Cordova support and now the output should look like the following:

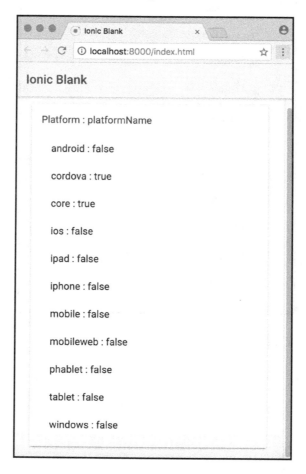

If we notice carefully, we can see that in the preceding screenshot, that **cordova** is now set to **true**.

Using the preceding cross-section of platform names, we can easily customize the app and tailor the user experience.

 To find out more about the platform service, refer to `http://ionicframew ork.com/docs/api/platform/Platform/`

Storage service

In this section, we are going to take a look at the Storage service. The Storage class from Ionic helps us interact with various storage options that are available when the app runs in the native container.

Quoting the Ionic documentation:

> Storage is an easy way to store key/value pairs and JSON objects. Storage uses a variety of storage engines underneath, picking the best one available depending on the platform.

> When running in a native app context, Storage will prioritize using SQLite, as it's one of the most stable and widely used file-based databases, and avoids some of the pitfalls of things like localstorage and IndexedDB, such as the OS deciding to clear out such data in low disk-space situations.

> When running in the web or as a Progressive Web App, Storage will attempt to use IndexedDB, WebSQL, and localstorage, in that order.

Now, to start working with the Storage class, we will create a new app. Run the following:

```
ionic start -a "Example 12" -i app.example.twelve example12 blank --v2
```

And then run `ionic serve` to launch it in the browser.

To understand how to use Storage, we will be building a simple user management app. In this app, we can add a user, persist that data in storage, and then remove it later on. The main purpose of this app is to explore the storage class.

The final app will look something like the following:

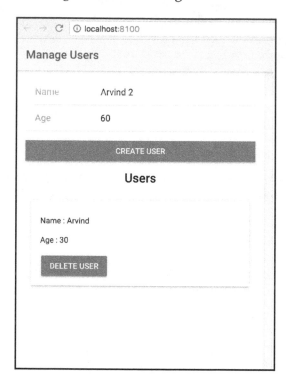

Before we start working with the `Storage` class, we need to add it to our `Ionic` project. Run the following:

```
npm install --save @ionic/storage
```

Next, we need to add it as a provider. Update `example12/src/app/app.module.ts` as shown here:

```
import { BrowserModule } from '@angular/platform-browser';
import { ErrorHandler, NgModule } from '@angular/core';
import { IonicApp, IonicErrorHandler, IonicModule } from 'ionic-angular';
import { SplashScreen } from '@ionic-native/splash-screen';
import { StatusBar } from '@ionic-native/status-bar';

import { MyApp } from './app.component';
import { HomePage } from '../pages/home/home';
import { IonicStorageModule } from '@ionic/storage';

@NgModule({
  declarations: [
```

```
      MyApp,
      HomePage
    ],
    imports: [
      BrowserModule,
      IonicModule.forRoot(MyApp),
      IonicStorageModule.forRoot()
    ],
    bootstrap: [IonicApp],
    entryComponents: [
      MyApp,
      HomePage
    ],
    providers: [
      StatusBar,
      SplashScreen,
      {provide: ErrorHandler, useClass: IonicErrorHandler}
    ]
})
export class AppModule {}
```

Next, we will build the interface. Open `example12/src/pages/home/home.html`. We will update the header first to the following:

```
<ion-header>
    <ion-navbar>
        <ion-title>
            Manage Users
        </ion-title>
    </ion-navbar>
</ion-header>
```

Next, in the content section, we will create two divisions, one for the form where the user will enter the name and age, and one more division for displaying the list of users:

```
<ion-content padding>
    <div>
        <ion-list>
            <ion-item>
                <ion-label fixed>Name</ion-label>
                <ion-input type="text" placeholder="Enter Name" #name>
                </ion-input>
            </ion-item>
            <ion-item>
                <ion-label fixed>Age</ion-label>
                <ion-input type="number" placeholder="Enter Age" #age>
                </ion-input>
            </ion-item>
```

```
        </ion-list>
        <button ion-button full color="primary" (click)="addUser(name,
        age)" [disabled]="!name.value || !age.value">Create
        User</button>
    </div>
    <div *ngIf="users.length > 0">
        <h3 style="text-align: center;" padding>Users</h3>
        <ion-card *ngFor="let user of users">
            <ion-card-content>
                <ion-label>Name : {{user.name}}</ion-label>
                <ion-label>Age : {{user.age}}</ion-label>
                <button ion-button color="danger"
                (click)="removeUser(user)">Delete User</button>
            </ion-card-content>
        </ion-card>
    </div>
</ion-content>
```

Next, we will start working with the logic. Update
`example12/src/pages/home/home.ts` as shown here

```typescript
import { Component } from '@angular/core';
import { NavController } from 'ionic-angular';
import { Storage } from '@ionic/storage';

@Component({
  selector: 'page-home',
  templateUrl: 'home.html'
})
export class HomePage {
  users: any[] = [];

  constructor(private navCtrl: NavController, private storage: Storage) {
    // get all the users from storage on load
    this.getUsers();
  }

  getUsers() {
    this.storage.ready().then(() => {
      this.storage.forEach((v, k, i) => {
        if (k.indexOf('user-') === 0) {
          this.users.push(v);
        }
      });
    });
  }

  addUser(name, age) {
```

```
      this.storage.ready().then(() => {
        let user = {
          id: this.genRandomId(),
          name: name.value,
          age: age.value
        };
        // save it to the storage
        this.storage.set('user-' + user.id, user);
        // update the inmemory variable to refresh the UI
        this.users.push(user);
        // reset the form
        name.value = '';
        age.value = '';
      });
    }

    removeUser(user) {
      this.storage.ready().then(() => {
        // remove from storage
        this.storage.remove('user-' + user.id);
        // update the inmemory variable to refresh the UI
        this.users.splice(this.users.indexOf(user), 1);
      });
    }

    genRandomId() {
      return Math.floor(Math.random() * 9999); // up to 4 digits random
  number
    }

  }
```

In the preceding code, first we have imported the `Storage` from `@ionic/storage`. Next, we have instantiated the same in the constructor.

We have created a class variable named `users` that will be used to store all the users we are creating in memory. Inside the constructor, we are invoking `getUsers()` to fetch the users from the storage on load. We have created two functions, `addUser()` and `removeUser()`, to add a user and remove a user.

Since the storage is a key value store, we are creating the keys of the user we are storing using the ID of the user. For instance, if the ID of the user is 1, we create the key as `user-1`. This way, we know that all keys in the storage belonging to our app start with *user*, in case there are other entities using Storage in the same app.

We are using `genRandomId()` to generate a random number between 1 and 9,999.

If we save all the files, go back to the browser, and open the console, we should see something like the following:

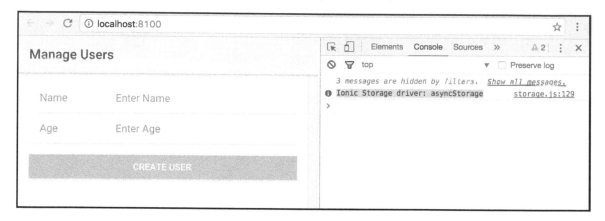

Do notice the message in the console. This message shows us the data will be stored in **asynStorage**. So, in Chrome, it would be IndexedDB.

So, in Chrome, if we click on the **Applications** tab in the development tools and navigate to IndexedDB, we should see something like the following:

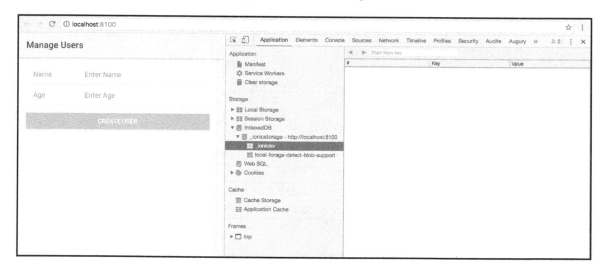

Now, let us add a user using the form. And the updated screen and storage should look like the following:

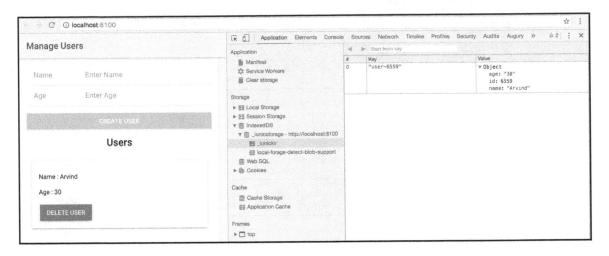

Now, on clicking on delete, we should see the storage cleared and the UI updated without any users.

So, using storage, we can easily start working with data persistence in our Ionic app, without worrying about the underlying implementation.

If needed, we can override `IonicStorageModule.forRoot()` as follows:

```
IonicStorageModule.forRoot({
  name: 'appDB',
  driverOrder: ['indexeddb', 'sqlite', 'websql']
})
```

You can find more configurations and properties here: `https://ionicframework.com/docs /storage/`

With this, we complete the overview of Storage in Ionic.

Summary

In this chapter, we have gone through the two main decorators of Ionic. Then we have gone through the config and platform services and seen how we can customize the app based on the platform and configuration. After that, we have gone through the Storage API in Ionic. Refer to `Chapter 11`, *Ionic 3*, to take a look at the all new `IonicPage` directive and `IonicPage` module.

In the next chapter, we will be working with theming Ionic apps.

5
Ionic and SCSS

In this chapter, we will take a look at theming with Ionic. Theming in Ionic is simple and easy to implement. The Ionic team has taken great efforts in simplifying and modularizing theming in Ionic. In a nutshell, theming in Ionic happens at component level, as well as platform level (iOS, Android, and WP). Ionic uses SCSS to work with theming. We will be going through the following topics in this chapter:

- Sass versus SCSS
- Working with SCSS variables
- Platform-level and page/component-level overrides

What is Sass?

Quoting from the Sass documentation:

> *"Sass is an extension of CSS that adds power and elegance to the basic language."*

It allows us to use variables, nested rules, mixins, inline imports, and more, all with a fully CSS-compatible syntax. Sass helps keep large stylesheets well organized, and get small stylesheets up and running quickly.

In simpler terms, Sass makes CSS programmable. But the chapter is titled SCSS; why are we talking about Sass? Well, Sass and SCSS are pretty much the same CSS preprocessor, each with its own way of writing the pre-CSS syntax.

SCSS was developed as part of another preprocessor named HAML (`http://haml.info/`) by Ruby developers, so it inherited a lot of syntax style from Ruby, such as indentation, no braces, and no semicolons.

A sample Sass file would look like this:

```
// app.sass

brand-primary= blue

.container
    color= !brand-primary
    margin= 0px auto
    padding= 20px

=border-radius(!radius)
    -webkit-border-radius= !radius
    -moz-border-radius= !radius
    border-radius= !radius


*

    +border-radius(0px)
```

When ran through the Sass compiler, it would return the following code:

```
.container {
  color: blue;
  margin: 0px auto;
  padding: 20px;
}

* {
  -webkit-border-radius: 0px;
  -moz-border-radius: 0px;
  border-radius: 0px;
}
```

Good old CSS. But did you notice that `brand-primary` acting as a variable, substituting its value inside the container class? And the `border-radius` acting as a function (also called a mixin), generating the required CSS rules when called with an argument? Yes, the missing piece in CSS programming. You can try out the preceding conversion: `http://sasstocss.appspot.com/` and check out how Sass gets compiled to CSS.

People who are used to the bracket-based coding languages find this way of writing code a bit difficult. So, enter SCSS.

Sass stands for **Syntactically Awesome Style Sheets** and SCSS stands for **Sassy CSS**. So SCSS is pretty much the same as Sass, except for the CSS-like syntax. The preceding Sass code, would look like this when written in SCSS:

```scss
$brand-primary: blue;

.container{
    color: !brand-primary;
    margin: 0px auto;
    padding: 20px;
}

@mixin border-radius($radius) {
    -webkit-border-radius: $radius;
    -moz-border-radius: $radius;
    border-radius: $radius;
}

* {
    @include border-radius(5px);
}
```

This looks a lot closer to CSS itself, right? And it is expressive. And Ionic uses SCSS to style its components.

If you want to know more about SCSS versus Sass, you can look at:
`http://thesassway.com/editorial/sass-vs-scss-which-syntax-is-better`.

Now that we have a basic understanding of what SCSS and Sass are and how to use them, we will leverage them in our Ionic app to maintain and theme our components.

Ionic and SCSS

By default, Ionic is packed with SCSS. Unlike the earlier version, where one had to set up SCSS in a project, in Ionic 2 the theming has become more modular and simpler. There are two levels at which theming can happen:

- At the platform level
- At the page/component level

App-level theming is almost always what we need. We would change the colors of our app based on our brand, and since Ionic uses a SCSS map, the colors are inherited directly by the components. Also, we can add, rename, and remove colors as needed. The primary color is the only required color in the map. iOS, MD, and WP colors can be further customized if colors are different per mode.

Page/component-level theming is very helpful if we would like to keep our styles isolated and specific to those pages/components.

This is one of the biggest advantages of the component-based approach to app development. We can keep our components modular and manageable, and at the same time keep the styles and functionality from leaking from one to another, unless intended.

To get the hang of theming in Ionic, we will scaffold a new tabs app and theme the same. Create a new folder if needed, named `chapter5`, and then open a new command prompt/terminal. Run the following:

```
ionic start -a "Example 13" -i app.example.thirteen example13 tabs
--v2
```

Once the app is scaffolded, run `ionic serve` to view the app in the browser. The first thing we are going to work with is the colors. Open `example13/src/theme/variables.scss` and we should see a variable map named `$colors`.

To quickly test the color scheme, change the value of the primary variable inside the `$colors` map from `#387ef5` to `red`. We should see the following:

As mentioned earlier, primary is the only mandatory value.

The colors map can be extended to add our own colors as well. For instance, on `example13/src/pages/home/home.html`, let us add a button with an attribute name `purple`, which would look something like this:

```
<ion-content padding>
    <button ion-button color="purple">A Purple Button</button>
</ion-content>
```

Inside the `$colors` map, add a new key value: `purple: #663399`. The complete map would look like this:

```
$colors: (
   primary:     red,
   secondary:   #32db64,
   danger:      #f53d3d,
   light:       #f4f4f4,
   dark:        #222,
   purple:      #663399
);
```

Now, if we go back to the page, we should see the following:

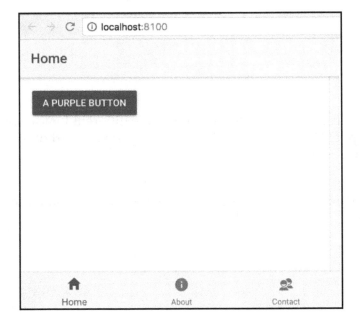

It is indeed that simple to add new colors to our app.

We can further customize the theme colors by adding in a base and a contrast property. The base will be the background of the element and the contrast will be the text color.
To test the preceding feature, open example13/src/pages/about/about.html and add a floating action button as mentioned in the following code:

```
<ion-content padding>
  <button ion-fab color="different">FAB</button>
</ion-content>
```

In the preceding snippet, we have added color=different to the FAB. We will be using this variable name to apply styles.

Our updated $colors map would be as follows:

```
$colors: (
  primary:     red,
  secondary:   #32db64,
  danger:      #f53d3d,
  light:       #f4f4f4,
  dark:        #222,
  purple:      #663399,
  different: (
    base: #4CAF50,
    contrast: #F44336
  )
);
```

Note: This will generate styles for all the different Ionic components. Do not put SCSS variables in the map if they are not part of the root component.

When we navigate to the **About** tab after saving all the files, we should see the following:

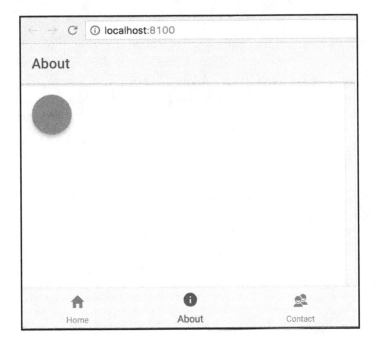

Isn't theming simple?

Page-level overrides

We can take the same theming to the next level by applying different styles to the same component in two different pages. For instance, we will make a label look different in the **About** page and the **Contact** page. This is how we will achieve it.

In `example13/src/pages/about/about.html`, we will add a new label inside the `ion-content` section, as shown in the following code:

```
<ion-content padding>
  <button ion-fab color="different">FAB</button>
  <label>This is a label that looks different from the one on Contact
Page</label>
</ion-content>
```

We will add the required styles in `example13/src/pages/about/about.scss`, as shown in the following code:

```
page-about {
    label {
        border: 2px solid #FF5722;
```

```
            background: #FF5722;
        }
    }
```

Similarly, we will add another label in `example13/src/pages/contact/contact.html` inside the `ion-content` section, as shown in the following code:

```
<ion-content>
    <label>This is a label that looks different from the one on About
Page</label>
</ion-content>
```

We will add the required styles inside `example13/src/pages/contact/contact.scss`, as shown in the following code:

```
page-contact {
    label {
        border: 2px solid #009688;
        background: #009688;
        margin: 20px;
        margin-top: 100px;
        display: block;
    }
}
```

Now, if we save all the files and go back to the **About** page in the browser, we should see the following:

And the **Contact** page will look like this:

As we can see from the preceding image, we are using page-level styling to differentiate between the two components. The preceding screenshot is a simple example of how we can have multiple styles for the same component in different pages.

Platform-level overrides

Now that we have seen how to apply styles at page level, let us see how Ionic theming makes it so simple to manage styles at platform level. Platform-level styles are applicable when the same app is viewed in multiple devices, which have their own distinct styles.

While working with Ionic, we define modes, where a mode is the platform in which the app is running. By default, Ionic adds a class name, which is the same as the mode on the ion-app element. For instance, if we are viewing the app on Android, the body will have a class named md, where md stands for **material design**.

To quickly check this out, we will open `http://localhost:8100/?ionicplatform=ios` and then inspect the body element in the developer tools. We should see the `ion-app` element with a class named `ios`, among other classes:

If we open `http://localhost:8100/?ionicplatform=android`, we should see the following:

And if we open `http://localhost:8100/?ionicplatform=windows`, we should see the following:

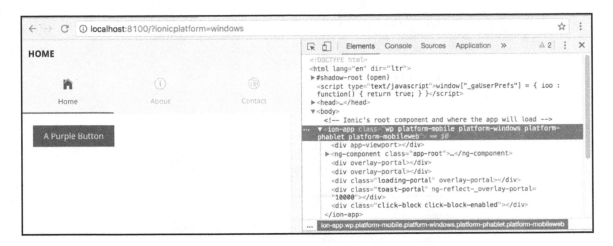

As of today, there are three modes in Ionic:

Platform	Mode	Description
iOS	ios	Applies iOS styling to all components
Android	md	Applies material design styling to all components
Windows	wp	Applies Windows styling to all components
Core	md	If we are not on one of the aforementioned devices, the app will get material design styling by default

Refer here for more information: `http://ionicframework.com/docs/theming/platform-specific-styles/`.

We will be defining platform-specific styles inside the `example13/src/theme/variables.scss` file in the sections provided by comments.

To understand platform-specific styles, we will be applying different background colors to the `navbar` and changing the text color.

Open `example13/src/theme/variables.scss` and add the following styles under the section that says `App Material Design Variables` in comments:

```
// App Material Design Variables
// --------------------------------------------------


// Material Design only Sass variables can go here
.md{
```

```
ion-navbar .toolbar-background {
    background: #FF5722;
}

ion-navbar .toolbar-title {
    color: #fff;
}
}
```

Now, when we save the file and navigate to
`http://localhost:8100/?ionicplatform=android`, we should see the following:

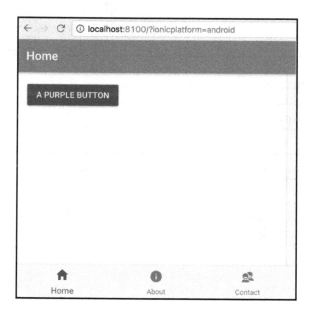

Do note the `.md` class, inside which the styles are nested. This is what makes the styles platform specific.

Similarly, we update the `App iOS Variables` section:

```
// App iOS Variables
// ---------------------------------------------------
// iOS only Sass variables can go here
.ios{
  ion-navbar .toolbar-background {
      background: #2196F3;
  }

  ion-navbar .toolbar-title {
      color: #fff;
```

```
      }
   }
```

Then we should see the following:

Finally, for Windows, we will update the `App Windows Variables`, section as mentioned in the following code:

```
// App Windows Variables
// ----------------------------------------------
// Windows only Sass variables can go here
.wp{
  ion-navbar .toolbar-background {
      background: #9C27B0;
  }

  ion-navbar .toolbar-title {
      color: #fff;
  }
}
```

We should see the following:

 We have already seen in Chapter 4, *Ionic Decorators and Services*, how we can change the mode of the app to either md, ios, or wp using the config properties.

We can also set the platform dynamically and apply styles.
To understand this, we will work with the badge component. Only on Windows platform, the badge component will not have any border radius, but we would like to override that behavior using dynamic attributes.

In our existing example13/src/pages/contact/contact.html, we will add the following snippet inside the ion-content section:

```
<ion-item>
        <ion-icon name="logo-dropbox" item-left></ion-icon>
        Files
        <ion-badge item-right [attr.round-badge]="isWindows ? '' :
null">175</ion-badge>
    </ion-item>
```

If we notice that on `ion-badge`, we have a conditional attribute `[attr.round-badge]="isWindows ? '' : null"`. If the platform is Windows, we will add a new attribute named `round-badge`, and we will update our `example13/src/pages/contact/contact.ts` as mentioned in the following code:

```
import { Component } from '@angular/core';
import { Platform } from 'ionic-angular';

@Component({
  selector: 'page-contact',
  templateUrl: 'contact.html'
})
export class ContactPage {
  isWindows: Boolean;

  constructor(public platform: Platform) {
    this.isWindows = platform.is('windows');
  }
}
```

We have defined the value for `isWindows` inside the constructor. Now, if we save all the files and navigate to `http://localhost:8100/?ionicplatform=windows`, we should see the following:

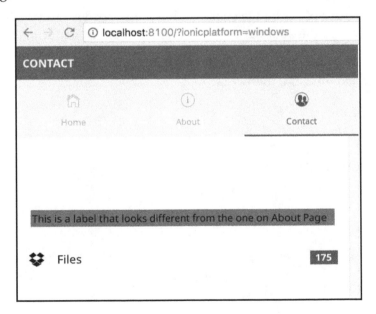

If we inspect the badge, we should see the attribute `round-badge` added:

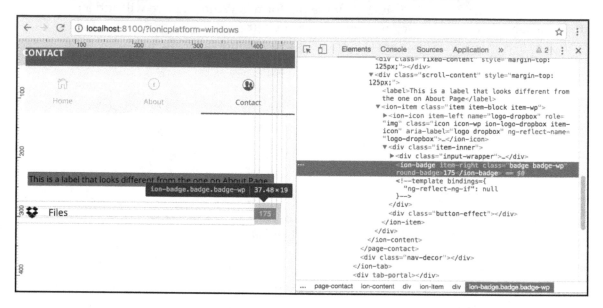

We can navigate to other platforms and validate the same.

If we observe, the border of the badge container has a `0px` border radius. Now we will add the required overrides to the `example13/src/theme/variables.scss` in the App Windows Variables section.

The snippet would look like the following:

```
.wp{
  // snipp

  ion-badge[round-badge]{
    border-radius: 12px;
  }
}
```

Now, even for the Windows platform, we can see the `border-radius` being applied:

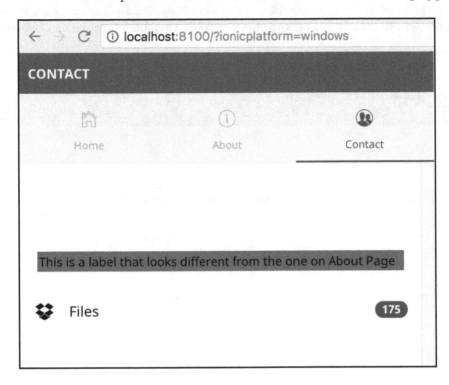

This is another way we can achieve platform-specific overrides.

Component-level overrides

Whatever customizations we have seen so far are mostly at the page and platform level. What if we want to customize the components that are provided by Ionic to match our brand's look and feel?

This can also be achieved quite easily thanks to the Ionic team, who have gone the extra mile in exposing the variable names to customize the properties.

If we navigate to
`http://ionicframework.com/docs/theming/overriding-ionic-variables/`, we will see a
filterable table where we can find component-specific variables that we can override:

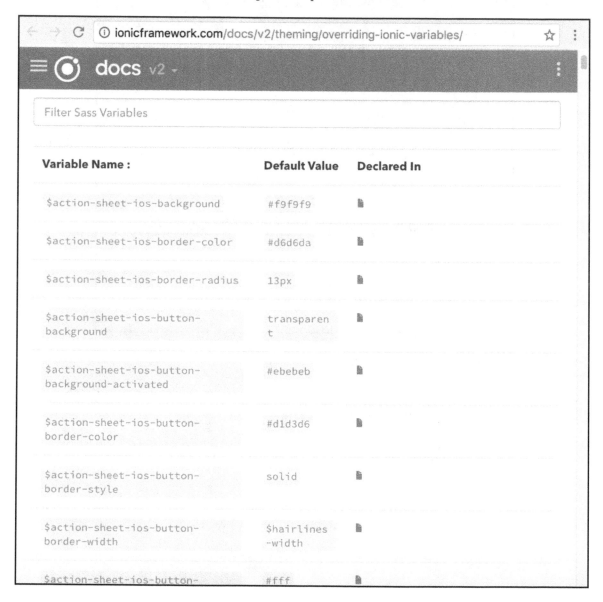

Theme a sample component

To quickly check this out, we will implement the overlay loading bar on the home page of our current app. When a user lands on this tab, we will programmatically trigger the loading popup, and depending on the platform, we will customize the look and feel of the component to show that components can be customized as we please.

Update `example13/src/pages/home/home.ts` as mentioned in the following code:

```
import { Component } from '@angular/core';
import { LoadingController } from 'ionic-angular';

@Component({
  selector: 'page-home',
  templateUrl: 'home.html'
})
export class HomePage {

  constructor(public loadingCtrl: LoadingController) {
    this.presentLoading();
  }

  presentLoading() {
    let loader = this.loadingCtrl.create({
      content: "Please wait...",
      duration: 3000
    });
    loader.present();
  }
}
```

We have defined a function named `presentLoading` and invoked it inside the constructor. This will show the loading bar on page load.

If we save this page and navigate to the three different platforms, we will see styles specific to that particular platform. In this example, we are going to make all the loading bars look (almost) alike, irrespective of the platform. We are going to achieve the same by messing with the SCSS variables.

If we navigate to `http://ionicframework.com/docs/theming/overriding-ionic-variables/` and filter `loading-ios`, we will see a bunch of SCSS variables that are related to the loading popup styling. Similarly, if we search for `loading-md`, we will find SCSS variables related to Android. Finally, if we search for `loading-wp`, we find SCSS variables for the Windows platform.

We will use the preceding variable names and customize the look and feel. Open example13/src/theme/variables.scss. After @import 'ionic.globals'; is defined and before the colors map is defined, we will add the component-level overrides. If you are looking at the commented SCSS file, you will see a section named Shared Variables. This is where we add our variable overrides.

We have taken a few SCSS variables and modified their properties for each platform, as shown in the following code:

```scss
// Overriding Loading Popup for iOS
// >> Start
$loading-ios-background: #2196F3;
$loading-ios-border-radius: 0px;
$loading-ios-text-color: #fff;
$loading-ios-spinner-color: #eee;
// >> End

// Overriding Loading Popup for Android
// >> Start
$loading-md-background: #2196F3;
$loading-md-border-radius: 0px;
$loading-md-text-color: #fff;
$loading-md-spinner-color: #eee;
// >> End

// Overriding Loading Popup for Windows
// >> Start
$loading-wp-background: #2196F3;
$loading-wp-border-radius: 0px;
$loading-wp-text-color: #fff;
$loading-wp-spinner-color: #eee;
// >> End
```

Now, if we navigate to `http://localhost:8100/?ionicplatform=ios`, we should see the following:

If we navigate to `http://localhost:8100/?ionicplatform=android`, we should see the following:

And finally, if we navigate to `http://localhost:8100/?ionicplatform=windows`, we should see the following:

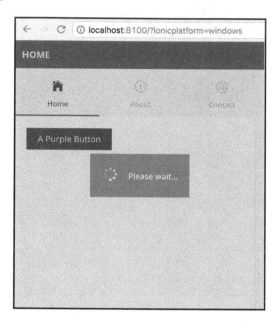

We can add custom CSS as well, to make all three of them look alike.

With this, we complete our overview of theming Ionic apps at platform level and page/component-level.

Summary

In this chapter, we have seen how to theme Ionic apps. We have also seen how we can easily implement styling at platform level and page/component-level.

In the next chapter, we will be looking at Ionic Native. Ionic Native is what ngCordova is to Ionic 1. We will dig deeper into integrating device features with an Ionic app.

6
Ionic Native

In this chapter, we are going to look at integrating device-specific features, such as network, battery status, camera, and so on into an Ionic app. To start exploring this, we will first look at Cordova plugins, and then work with Ionic Native.

In this chapter, we will take a look at:

- Setting up a platform-specific SDK
- Working with the Cordova plugin API
- Working with Ionic Native
- Testing a few Ionic Native plugins

Setting up a platform-specific SDK

Before we start interacting with the device-specific features, we need to have the SDK for that device's operating system set up on our local machine. Officially, Ionic supports iOS, Android, and Windows phone platforms. Nevertheless, Ionic can be used on any device, which can run HTML, CSS, and JavaScript.

The following are links on how to set up a mobile SDK on our local machine. Unfortunately, we cannot proceed further in this chapter (and book) without setting that up. Let's look at the following links:

- **Android**:
  `https://cordova.apache.org/docs/en/latest/guide/platforms/android/`
- **iOS**: `https://cordova.apache.org/docs/en/6.x/guide/platforms/ios/`
- **Windows**: `https://cordova.apache.org/docs/en/6.x/guide/platforms/wp8/`

 Note: For other supported OS, you can check out
`https://cordova.apache.org/docs/en/6.x/guide/overview/`.

In this book, we will work with Android and iOS only. You can follow a similar approach for other mobile platforms as well. Before we proceed further, we need to make sure the setup is completed, and is working as expected.

The Android setup

Make sure you have the SDK installed and Android tools are in your path:

- From anywhere on your machine in a command prompt/terminal, run: `android`. This will launch the Android SDK manager. Make sure that you have the latest version of Android, or any specific version you are targeting installed.
- Run the following command:

```
android avd
```

- This will launch the Android Virtual Device manager. Make sure you have at least one AVD set up. If this isn't yet the case, you can easily do so by clicking on the **Create** button. You can fill the options as follows:

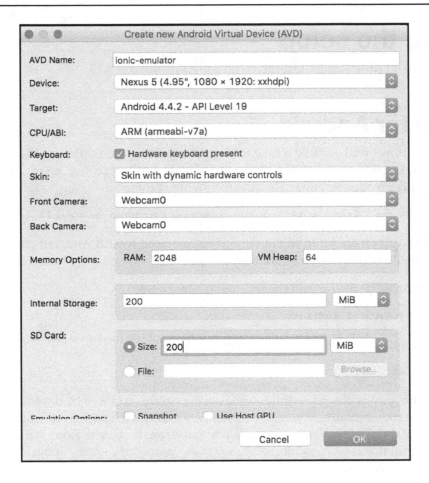

The iOS setup

Make sure you have Xcode and the required tools installed, and also have `ios-sim` and `ios-deploy` installed globally:

```
npm install -g ios-sim
npm install -g ios-deploy
```

 iOS setup can be done only on an Apple machine. Windows developers cannot deploy iOS apps from Windows machines, as Xcode is required to do so.

Testing the setup

Let's take a look at how we can test the setup for Android and iOS.

Testing for Android

To test the setup, we will scaffold a new Ionic app, and emulate that using the Android and iOS emulators. We will first scaffold a tabs app. Create a folder named `chapter6` and open a new command prompt/terminal. Run the following command:

```
ionic start -a "Example 14" -i app.example.fourteen example14 tabs --v2
```

To emulate the app on an Android emulator, first we need to add Android platform support for this project and then emulate it:

To add the Android platform, run the following command:

```
ionic platform add android
```

Once that is done, run the following command:

```
ionic emulate android
```

After some time, you will see the emulator launch, and the app will be deployed and executed inside the emulator. If you have already worked with native Android apps, you know how slow the Android emulator is. If you have not, it is quite slow. An alternative to the Android emulator is Genymotion (`https://www.genymotion.com`). Ionic is nicely integrated with Genymotion as well.

Genymotion has two flavors, one free and the other for commercial use. The free version has minimal features and is supposed to be for personal use only.

 You can download a copy of Genymotion from:
`https://www.genymotion.com/#!/store`.

Once you have installed Genymotion, create a new virtual device with your preferred Android SDK. My config looks like this:

Next, we launch the emulator and let it run in the background. Now that we have Genymotion running, we need to tell Ionic to emulate the app using Genymotion and not the Android emulator. For that we use the following command:

```
ionic run android
```

Instead of this: `ionic emulate android`.

This will deploy the app to the Genymotion emulator and you can see the app immediately, unlike with the Android emulator:

Make sure Genymotion is running in the background before you run the app.

If Genymotion seems a bit large for your pocket, you can simply connect your Android mobile phone to your machine and run this:

```
ionic run android
```

This will deploy the app to the actual device.

To set up Android USB debugging, please refer to:
`https://developer.android.com/studio/run/device.html`.

The earlier screenshots of Genymotion are taken from a personal edition, as I do not have a license for it. I generally use the iOS emulator in tandem with my Android mobile phone during the development phase. Once the entire development is completed, I purchase device time from device farms, and test on the targeted devices.

If you are facing an issue while connecting your Android mobile phone to your computer, please check if you are able to run `adb device` in the command prompt/terminal and are able to see your device listed here. You can find more information on **Android Debug Bridge (ADB)** at: `https://developer.android.com/studio/command-line/adb.html`.

Testing for iOS

To test for iOS, we will first add iOS platform support as we did for Android, and then emulate it.

Run the following command:

```
ionic platform add ios
```

Then, run this: `ionic emulate ios`.

You should see the default emulator launch and, finally, the app will appear in the emulator as shown in the following screenshot:

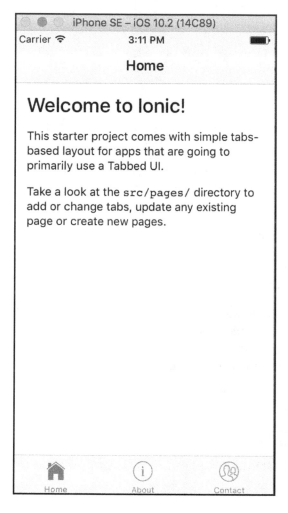

To deploy onto an Apple device, you can run the following command:

```
ionic run ios
```

Make sure you are able to emulate/run the app before moving further.

Getting started with Cordova plugins

According to the Cordova documentation:

> *"A plugin is a package of injected code that allows the Cordova WebView within which the app renders to communicate with the native platform on which it runs. Plugins provide access to device and platform functionality that is ordinarily unavailable to web-based apps. All the main Cordova API features are implemented as plugins, and many others are available that enable features such as bar code scanners, NFC communication, or to tailor calendar interfaces..."*

In other words, Cordova plugins are windows to the device-specific features. The Cordova team has already built the needed plugins to work with almost all device-specific features. There are community-contributed plugins as well that can provide customization wrappers around device-specific features.

 You can search for existing plugins here:
`https://cordova.apache.org/plugins/`.

During the course of this chapter, we will be exploring a few plugins. Since we are focusing on Ionic-specific development, we will add plugins using the Ionic CLI. Under the hood, Ionic CLI calls the Cordova CLI to execute the necessary actions.

The Ionic plugin API

There are four main commands that we will be using while dealing with plugins.

Add a plugin

This CLI command is used to add a new plugin to the project:

```
ionic plugin add org.apache.cordova.camera
```

Also, you can use this:

```
ionic plugin add cordova-plugin-camera
```

Remove a plugin

This CLI command is used to remove a plugin from the project:

```
ionic plugin rm org.apache.cordova.camera
```

Also, you can use this:

```
ionic plugin rm cordova-plugin-camera
```

List added plugins

This CLI command is used to list all the plugins in the project, for example:

```
ionic plugin ls
```

Search plugins

This CLI command is used to search plugins from the command line, for example:

```
ionic plugin search scanner barcode
```

Ionic Native

Now that we have the lay of the land on how to work with Cordova plugins, we will scaffold a new project and work with integrating Cordova plugins with our Ionic app.

Ionic provides us a simple wrapper to work with Cordova plugins in a TypeScript fashion. Until all the plugins adopt the ES6/TS approach, we will need a way to work with these plugins inside our Ionic app.

Enter Ionic Native. Ionic Native is an ES6/TypeScript implementation of today's ES5 Cordova plugins, so you can import the plugins you need and use them in TypeScript. The Ionic team has done a great job in making the plugins available to us in the form of TypeScript bindings.

Ionic Native test drive

To test, we will scaffold a new project and execute the following commands:

1. Run the following command:

    ```
    ionic start -a "Example 15" -i app.example.fifteen
    example15 blank --v2
    ```

    And `cd` into the `example15` folder.

2. Let's search for the battery status plugin and add it to our project. Run the following command:

    ```
    ionic plugin search battery status
    ```

3. This will launch the default browser and will navigate you to: `http://cordova.apache.org/plugins/?q=battery%20status`. Depending on what plugin name you find, you can add that plugin to the project. So, in our case, to add the battery status plugin to the project, we would run this:

    ```
    ionic plugin add cordova-plugin-battery-status.
    ```

    This will add the battery status plugin (`https://github.com/apache/cordova-plugin-battery-status`) to our current project. The same can be found from the Ionic Native's documentation here: `https://ionicframework.com/docs/native/battery-status/`.

To view all the plugins that were installed, run the following command:

```
ionic plugin ls
```

Then, you should see the following screenshot:

```
[→  example15 ionic plugin ls
cordova-plugin-battery-status 1.2.3 "Battery"
cordova-plugin-console 1.0.5 "Console"
cordova-plugin-device 1.1.4 "Device"
cordova-plugin-splashscreen 4.0.2 "Splashscreen"
cordova-plugin-statusbar 2.2.1 "StatusBar"
cordova-plugin-whitelist 1.3.1 "Whitelist"
ionic-plugin-keyboard 2.2.1 "Keyboard"
```

Apart from adding the Cordova plugin, we need to add the required Ionic Native module for battery status. Run the following command:

```
npm install --save @ionic-native/battery-status
```

After adding the module, we need to mark it as a provider in
`example15/src/app/app.module.ts`. Open `example15/src/app/app.module.ts` and
update it as shown:

```
import { NgModule, ErrorHandler } from '@angular/core';
import { IonicApp, IonicModule, IonicErrorHandler } from 'ionic-angular';
import { MyApp } from './app.component';
import { HomePage } from '../pages/home/home';

import { StatusBar } from '@ionic-native/status-bar';
import { SplashScreen } from '@ionic-native/splash-screen';
import { BatteryStatus } from '@ionic-native/battery-status';

@NgModule({
  declarations: [
    MyApp,
    HomePage
  ],
  imports: [
    IonicModule.forRoot(MyApp)
  ],
  bootstrap: [IonicApp],
  entryComponents: [
    MyApp,
    HomePage
  ],
  providers: [
    StatusBar,
    SplashScreen,
    BatteryStatus,
    {provide: ErrorHandler, useClass: IonicErrorHandler}
  ]
})
export class AppModule {}
```

Now, we can start consuming the battery status plugin. Open
`example15/src/pages/home/home.ts` and update it with the following code:

```
import { Component } from '@angular/core';
import { BatteryStatus } from 'ionic-native';
import { Platform } from 'ionic-angular';

@Component({
  selector: 'page-home',
  templateUrl: 'home.html'
})
export class HomePage {
  level: Number;
```

```
    isPlugged: Boolean;

    constructor(platform: Platform) {
      platform.ready().then(() => {
        BatteryStatus.onChange().subscribe(
          (status) => {
            this.level = status.level;
            this.isPlugged = status.isPlugged;
          }
        );
      });
    }
}
```

This is how Ionic Native exposes `BatteryStatus`.

Next, update the `ion-content` section of `example15/src/pages/home/home.html` as shown:

```
<ion-header>
    <ion-navbar>
        <ion-title>
            Battery Status
        </ion-title>
    </ion-navbar>
</ion-header>
<ion-content padding>
    <h2>level : {{level}}</h2>
    <h2>isPluggedIn : {{isPlugged}}</h2>
</ion-content>
```

Now run the following command:

```
ionic serve
```

You will not see any output on the page and, if you open the development tools, you will see a warning in the console that says:

```
Native: tried calling StatusBar.styleDefault, but Cordova is not
available.
Make sure to include cordova.js or run in a device/simulator
```

This means that we cannot run the plugins directly in the browser; they need an environment to execute such as Android, iOS, or Windows.

To test the app (and plugin), we will add either an Android platform or an iOS platform:

```
ionic platform add android
```

You can also use the following command:

```
ionic platform add ios
```

Then execute any one of the following commands:

- ionic emulate android
- ionic emulate ios
- ionic run android
- ionic run ios

Running any one of the preceding command would display the following output:

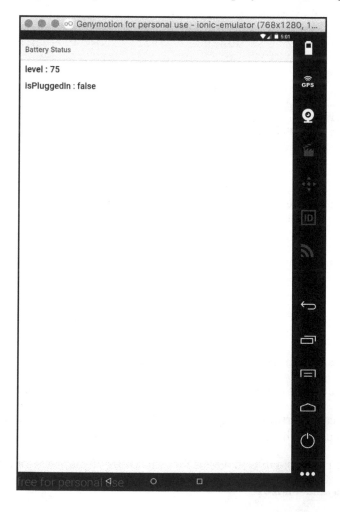

Now you know how to add Cordova plugins to your Ionic app and test them. In the next section, we will be working with a few more plugins. The preceding screenshots from Genymotion are from my personal use license. These images are for illustration purposes only.

The Cordova whitelist plugin

Before we go ahead and start working with Ionic Native, we are going to spend a moment on one of the key Cordova plugins -- the whitelist plugin: `https://github.com/apache/cordova-plugin-whitelist`.

From the Cordova documentation on the whitelist plugin:

> *"Domain whitelisting is a security model that controls access to external domains over which your application has no control. Cordova provides a configurable security policy to define which external sites may be accessed."*

So, if we want to have more control over how our app should behave when dealing with content from other sources, we should be working with the whitelist plugin. As you may have noticed, this plugin is already added to our Ionic app. If this plugin is not added to the Ionic/Cordova app, you can do so easily by running:

```
ionic plugin add https://github.com/apache/cordova-plugin-
whitelist.git
```

Once the plugin is added, you can update the `config.xml` file with the navigation whitelist -- the links that your app is allowed to open inside WebView to allow links to `example.com`.

You will be adding the following code:

```
<allow-navigation href="http://example.com/*" />
```

If you want your WebView to link to any website, you need to add this:

```
<allow-navigation href="http://*/*" />
<allow-navigation href="https://*/*" />
<allow-navigation href="data:*" />
```

You can also add an Intent whitelist, where you can specify the list of links that are allowed to be browsed on the device. For instance, open the SMS app from our custom app:

```
<allow-intent href="sms:*" />
```

Or simple web pages:

```
<allow-intent href="https://*/*" />
```

You can also enforce a **Content Security Policy (CSP)** (http://content-securitypolicy.com/) on your app as well using this plugin. All you need to do is add a meta tag to the www/index.html file, as follows:

```
<!-- Allow XHRs via https only -->
<meta http-equiv="Content-Security-Policy" content="default-src 'self'
https:">
```

This was a quick tour of the Whitelist plugin. This plugin is applicable to:

- Android 4.0.0 or above
- iOS 4.0.0 or above

 Do remember to add this plugin and configure it; otherwise, external links will not work.

Working with Cordova plugins using Ionic Native

In the earlier example, we have already seen how we can integrate a device feature such as battery status with our Ionic app. Now, we are going to explore a few more such plugins and see how we can implement them.

Device

The first plugin we are going to look at in this section is the device plugin. This plugin describes the device's hardware and software specifications.

You can know more about this plugin here:
`https://github.com/apache/cordova-plugin-device` or
`https://ionicframework.com/docs/native/device/`.

Let us scaffold a new blank app and then add the device plugin to it:

```
ionic start -a "Example 16" -i app.example.sixteen example16 blank --v2
```

Once the app is scaffolded, `cd` into the `example16` folder. Now we will add the device plugin, run the following command:

```
ionic plugin add cordova-plugin-device
```

This will add the device plugin. Once that is done, we will add the Ionic native device module. Run the following command:

```
npm install --save @ionic-native/device
```

Once the module is added, we need to mark it as a provider in `example16/src/app/app.module.ts`. Update `example16/src/app/app.module.ts` as shown:

```
import { NgModule, ErrorHandler } from '@angular/core';
import { IonicApp, IonicModule, IonicErrorHandler } from 'ionic-angular';
import { MyApp } from './app.component';
import { HomePage } from '../pages/home/home';

import { StatusBar } from '@ionic-native/status-bar';
import { SplashScreen } from '@ionic-native/splash-screen';
import { Device } from '@ionic-native/device';

@NgModule({
  declarations: [
    MyApp,
    HomePage
  ],
  imports: [
    IonicModule.forRoot(MyApp)
  ],
  bootstrap: [IonicApp],
  entryComponents: [
    MyApp,
    HomePage
  ],
  providers: [
    StatusBar,
    SplashScreen,
```

```
    Device,
    { provide: ErrorHandler, useClass: IonicErrorHandler }
  ]
})
export class AppModule { }
```

Next, we will add either the iOS or the Android platform by running `ionic platform add ios` or `ionic platform add android`.

Now, we will add the code relevant to the device plugin. Open `example16/src/pages/home/home.ts` and update the class as follows:

```
import { Component } from '@angular/core';
import { Device } from '@ionic-native/device';
import { Platform } from 'ionic-angular';

@Component({
  selector: 'page-home',
  templateUrl: 'home.html'
})
export class HomePage {
  cordova: String;
  model: String;
  devicePlatform: String;
  uuid: String;
  version: String;
  manufacturer: String;
  isVirtual: Boolean;
  serial: String;

  constructor(private platform: Platform,
    private device: Device) {
    platform.ready().then(() => {
      let device = this.device;
      this.cordova = device.cordova;
      this.model = device.model;
      this.devicePlatform = device.platform;
      this.uuid = device.uuid;
      this.version = device.version;
      this.manufacturer = device.manufacturer;
      this.isVirtual = device.isVirtual;
      this.serial = device.serial;
    });
  }
}
```

Next, update example16/src/pages/home/home.html as shown:

```
<ion-header>
  <ion-navbar>
    <ion-title>
      Ionic Blank
    </ion-title>
  </ion-navbar>
</ion-header>

<ion-content padding>
  <table>
    <tr>
      <td>cordova</td>
      <td>{{cordova}}</td>
    </tr>
    <tr>
      <td>model</td>
      <td>{{model}}</td>
    </tr>
    <tr>
      <td>platform</td>
      <td>{{platform}}</td>
    </tr>
    <tr>
      <td>uuid</td>
      <td>{{uuid}}</td>
    </tr>
    <tr>
      <td>version</td>
      <td>{{version}}</td>
    </tr>
    <tr>
      <td>manufacturer</td>
      <td>{{manufacturer}}</td>
    </tr>
    <tr>
      <td>isVirtual</td>
      <td>{{isVirtual}}</td>
    </tr>
    <tr>
      <td>serial</td>
      <td>{{serial}}</td>
    </tr>
  </table>
</ion-content>
```

Save all the files and, finally, run `ionic emulate ios` or `ionic emulate android`. We should see the following output:

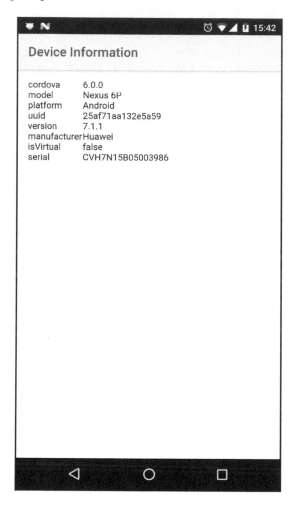

As you can see from the preceding screenshot, the device is a Nexus 6P.

Toast

The next plugin we are going to work with is the Toast plugin. This plugin shows text popups that do not block the user's interaction with the app.

You can learn more about this plugin here:
`https://github.com/EddyVerbruggen/Toast-PhoneGap-Plugin` or
`https://ionicframework.com/docs/native/toast/`.

We will scaffold a new blank app using the following command:

```
ionic start -a "Example 17" -i
app.example.seventeen example17 blank --v2
```

Once the app is scaffolded, `cd` into the `example17` folder. Now we will add the Toast plugin, run:

```
ionic plugin add cordova-plugin-x-toast
```

Then we will add the Ionic Native Toast module:

```
npm install --save @ionic-native/toast
```

Next, we will add Toast as a provider in `example17/src/app/app.module.ts`. Update `example17/src/app/app.module.ts` as shown:

```
import { NgModule, ErrorHandler } from '@angular/core';
import { IonicApp, IonicModule, IonicErrorHandler } from 'ionic-angular';
import { MyApp } from './app.component';
import { HomePage } from '../pages/home/home';

import { StatusBar } from '@ionic-native/status-bar';
import { SplashScreen } from '@ionic-native/splash-screen';
import { Toast } from '@ionic-native/toast';

@NgModule({
  declarations: [
    MyApp,
    HomePage
  ],
  imports: [
    IonicModule.forRoot(MyApp)
  ],
  bootstrap: [IonicApp],
  entryComponents: [
    MyApp,
    HomePage
  ],
  providers: [
    StatusBar,
    SplashScreen,
    Toast,
    {provide: ErrorHandler, useClass: IonicErrorHandler}
```

```
    ]
  })
export class AppModule {}
```

Once that is done, add either the iOS or the Android platform by running:

```
ionic platform add ios
```

Or:

```
ionic platform add android
```

Now, we will add the code relevant to the Toast plugin. Open
example17/src/pages/home/home.ts and update as the file shown:

```
import { Component } from '@angular/core';
import { Toast } from '@ionic-native/toast';
import { Platform } from 'ionic-angular';

@Component({
  selector: 'page-home',
  templateUrl: 'home.html'
})
export class HomePage {

  constructor(private platform: Platform, private toast: Toast) {
    platform.ready().then(() => {
      toast.show("I'm a toast", '5000', 'center').subscribe(
        (toast) => {
          console.log(toast);
        }
      );
    });
  }

}
```

Save all the files and run:

```
ionic emulate ios or ionic emulate android
```

And you should see the following output:

To know more about the Toast plugin API methods, refer to:
`http://ionicframework.com/docs/native/toast/`.

Dialogs

The next plugin we are going to work with is the dialogs plugin. This triggers the alert, confirm, and prompt windows.

You can learn more about the plugin from here:
`https://github.com/apache/cordova-plugin-dialogs` and
`https://ionicframework.com/docs/native/dialogs/`.

First, scaffold a new blank app for the dialogs plugin:

```
ionic start -a "Example 18" -i app.example.eightteen example18 blank --v2
```

Once the app is scaffolded, `cd` into the `example18` folder. Now we will add the dialogs plugin, run:

```
ionic plugin add cordova-plugin-dialogs
```

After that, we will add the Ionic Native module for dialogs. Run the following command:

```
npm install --save @ionic-native/dialogs
```

Next, add Dialogs as a provider. Update `example18/src/app/app.module.ts` as mentioned:

```
import { NgModule, ErrorHandler } from '@angular/core';
import { IonicApp, IonicModule, IonicErrorHandler } from 'ionic-angular';
import { MyApp } from './app.component';
import { HomePage } from '../pages/home/home';

import { StatusBar } from '@ionic-native/status-bar';
import { SplashScreen } from '@ionic-native/splash-screen';
import { Dialogs } from '@ionic-native/dialogs';

@NgModule({
  declarations: [
    MyApp,
    HomePage
  ],
  imports: [
    IonicModule.forRoot(MyApp)
  ],
  bootstrap: [IonicApp],
  entryComponents: [
    MyApp,
    HomePage
  ],
```

```
  providers: [
    StatusBar,
    SplashScreen,
    Dialogs,
    {provide: ErrorHandler, useClass: IonicErrorHandler}
  ]
})
export class AppModule {}
```

Once that is done, add either the iOS or the Android platform by running:

```
ionic platform add ios
```

Or:

```
ionic platform add android
```

Now, we will add the code relevant to the Dialog plugin. Open example18/src/pages/home/home.ts and update as the file with the code mentioned:

```
import { Component } from '@angular/core';
import { Dialogs } from '@ionic-native/dialogs';
import { Platform } from 'ionic-angular';

@Component({
  selector: 'page-home',
  templateUrl: 'home.html'
})
export class HomePage {
  name: String;

  constructor(private dialogs: Dialogs, private platform: Platform) {
    platform.ready().then(() => {
      dialogs
        .prompt('Name Please?', 'Identity', ['Cancel', 'Ok'], 'John
        McClane')
        .then((result) => {
          if (result.buttonIndex == 2) {
            this.name = result.input1;
          }
        });
    });
  }
}
```

Next, we will update `example18/src/pages/home/home.html` as shown:

```
<ion-header>
    <ion-navbar>
        <ion-title>
            Reveal Your Identity
        </ion-title>
    </ion-navbar>
</ion-header>
<ion-content padding>
    Hello {{name}}!!
</ion-content>
```

Save all the files and, finally, run the following command:

ionic emulate ios or ionic emulate android

We should see the following output:

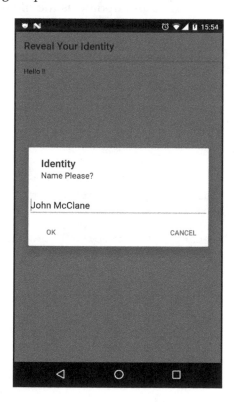

To learn more about the dialogs plugin API methods, refer to:
`https://ionicframework.com/docs/native/dialogs/`.

Local notifications

The next plugin we are going to work with is the local notification plugin. This plugin is primarily used to notify or remind users about an activity related to an app. Sometimes, notifications are also shown when a background activity is going on such as, a large file upload.

You can learn more about the plugin from here: `https://github.com/katzer/cordova-plugin-local-notifications` and `https://ionicframework.com/docs/native/local-notifications/`.

First, scaffold a new blank app for the local notification plugin:

```
ionic start -a "Example 19" -i
app.example.nineteen example19 blank --v2
```

Once the app is scaffolded, `cd` into the `example19` folder. Now, we will add the local notification plugin, run the following command:

```
ionic plugin add de.appplant.cordova.plugin.local-notification
```

Next, add the Ionic Native module:

```
npm install --save @ionic-native/local-notifications
```

And update the providers in `example19/src/app/app.module.ts`:

```
import { NgModule, ErrorHandler } from '@angular/core';
import { IonicApp, IonicModule, IonicErrorHandler } from 'ionic-angular';
import { MyApp } from './app.component';
import { HomePage } from '../pages/home/home';

import { StatusBar } from '@ionic-native/status-bar';
import { SplashScreen } from '@ionic-native/splash-screen';
import { LocalNotifications } from '@ionic-native/local-notifications';

@NgModule({
  declarations: [
    MyApp,
    HomePage
  ],
  imports: [
    IonicModule.forRoot(MyApp)
  ],
  bootstrap: [IonicApp],
  entryComponents: [
    MyApp,
```

```
      HomePage
    ],
    providers: [
      StatusBar,
      SplashScreen,
      LocalNotifications,
      {provide: ErrorHandler, useClass: IonicErrorHandler}
    ]
  })
  export class AppModule {}
```

Once that is done, add either the iOS or the Android platform by running:

```
ionic platform add ios
```

Or:

```
ionic platform add android
```

Now, we will add the code relevant to the local notifications plugin. Open example19/src/pages/home/home.ts and update as shown:

```
import { Component } from '@angular/core';
import { LocalNotifications } from '@ionic-native/local-notifications';
import { Platform } from 'ionic-angular';

@Component({
  selector: 'page-home',
  templateUrl: 'home.html'
})
export class HomePage {
  defaultText: String = 'Hello World';

  constructor(private localNotifications: LocalNotifications, private
platform: Platform) { }

  triggerNotification(notifText) {
    this.platform.ready().then(() => {

      notifText = notifText || this.defaultText;
      this.localNotifications.schedule({
        id: 1,
        text: notifText,
      });
    });
  }
```

```
}
```

Next, we will update `example19/src/pages/home/home.html` as shown:

```html
<ion-header>
    <ion-navbar>
        <ion-title>
            Local Notification
        </ion-title>
    </ion-navbar>
</ion-header>
<ion-content padding>
    <div class="list">
        <label class="item item-input">
            <span class="input-label">Enter Notification text</span>
            <input type="text" #notifText [ngModel]="defaultText">
        </label>
        <label class="item item-input">
            <button ion-button color="dark" (click)="
            triggerNotification(notifText.value)">Notify</button>
        </label>
    </div>
</ion-content>
```

Save all the files and run the following command:

```
ionic server android
```

Or:

```
ionic server ios
```

We should see the following output:

Now, when we look at that notification bar, we should see the local notification:

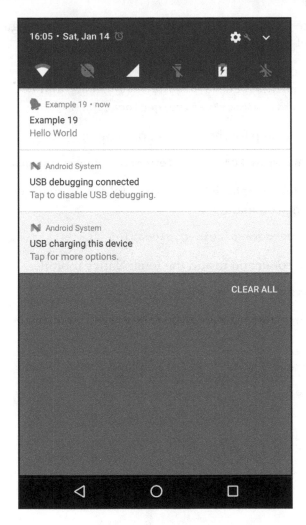

To learn more about the dialogs plugin API methods, refer to:
`https://ionicframework.com/docs/native/local-notifications/`.

Geolocation

The final plugin we are going to take a look at is the Geolocation plugin, which helps to fetch the coordinates of the device.

You can know more about the plugin from here:
`https://github.com/apache/cordova-plugin-geolocation` and
`https://ionicframework.com/docs/native/geolocation/`.

First, scaffold a new blank app for the Geolocation plugin:

```
ionic start -a "Example 20" -i app.example.twenty example20 blank --v2
```

Once the app is scaffolded, `cd` into the `example20` folder. Now we will add the Geolocation plugin, run the following command:

```
ionic plugin add cordova-plugin-geolocation
```

Next, run the following command to add the Ionic Native module:

```
npm install --save @ionic-native/geolocation
```

Now, we register the provider. Update `example20/src/app/app.module.ts`:

```typescript
import { NgModule, ErrorHandler } from '@angular/core';
import { IonicApp, IonicModule, IonicErrorHandler } from 'ionic-angular';
import { MyApp } from './app.component';
import { HomePage } from '../pages/home/home';

import { StatusBar } from '@ionic-native/status-bar';
import { SplashScreen } from '@ionic-native/splash-screen';
import { Geolocation } from '@ionic-native/geolocation';

@NgModule({
  declarations: [
    MyApp,
    HomePage
  ],
  imports: [
    IonicModule.forRoot(MyApp)
  ],
  bootstrap: [IonicApp],
  entryComponents: [
    MyApp,
    HomePage
  ],
  providers: [
```

```
      StatusBar,
      SplashScreen,
      Geolocation,
      {provide: ErrorHandler, useClass: IonicErrorHandler}
   ]
})
export class AppModule {}
```

Once that is done, add either the iOS or the Android platform by running:

ionic platform add ios

Or:

ionic platform add android

Now, we will add the code relevant to the Geolocation plugin. Open example20/src/pages/home/home.ts and update with the following:

```
import { Component } from '@angular/core';
import { Platform } from 'ionic-angular';
import { Geolocation } from '@ionic-native/geolocation';

@Component({
  selector: 'page-home',
  templateUrl: 'home.html'
})
export class HomePage {
  latitude: Number = 0;
  longitude: Number = 0;
  accuracy: Number = 0;

  constructor(private platform: Platform,
    private geolocation: Geolocation) {
    platform.ready().then(() => {
      geolocation.getCurrentPosition().then((position) => {
        this.latitude = position.coords.latitude;
        this.longitude = position.coords.longitude;
        this.accuracy = position.coords.accuracy;
      });
    });
  }
}
```

Next, update `example20/src/pages/home/home.html` as shown in the following code:

```
<ion-header>
    <ion-navbar>
        <ion-title>
            Ionic Blank
        </ion-title>
    </ion-navbar>
</ion-header>
<ion-content padding>
    <ul class="list">
        <li class="item">
            Latitude : {{latitude}}
        </li>
        <li class="item">
            Longitude : {{longitude}}
        </li>
        <li class="item">
            Accuracy : {{accuracy}}
        </li>
    </ul>
</ion-content>
```

Save all the files and finally run the following command:

```
ionic emulate ios
```

Or:

```
ionic emulate android
```

We should see the following output:

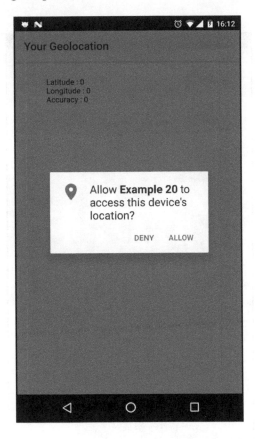

Once the permission is provided, we should see the values as shown in the following screenshot:

My Google Nexus 6P runs Android Nougat, which has a new feature called runtime permissions. This allows a user to give permission at runtime rather than while installing the app. You can learn more about that feature here:

`https://developer.android.com/training/permissions/requesting.html`.

To learn more about the Geolocation plugin API methods, refer to:

`https://ionicframework.com/docs/native/geolocation/`.

The preceding examples should have provided a good insight into how you can use Ionic Native.

Summary

In this chapter, we have seen what Cordova plugins are, and how they can be used in an existing Ionic app. We started off by setting up a local development environment for Android and iOS, and then we learned how to emulate and run an Ionic app. Next, we explored how to add Cordova plugins to an Ionic project and use them. Finally, with the aid of Ionic Native, we injected plugins in our Ionic app and worked with them.

In the next chapter, we are going to use the knowledge we have gained so far in building an app named Riderr. Using the public API exposed by Uber, we will be building an app using which a rider can book an Uber ride.

7
Building the Riderr App

With the knowledge we have gained so far, we will be building an app that helps users to book a ride. This app consumes the API exposed by Uber (`https://uber.com/`), a popular ride-hailing service provider, and integrates the same with an Ionic app. In this app, we are going to work on the following:

- Integrating with Uber OAuth 2.0
- Integrating REST APIs
- Interacting with device features
- Working with Google APIs
- And finally, booking a ride

The main purpose of this chapter is to show how one could use both REST APIs as well as device features such as Geolocation and InappBrowser, to build real-world apps using Ionic.

App overview

The app we are going to build is named Riderr. Riderr helps users to book a cab between two points. This app uses the APIs provided by Uber (`https://uber.com/`) to book a ride. In this app, we are not going to integrate all the APIs of Uber. We will be implementing a few endpoints that display the user's information as well as the user's ride information, and a few endpoints that help us book a ride, view the current ride, and cancel a ride.

To achieve this, we will be using Uber's OAuth to authenticate the user so that we can display the user's information as well as book a ride on behalf of the user.

Here is a quick preview of what the app is going to look like once we are done building the app:

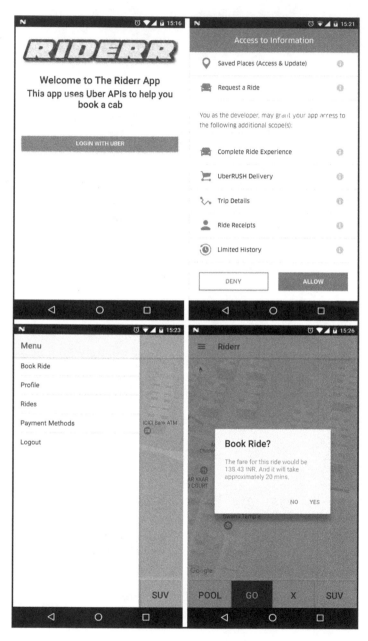

Note: Neither the book publication company nor I take any responsibility for loss of money or account ban from Uber. Please read the API instructions clearly before using Uber Production APIs.

Uber APIs

In this section, we are going to go over the various APIs that we are going to consume in the Riderr app. We will also be generating a Client ID, a Client Secret, and a Server Token that we are going to use while making the requests.

Authentication

There are three authentication mechanisms for accessing the Uber API:

- Server Token
- Single sign-on (SSO)
- OAuth 2.0

For us to make requests on behalf of a user, access the user's personal information, and book rides on the user's behalf, we need an OAuth 2.0 access token. Hence we will be following the OAuth 2.0 mechanism.
If you are new to the OAuth 2.0 mechanism, take a look at
`http://www.bubblecode.net/en/2016/01/22/understanding-oauth2/` or
`https://www.digitalocean.com/community/tutorials/an-introduction-to-oauth-2`.

Registering with Uber

Before we proceed further, we need to have an Uber account to log in and register a new app with Uber. If you don't have an account, you can create one quite easily using the Uber app.

Once you have created an Uber account, navigate to
`https://developer.uber.com/dashboard/create`, log in, and fill in the form, which is as
follows:

Then click on **Create**. This will register a new app with Uber and will create a Client ID,
Client Secret, and Server Token for this app. Next, click on the **Authorization** tab on the
same page (where we find the Client ID). Update the Redirect URL to
`http://localhost/callback`. This is very important. If we don't, Uber does not know
where to send the user after authentication.

Using a combination of Client ID and Client Secret, we request an Access Token. Then,
using this access token, we will be accessing Uber resources on behalf of a user.

To proceed further, you need to have a decent understanding of OAuth 2.0, as we will be
implementing the same in our application.

API

In this app, we are going to consume the following APIs from Uber:

- `/authorize`: `https://developer.uber.com/docs/riders/references/api/v2/authorize-get`. This endpoint allows the app to redirect the user to the authorization page. We will go deeper into this endpoint when we start working with the app.
- `/token`: This endpoint uses the code returned by the `/authorize` endpoint and requests the access token. This token is then used to make further requests. API Doc: `https://developer.uber.com/docs/riders/references/api/v2/token-post`.
- `/me`: This endpoint returns the user information, taking the access token as the input. API Doc: `https://developer.uber.com/docs/riders/references/api/v1.2/me-get`.
- `/history`: This endpoint returns the Uber ride history of the user. This endpoint requires special permissions (Privileged Scope). But, for our example, since this is a development app, we will be using this endpoint with Full Access scope. But if you would like to make a production deployment of the app, refer to `https://developer.uber.com/docs/riders/guides/scopes` for more information. API Doc: `https://developer.uber.com/docs/riders/references/api/v1.2/history-get`.
- `/payment-methods`: This endpoint returns the available payment options for the user. This endpoint also requires privileged scope. API Doc: `https://developer.uber.com/docs/riders/references/api/v1.2/payment-methods-get`.
- `/products`: This endpoint returns the list of products supported in a given location. In the place where I live - Hyderabad, India - Uber offers Uber Pool, Uber Go, Uber X, and Uber SUV. These vary from place to place within the city as well. In some parts of the city, I have access to Uber Moto as well. Using this endpoint, we will fetch the products supported at a given location. API Doc: `https://developer.uber.com/docs/riders/references/api/v1.2/products-get`.
- `/request/estimate`: Before we request a ride, we need to get a fare estimate from Uber. If the user is fine with the fare estimate, we will make the actual request. This endpoint accepts the required information and responds with a fare object. API Doc: `https://developer.uber.com/docs/riders/references/api/v1.2/requests-estimate-post`.
- `/requests`: This endpoint accepts the fare id, product id, from location, and to location, and books a ride. API Doc: `https://developer.uber.com/docs/riders/references/api/v1.2/requests-post`.

- `/requests/current`: This endpoint will return the details of the current ride if any. API Doc: `https://developer.uber.com/docs/riders/references/api/v1.2/requests-current-get`.

- `/requests/current`: This endpoint will cancel/delete the current ride. API Doc: `https://developer.uber.com/docs/riders/references/api/v1.2/requests-current-delete`.

 Note: You can refer to `https://developer.uber.com/docs/riders/introduction` for other available APIs.

Building Riderr

Now that we have an understanding of the list of APIs, we will start working with the Ionic app.

Scaffolding the app

The next step in this chapter is to scaffold a new Ionic blank app and start integrating the Uber API with it.

Create a new folder named `chapter7`, open a new command prompt/terminal inside the `chapter7` folder, and run the following:

```
ionic start -a "Riderr" -i app.example.riderr riderr blank --v2
```

This will scaffold a new blank project.

Uber API service

In this section, we are going to start working with the service layer that interfaces with the Uber API. We will be implementing the aforementioned endpoints inside the Ionic app.

Once the app has been scaffolded, navigate into the `src` folder and create a new folder named `services`. Inside the `services` folder, create a file named `uber.service.ts`. We will be writing all the Uber integration logic here.

Open the `riderr` project inside your favorite text editor and navigate to `riderr/src/services/uber.service.ts`. The first thing we are going to do is add the required imports. Add the following to the top of the `uber.services.ts` file:

```
import { Injectable } from '@angular/core';
import { LoadingController } from 'ionic-angular';
import { Http, Headers, Response, RequestOptions } from '@angular/http';
import { InAppBrowser } from '@ionic-native/in-app-browser';
import { Storage } from '@ionic/storage';
import { Observable } from 'rxjs/Observable';
```

We have included

- `Injectable`: To mark the current class as a provider
- `LoadingController`: To show messages while making network requests; `Http`, `Headers`, `Response`, and `RequestOptions` for processing `http` requests
- `InAppBrowser`: To achieve OAuth 2.0 without using a server to get the access token
- `Storage`: For storing the access token
- `Observable`: For better processing of asynchronous requests

Next, we will define the class and class level variables:

```
@Injectable()
export class UberAPI {
  private client_secret: string =
'igVTjJAByDAVfKYgaNGX1MgvoWNmsuTI_OYJz7eq';
  private client_id: string = '9i2dK88Ovw0WvH3wmS-H0JA6ZF5Z2GP1';
  private redirect_uri: string = 'http://localhost/callback';
  private scopes: string = 'profile history places request';
  // we will be using the sandbox URL for our app
  private UBERSANDBOXAPIURL = 'https://sandbox-api.uber.com/v1.2/';
  // private UBERAPIURL = 'https://api.uber.com/v1.2/';
  private TOKENKEY = 'token'; // name of the key in storage
  private loader; // reference to the loader
  private token; // copy of token in memory
}
```

In the preceding code snippet, update `client_secret` and `client_id` from the new app you have registered with Uber. Do notice the `scopes` variable. It is here that we are requesting permission to access privileged content from Uber on the user's behalf.

Note: I will be deleting the preceding registered app once I am done with this example. So, please make sure you have your own `client_secret` and `client_id`.

Next comes the constructor:

```
//snipp -> Inside the class
    constructor(private http: Http,
    private storage: Storage,
    private loadingCtrl: LoadingController,
    private inAppBrowser: InAppBrowser) {
      // fetch the token on load
      this.storage.get(this.TOKENKEY).then((token) => {
        this.token = token;
      });
    }
```

In the `constructor`, we have instantiated `Http`, `Storage`, and `LoadingController` classes, we are also fetching the access token stored in memory and saving it in-memory for future use.

For every single request that we make to the Uber API (except for the authentication ones), we need to send the access token as part of the headers. We have the following method that will help us with this:

```
// snipp
  private createAuthorizationHeader(headers: Headers) {
    headers.append('Authorization', 'Bearer ' + this.token);
    headers.append('Accept-Language', 'en_US');
    headers.append('Content-Type', 'application/json');
  }
```

Next, we need a method that returns a Boolean indicating whether the user is authenticated and we have a token to make requests to the Uber API:

```
// snipp
  isAuthenticated(): Observable<boolean> {
    this.showLoader('Autenticating...');
    return new Observable<boolean>((observer) => {
      this.storage.ready().then(() => {
        this.storage.get(this.TOKENKEY).then((token) => {
          observer.next(!!token); // !! -> converts truthy falsy to
          boolean.
          observer.complete();
          this.hideLoader();
        });
```

```
        });
      });
    }
```

This method will query the storage for the existence of the token. If the token exists, the `observer` returns `true`, else `false`. We will be implementing `showLoader()` and `hideLoader()` at the end of all the APIs.

If the user is authenticated, the user is logged in. That means we need to have an option where the user logs out. Since the API server is stateless, it does not maintain any session information to invalidate. Hence, by clearing the token from our storage, we invalidate the session from the client side:

```
// snipp
  logout(): Observable<boolean> {
    return new Observable<boolean>((observer) => {
      this.storage.ready().then(() => {
        this.storage.set(this.TOKENKEY, undefined);
        this.token = undefined;
        observer.next(true);
        observer.complete();
      });
    });
  }
```

Now we are going to write our first API method that interacts with the Uber API. This is the authentication method:

```
// snipp
auth(): Observable<boolean> {
    return new Observable<boolean>(observer => {
      this.storage.ready().then(() => {
        let browser =
        this.inAppBrowser.create
        (`https://login.uber.com/oauth/v2/authorize?
        client_id=${this.client_id}&
        response_type=code&scope=${this.scopes}
        &redirect_uri=${this.redirect_uri}`, '_blank',
        'location=no,clearsessioncache=yes,clearcache=yes');
        browser.on('loadstart').subscribe((event) => {
          let url = event.url;

          // console.log(url);
          // URLS that get fired

          // 1. https://login.uber.com/oauth/v2/authorize?
          client_id=9i2dK88Ovw0WvH3wmS-
```

```
H0JA6ZF5Z2GP1&response_type=
code&scope=profile%20history%20places%20request

// 2. https://auth.uber.com/login/?
next_url=https%3A%2F%2Flogin.uber.com
%2Foauth%...520places%2520request
&state=Pa2ONzlEGsB4M41VLKOosWTlj9snJqJREyCFrEhfjx0%3D

// 3. https://login.uber.com/oauth/v2/authorize?
client_id=9i2dK88Ovw0WvH3wmS-
H0JA...ry%20places%20request&
state=Pa2ONzlEGsB4M41VLKOosWTlj9snJqJREyCFrEhfjx0%3D

// 4. http://localhost/callback?state=
Pa2ONzlEGsB4M41VLKOosWTlj9snJqJREyCFrEhfjx0%3D&
code=9Xu6ueaNhUN1uZVvqvKyaXPhMj8Bzb#_

// we are interested in #4
if (url.indexOf(this.redirect_uri) === 0) {
  browser.close();
  let resp = (url).split("?")[1];
  let responseParameters = resp.split("&");
  var parameterMap: any = {};

  for (var i = 0; i < responseParameters.length; i++) {
    parameterMap[responseParameters[i].split("=")[0]] =
    responseParameters[i].split("=")[1];
  }

  // console.log('parameterMap', parameterMap);
  /*
    {
      "state":
      "W9Ytf2cicTMPMpMgwh9HfojKv7gQxxhrcOgwffqdrUM%3D",
      "code": "HgSjzZHfF4GaG6x1vzS3D96kGtJFNB#_"
    }
  */

  let headers = new Headers({
    'Content-Type': "application/x-www-form-urlencoded"
  });
  let options = new RequestOptions({ headers: headers });
  let data =
  `client_secret=${this.client_secret}
  &client_id=${this.client_id}&grant_type=
  authorization_code&redirect_uri=
  ${this.redirect_uri}&code=${parameterMap.code}`;
```

```
              return
              this.http.post
              ('https://login.uber.com/oauth/v2/token', data, options)
                .subscribe((data) => {
                  let respJson: any = data.json();
                  // console.log('respJson', respJson);
                  /*
                    {
                      "last_authenticated": 0,
                      "access_token": "snipp",
                      "expires_in": 2592000,
                      "token_type": "Bearer",
                      "scope": "profile history places request",
                      "refresh_token": "26pgA43ZvQkxEQi7qYjMASjfq6lg8F"
                    }
                  */

                  this.storage.set(this.TOKENKEY, respJson.access_token);
                  this.token = respJson.access_token; // load it up in
                  memory
                  observer.next(true);
                  observer.complete();
                });
            }
          });
        });
      });
    }
```

There is a lot happening in this method. We are using the Ionic Native's InAppBrowser
(https://ionicframework.com/docs/native/in-app-browser/) plugin to redirect the user
to the Authorize endpoint. The Authorize endpoint
(https://login.uber.com/oauth/v2/authorize?client_id=${this.client_id}&
response_type=code&scope=${this.scopes}&redirect_uri=${this.redirect_ur
i}) takes the Client ID, scopes, and the redirect URL.

The redirect_uri is an important parameter, as the Uber API redirects the app to that
URL after authentication. And inside our app, we are listening for the URL change event
via browser.on('loadstart'). And we are looking for a URL that starts with
http://localhost/callback. If this URL is matched, we close the browser and extract
the code from the URL.

Once we have the code, we need to exchange the same for an Access Token. That would be the next part of the auth(), to fetch the token from
https://login.uber.com/oauth/v2/token by passing in the client_secret, client_id, redirect_uri, and code. Once we receive the access token, we save it to the storage.

 Note: To find out more about storage, refer to
https://ionicframework.com/docs/storage/ or the *Storage service* section in *Chapter 4, Ionic Decorators and Services.*

Now that we have the access token, we will be making a request to Uber APIs to get, post, and delete data.

The first API method we are going to implement is going to fetch the user's information:

```
// snipp
  getMe(): Observable<Response> {
    this.showLoader();
    let headers = new Headers();
    this.createAuthorizationHeader(headers);
    return this.http.get(this.UBERSANDBOXAPIURL + 'me', {
      headers: headers
    });
  }
```

Do notice that I am making the API request to the Uber Sandbox API URL and not to the production service. This is always a good idea till you are confident in your implementation. The Uber Sandbox API and Uber API have a very similar implementation, except the data in the Sandbox environment is not real-time, it follows the same rules as the Uber API. When in production, do remember to update the API base.

Next, comes the history API:

```
// snipp
  getHistory(): Observable<Response> {
    this.showLoader();
    let headers = new Headers();
    this.createAuthorizationHeader(headers);
    return this.http.get(this.UBERSANDBOXAPIURL + 'history', {
      headers: headers
    });
  }
```

The headers will be passed to every request that will need an access token to process the request.

Next, comes the payment methods endpoint:

```
// snipp
  getPaymentMethods(): Observable<Response> {
    this.showLoader();
    let headers = new Headers();
    this.createAuthorizationHeader(headers);
    return this.http.get(this.UBERSANDBOXAPIURL + 'payment-methods', {
      headers: headers
    });
  }
```

The preceding three endpoints will return the user and user ride information. The next endpoint will return the list of products supported at a given location:

```
// snipp
  getProducts(lat: Number, lon: Number): Observable<Response> {
    this.showLoader();
    let headers = new Headers();
    this.createAuthorizationHeader(headers);
    return this.http.get(this.UBERSANDBOXAPIURL + 'products?latitude='
    + lat + '&longitude=' + lon, {
      headers: headers
    });
  }
```

This method will be used to display the list of products or ride types available.

Before making the actual ride booking, we need to first get a fare estimate. We will be using the `requestRideEstimates()` method for this:

```
//snipp
  requestRideEstimates(start_lat: Number, end_lat: Number, start_lon:
Number, end_lon: Number): Observable<Response> {
    this.showLoader();
    // before booking
    let headers = new Headers();
    this.createAuthorizationHeader(headers);
    return this.http.post(this.UBERSANDBOXAPIURL + 'requests/estimate', {
      "start_latitude": start_lat,
      "start_longitude": start_lon,
      "end_latitude": end_lat,
      "end_longitude": end_lon
    }, { headers: headers });
  }
```

Once we get the fare estimate and the user accepts it, we will be initiating a booking request using `requestRide()`:

```
// snipp
  requestRide(product_id: String, fare_id: String, start_lat: Number,
end_lat: Number, start_lon: Number, end_lon: Number): Observable<Response>
{
    this.showLoader();
    let headers = new Headers();
    this.createAuthorizationHeader(headers);
    return this.http.post(this.UBERSANDBOXAPIURL + 'requests', {
      "product_id": product_id,
      "fare_id": fare_id,
      "start_latitude": start_lat,
      "start_longitude": start_lon,
      "end_latitude": end_lat,
      "end_longitude": end_lon
    }, { headers: headers });
  }
```

This method returns the status of the booking. In the sandbox environment, no ride will be booked. If you are serious about booking an actual ride, you can change the API URL and initiate an actual booking. Do remember that an Uber driver will actually call you for your ride. And if you cancel the ride, appropriate cancellation fees will apply.

Note: Neither the book publication company nor I take any responsibility towards loss of money or account ban from Uber. Please read the API instructions clearly before using Uber Production APIs.

Since Uber allows only one ride to be booked at a time from an account, we can get the current ride using `getCurrentRides()`:

```
//snipp
  getCurrentRides(lat: Number, lon: Number): Observable<Response> {
    this.showLoader();
    let headers = new Headers();
    this.createAuthorizationHeader(headers);
    return this.http.get(this.UBERSANDBOXAPIURL + 'requests/current', {
      headers: headers
    });
  }
```

And finally, to cancel a ride, we will make a delete request using `cancelCurrentRide()`:

```
// snipp
  cancelCurrentRide(): Observable<Response> {
    this.showLoader();
    let headers = new Headers();
    this.createAuthorizationHeader(headers);
    return this.http.delete(this.UBERSANDBOXAPIURL +
    'requests/current', {
      headers: headers
    });
  }
```

The two utility methods that show and hide the processing loader are as follows:

```
// snipp
private showLoader(text?: string) {
    this.loader = this.loadingCtrl.create({
      content: text || 'Loading...'
    });
    this.loader.present();
  }

  public hideLoader() {
    this.loader.dismiss();
  }
```

With this, we have added all the required APIs that we are going to use to interact with Uber APIs.

Integration

Now that we have the required API services available, we will be creating the required views to represent that data.

When we scaffold the app, a page named home will be created for us. But since, in our app, everything starts with the authentication, we will first generate a login page. Then we will make that the first page of the app. To generate a new page, run the following:

```
ionic generate page login
```

Next, we need to update the page reference in `riderr/src/app/app.module.ts`. Update the `@NgModule` as shown:

```
import { NgModule, ErrorHandler } from '@angular/core';
import { IonicApp, IonicModule, IonicErrorHandler } from 'ionic-angular';
import { MyApp } from './app.component';
import { HomePage } from '../pages/home/home';
import { LoginPage } from '../pages/login/login';

import { UberAPI } from '../services/uber.service';
import { IonicStorageModule } from '@ionic/storage';

import { StatusBar } from '@ionic-native/status-bar';
import { SplashScreen } from '@ionic-native/splash-screen';

@NgModule({
  declarations: [
    MyApp,
    HomePage
    LoginPage
  ],
  imports: [
    IonicModule.forRoot(MyApp),
    IonicStorageModule.forRoot()
  ],
  bootstrap: [IonicApp],
  entryComponents: [
    MyApp,
    HomePage,
    LoginPage
  ],
  providers: [{ provide: ErrorHandler, useClass: IonicErrorHandler },
      UberAPI,
    StatusBar,
    SplashScreen,
  ]
})
export class AppModule { }
```

We will generate and add the remaining pages as we go along.

> Note: As Ionic keeps evolving, class names, and structures of pages might change. But the gist of developing an app in Ionic will remain the same.

Next, we will update `app.component.ts` to load the login page as the first one. Update `riderr/src/app/app.component.ts` as shown:

```
import { Component } from '@angular/core';
import { Platform } from 'ionic-angular';
import { StatusBar } from '@ionic-native/status-bar';
import { SplashScreen } from '@ionic-native/splash-screen';

import { LoginPage } from '../pages/login/login';

@Component({
  templateUrl: 'app.html'
})
export class MyApp {
  rootPage = LoginPage;

  constructor(platform: Platform, statusBar: StatusBar, splashScreen:
SplashScreen) {
    platform.ready().then(() => {
      statusBar.styleDefault();
      splashScreen.hide();
    });
  }
```

Now we will update the `LoginPage` component. First, the `login.html` page. Update `riderr2/src/pages/login/login.html` as shown:

```
<ion-content padding text-center>
  <img src="assets/icon/logo.png" alt="Riderr Logo">
  <h2>Welcome to The Riderr App</h2>
  <h3>This app uses Uber APIs to help you book a cab</h3>
  <br><br><br>
    <button ion-button color="primary" full (click)="auth()">Login with
Uber</button>
</ion-content>
```

You can find the `logo.png` here:
`https://www.dropbox.com/s/8tdfgizjm24l3nx/logo.png?dl=0`. Once downloaded, move the image to the `assets/icon` folder.

Next, update `riderr/src/pages/login/login.ts` as shown:

```
import { Component } from '@angular/core';
import { NavController } from 'ionic-angular';
import { UberAPI } from '../../services/uber.service';
import { HomePage } from '../home/home';
```

```
@Component({
  selector: 'page-login',
  templateUrl: 'login.html'
})
export class LoginPage {

  constructor(private api: UberAPI, private navCtrl: NavController) {
    // check if the user is already authenticated
    this.api.isAuthenticated().subscribe((isAuth) => {
      if (isAuth) {
        this.navCtrl.setRoot(HomePage);
      }
      // else relax!
    });
  }

  auth() {
    this.api.auth().subscribe((isAuthSuccess) => {
      this.navCtrl.setRoot(HomePage);
    }, function(e) {
      // handle this in a user friendly way.
      console.log('Fail!!', e);
    });
  }
}
```

In the preceding code, we are including the required dependencies. In the constructor, we are checking whether the user is already authenticated using the isAuthenticated() that we created in the UberAPI class. If the user clicks on the **Login with Uber** button, we call the auth(), which in turn invokes the auth() of the UberAPI class.

If the user is successfully authenticated, we redirect the user to the home page. Else we don't do anything.

Assuming that the user has been successfully authenticated, the user will be redirected to the Home page. We are going to make the home page side-menu-based. The side menu will have links to navigate to various pages in our app.

We will update riderr/src/pages/home/home.html as shown:

```
<ion-menu [content]="content" (ionClose)="ionClosed()"
(ionOpen)="ionOpened()">
    <ion-header>
        <ion-toolbar>
            <ion-title>Menu</ion-title>
        </ion-toolbar>
    </ion-header>
```

```
<ion-content>
    <ion-list>
        <button ion-item menuClose
        (click)="openPage(bookRidePage)">
            Book Ride
        </button>
        <button ion-item menuClose (click)="openPage(profilePage)">
            Profile
        </button>
        <button ion-item menuClose (click)="openPage(historyPage)">
            Rides
        </button>
        <button ion-item menuClose
        (click)="openPage(paymentMethodsPage)">
            Payment Methods
        </button>
        <button ion-item menuClose (click)="logout()">
            Logout
        </button>
    </ion-list>
</ion-content>
</ion-menu>
<ion-nav #content [root]="rootPage" swipeBackEnabled="false"></ion-nav>
```

The preceding code is self-explanatory. To find out more about the menu, refer to `https://ionicframework.com/docs/api/components/menu/Menu/`.

Next, we will update the `HomePage` class. Update `riderr2/src/pages/home/home.ts` as shown:

```
import { Component } from '@angular/core';
import { BookRidePage } from '../book-ride/book-ride';
import { ProfilePage } from '../profile/profile';
import { HistoryPage } from '../history/history';
import { PaymentMethodsPage } from '../payment-methods/payment-methods';
import { LoginPage } from '../login/login';
import { UberAPI } from '../../services/uber.service';
import { NavController, Events } from 'ionic-angular';
import { ViewChild } from '@angular/core';

@Component({
  selector: 'page-home',
  templateUrl: 'home.html'
})
export class HomePage {

  private rootPage;
  private bookRidePage;
```

```
    private profilePage;
    private historyPage;
    private paymentMethodsPage;

    @ViewChild(BookRidePage) bookRide : BookRidePage;

    constructor(private uberApi: UberAPI,
      private navCtrl: NavController,
      public events: Events) {
      this.rootPage = BookRidePage;

      this.bookRidePage = BookRidePage;
      this.profilePage = ProfilePage;
      this.historyPage = HistoryPage;
      this.paymentMethodsPage = PaymentMethodsPage;
    }

    // http://stackoverflow.com/a/38760731/1015046
    ionOpened() {
      this.events.publish('menu:opened', '');
    }

    ionClosed() {
      this.events.publish('menu:closed', '');
    }

    ngAfterViewInit() {
      this.uberApi.isAuthenticated().subscribe((isAuth) => {
        if (!isAuth) {
          this.navCtrl.setRoot(LoginPage);
          return;
        }
      });
    }

    openPage(p) {
      this.rootPage = p;
    }

    logout(){
      this.uberApi.logout().subscribe(() => {
        this.navCtrl.setRoot(LoginPage);
      });
    }
  }
```

Here, we have imported the required classes. We will be generating the missing pages in the next few steps. Do note the `@ViewChild()` decorator. We will be going through that and `ionOpened()` and `ionClosed()` when we work with Google Maps.

Once the view has been initialized, we check whether the user is authenticated. If not, we redirect the user to the login page. `openPage()` sets the root page as the selected page from the menu. `logout()` cleans up the token and redirects the user to the login page.

Now we will create the required pages.

First, the page where most of the action happens - the `bookRide` page. Run the following:

```
ionic generate page bookRide
```

This will generate a new page. Once the page has been created, open `riderr/src/app/app.module.ts` and add `BookRidePage` to the `declarations` and `entryComponents` properties of `@NgModule()`.

`BookRidePage` is one of the most complex pages in the entire app. First off, we show a Google Map with the user's current location. We fetch the available products for that user at their location and display them.

Before we proceed further, I need to mention a weird bug that happens when working with Google Maps and click events on the map, inside an Ionic app.

On the Google Map, we show a marker and an info window with the user's current location. Clicking on the marker or the info window will redirect the user to set the destination location to book a ride. For this, we need to listen to the click event on the map. This kind of causes a problem when working with click events on non-Google Map components such as side menus, alerts, and so on. You can read more about the issue here: `https://github.com/driftyco/ionic/issues/9942#issuecomment-280941997`.

So, to overcome this bug, wherever there is a click interaction other than Google Map components, we need to disable the click listener on the Google Map and, once we are done, we need to re-enable it.

Going back to the `ionOpened()` and `ionClosed()` in `riderr/src/pages/home/home.ts`, we are firing custom events from them whenever the menu is opened or closed. This way, we disable the click listener on the map when the menu is opened and enable the click listener after the user selects a menu item. In `ionOpened()` and `ionClosed()`, we have only fired the events. We will be handling the same in `riderr/src/pages/book-ride/book-ride.ts`.

Now that we are aware of the issue, we can proceed further. We will first implement the menu and the map HTML. Update `riderr/src/pages/book-ride/book-ride.html` as shown:

```html
<ion-header>
    <ion-navbar>
        <button ion-button menuToggle>
            <ion-icon name="menu"></ion-icon>
        </button>
        <ion-title>Riderr</ion-title>
        <ion-buttons end>
            <button *ngIf="isRideinProgress" ion-button color="danger"
            (click)="cancelRide()">
                Cancel Ride
            </button>
        </ion-buttons>
    </ion-navbar>
</ion-header>
<ion-content>
    <div #map id="map"></div>
    <div class="prods-wrapper">
        <div *ngIf="!isRideinProgress">
            <h3 *ngIf="!products">Fetching Products</h3>
            <ion-grid *ngIf="products">
                <ion-row>
                    <ion-col *ngFor="let p of products" [ngClass]="
                    {'selected' : p.isSelected}">
                        <div class="br" (click)="productClick(p)">
                            <h3>{{p.display_name.replace('uber', '')}}
                            </h3>
                        </div>
                    </ion-col>
                </ion-row>
            </ion-grid>
        </div>
        <div *ngIf="isRideinProgress">
            <h3 text-center>Ride In Progress</h3>
            <p text-center>Ideally the ride information would be
            displayed here.</p>
        </div>
    </div>
</ion-content>
```

In the header, we have a button to cancel an ongoing ride. We will be populating the `isRideinProgress` property on the `BookRidePage` class, that manages the page state shown here. The `ion-grid` component displays the list of products that are supported for the current user at their location.

Also notice that we have added `<div #map id="map"></div>`. This will be the place where the map appears.

To clean up the UI a bit, we will be adding few styles. Update `riderr/src/pages/book-ride/book-ride.scss` as shown:

```
page-book-ride {
    #map {
        height: 88%;
    }
    .prods-wrapper {
        height: 12%;
    }
    .br {
        padding: 3px;
        text-align: center;
    }
    ion-col.selected {
        color: #eee;
        background: #333;
    }
    ion-col {
        background: #eee;
        color: #333;
        border: 1px solid #ccc;
    }
    ion-col:last-child .br {
        border: none;
    }
}
```

Next, we are going to update the `BookRidePage` class. There are quite a few methods, so I will be sharing them in parts, in the sequence of execution.

In `riderr/src/pages/book-ride/book-ride.ts`, we will first update the required imports:

```
import { Component } from '@angular/core';
import { UberAPI } from '../../services/uber.service';
import {
  Platform,
  NavController,
  AlertController,
  ModalController,
  Events
} from 'ionic-angular';
import { Diagnostic } from '@ionic-native/diagnostic';
```

```
import { Geolocation } from '@ionic-native/geolocation';
import {
  GoogleMaps,
  GoogleMap,
  GoogleMapsEvent,
  LatLng,
  CameraPosition,
  MarkerOptions,
  Marker
} from '@ionic-native/google-maps';
import { AutocompletePage } from '../auto-complete/auto-complete';
```

The @Component decorator will be as is.

Next, we are going to declare some class-level variables:

```
// snipp
  private map: GoogleMap;
  private products;
  private fromGeo;
  private toGeo;
  private selectedProduct;
  private isRideinProgress: boolean = false;
  private currentRideInfo;
```

And then define the constructor:

```
// snipp
constructor(private uberApi: UberAPI,
    private platform: Platform,
    private navCtrl: NavController,
    private alertCtrl: AlertController,
    private modalCtrl: ModalController,
    private diagnostic: Diagnostic,
    private geoLocation: Geolocation,
    private googleMaps: GoogleMap,
    public events: Events) { }
```

Once the view has been initialized, using the ngAfterViewInit() hook, we will start fetching the user's Geolocation:

```
// snipp
ngAfterViewInit() {
    //https://github.com/mapsplugin/cordova-plugin-googlemaps/issues/1140
    this.platform.ready().then(() => {
      this.requestPerms();

      //https://github.com/driftyco/ionic/issues/9942#issuecomment-
```

```
280941997
this.events.subscribe('menu:opened', () => {
  this.map.setClickable(false);
});
this.events.subscribe('menu:closed', () => {
  this.map.setClickable(true);
});
});
}
```

But before we get the Geolocation, we need to request the user to permit us to access the location services.

Also do notice the listeners implemented for the `menu:opened` and `menu:closed` events. This is how we disable a click on the map and re-enable it based on the state of the side menu. Continuing with our development:

```
// snipp
private requestPerms() {
    let that = this;
    function success(statuses) {
      for (var permission in statuses) {
        switch (statuses[permission]) {
          case that.diagnostic.permissionStatus.GRANTED:
            // console.log("Permission granted to use " + permission);
            that.fetCords();
            break;
          case that.diagnostic.permissionStatus.NOT_REQUESTED:
            console.log("Permission to use " + permission + " has not
            been requested yet");
            break;
          case that.diagnostic.permissionStatus.DENIED:
            console.log("Permission denied to use " + permission + " -
            ask again?");
            break;
          case that.diagnostic.permissionStatus.DENIED_ALWAYS:
            console.log("Permission permanently denied to use " +
            permission + " - guess we won't be using it then!");
            break;
        }
      }
    }

    function error(e) {
      console.log(e);
    }

    this.diagnostic.requestRuntimePermissions([
```

```
      that.diagnostic.permission.ACCESS_FINE_LOCATION,
      that.diagnostic.permission.ACCESS_COARSE_LOCATION
   ]).then(success).catch(error);
}
```

Using the Diagnostic plugin from `@ionic-native/diagnostic`, we request runtime permissions. This shows a popup asking the user whether the app can access the user's Geolocation. If the user allows the app, we will receive `Diagnostic.permissionStatus.GRANTED` status in the success callback. Then, we will try and fetch the user's coordinates. Other cases can be handled gracefully if needed:

```
// snipp
  private isExecuted = false;
  private fetCords() {
    // this needs to be called only once
    // since we are requesting 2 permission
    // this will be called twice.
    // hence the isExecuted
    if (this.isExecuted) return;
    this.isExecuted = true;
    // maps api key : AzaSyCZhTJB1kFAP70RuwDts6uso9e3DCLdRWs
    // ionic plugin add cordova-plugin-googlemaps --variable
    API_KEY_FOR_ANDROID="AzaSyCZhTJB1kFAP70RuwDts6uso9e3DCLdRWs"
    this.geoLocation.getCurrentPosition().then((resp) => {
      // resp.coords.latitude
      // resp.coords.longitude
      // console.log(resp);
      this.fromGeo = resp.coords;
      // Get the products at this location
      this.uberApi.getProducts(this.fromGeo.latitude,
      this.fromGeo.longitude).subscribe((data) => {
        this.uberApi.hideLoader();
        this.products = data.json().products;
      });
      // Trip in progress?
      this
        .uberApi
        .getCurrentRides(this.fromGeo.latitude, this.fromGeo.longitude)
        .subscribe((crrRides) => {
          this.currentRideInfo = crrRides.json();
          this.isRideinProgress = true;
          this.uberApi.hideLoader();
          // check for existing rides before processing
          this.loadMap(this.fromGeo.latitude, this.fromGeo.longitude);
        }, (err) => {
          if (err.status === 404) {
            // no rides availble
```

```
            }
            this.isRideinProgress = false;
            this.uberApi.hideLoader();
            // check for existing rides before processing
            this.loadMap(this.fromGeo.latitude, this.fromGeo.longitude);
        });
    }).catch((error) => {
      console.log('Error getting location', error);
    });
  }
```

fetCords() will use the Geolocation Ionic Native plugin to fetch the user's coordinates. Once we receive the location, we will initiate a request to getProducts(), passing in the user's latitude and longitude. In parallel, we check whether there are any rides in progress using the getCurrentRides() on the Uber API.

Once the response arrives, we call loadMap() to draw the required map.

We will be installing all the required Cordova plugins and Ionic Native modules after completing the code walk-through:

```
// snipp
private loadMap(lat: number, lon: number) {
    let element: HTMLElement = document.getElementById('map');
    element.innerHTML = '';
    this.map = undefined;
    this.map = this.googleMaps.create(element);
    let crrLoc: LatLng = new LatLng(lat, lon);
    let position: CameraPosition = {
      target: crrLoc,
      zoom: 18,
      tilt: 30
    };

    this.map.one(GoogleMapsEvent.MAP_READY).then(() => {
      // move the map's camera to position
      this.map.moveCamera(position); // works on iOS and Android

      let markerOptions: MarkerOptions = {
        position: crrLoc,
        draggable: true,
        title: this.isRideinProgress ? 'Ride in Progess' : 'Select
        Destination >',
        infoClick: (() => {
          if (!this.isRideinProgress) {
            this.selectDestination();
          }
```

```
      }),
      markerClick: (() => {
        if (!this.isRideinProgress) {
          this.selectDestination();
        }
      })
    };

    this.map.addMarker(markerOptions)
      .then((marker: Marker) => {
        marker.showInfoWindow();
      });

    // a rare bug
    // loader doesn't hide
    this.uberApi.hideLoader();
  });
}
```

`loadMap()` takes the Geolocation of the user, creates a marker at the location, and pans to that point using the camera API. The marker has a simple info text, Select **Destination >**, which, when clicked, takes the user to a screen to enter a destination to book a ride.

`infoClick()` and `markerClick()` register a callback to execute `selectDestination()` only there is no ride in progress:

```
// snipp
  private productClick(product) {
    // console.log(product);
    // set the active product in the UI
    for (let i = 0; i < this.products.length; i++) {
      if (this.products[i].product_id === product.product_id) {
        this.products[i].isSelected = true;
      } else {
        this.products[i].isSelected = false;
      }
    }

    this.selectedProduct = product;
  }
```

To book a ride, the user should select a product. `productClick()` takes care of that by setting a product as a selected product based on the user's selection from the home page.

Once the product is selected and the user's location is available, we can ask the user to enter the destination location so we can check for fare estimates:

```
// snipp
private selectDestination() {
    if (this.isRideinProgress) {
        this.map.setClickable(false);
        let alert = this.alertCtrl.create({
            title: 'Only one ride!',
            subTitle: 'You can book only one ride at a time.',
            buttons: ['Ok']
        });
        alert.onDidDismiss(() => {
            this.map.setClickable(true);
        });
        alert.present();
    } else {
        if (!this.selectedProduct) {
            // since the alert has a button
            // we need to first stop the map from
            // listening. Then process the alert
            // then renable
            this.map.setClickable(false);
            let alert = this.alertCtrl.create({
                title: 'Select Ride',
                subTitle: 'Select a Ride type to continue (Pool or Go or X)',
                buttons: ['Ok']
            });
            alert.onDidDismiss(() => {
                this.map.setClickable(true);
            });
            alert.present();
        } else {
            this.map.setClickable(false);
            let modal = this.modalCtrl.create(AutoCompletePage);
            modal.onDidDismiss((data) => {
                this.map.setClickable(true);
                this.toGeo = data;
                this
                    .uberApi
                    .requestRideEstimates(this.fromGeo.latitude,
                    this.toGeo.latitude, this.fromGeo.longitude,
                    this.toGeo.longitude)
                    .subscribe((data) => {
                        this.uberApi.hideLoader();
                        this.processRideFares(data.json());
                    });
```

```
            });
        modal.present();
      }
    }
  }
```

`selectDestination()` takes care of destination selection as well as getting the ride estimates. The first if condition inside `selectDestination()` is to make sure that the user has only one ride in progress. The second if condition checks whether there is at least one `selectedProduct`. If everything is good, we invoke the `AutoCompletePage` as a modal, where the user searches for a place using the Google Places Service. Once a place is selected using this service, we fetch the Geolocation of the destination. Then pass the required information to `requestRideEstimates()` to fetch the estimates.

We will be working with `AutoCompletePage` once we are done with `BookRidePage`. When instead of once we get the fares from the `requestRideEstimates()`, we will be presenting the same to the user:

```
// snipp
private processRideFares(fareInfo: any) {
    // ask the user if the fare is okay,
    // if yes, book the cab
    // else, do nothing
    console.log('fareInfo', fareInfo);
    this.map.setClickable(false);
    let confirm = this.alertCtrl.create({
      title: 'Book Ride?',
      message: 'The fare for this ride would be '
      + fareInfo.fare.value
      + ' ' + fareInfo.fare.currency_code + '.\n And it will take
      approximately ' +
      (fareInfo.trip.duration_estimate / 60) + ' mins.',
      buttons: [
        {
          text: 'No',
          handler: () => {
            this.map.setClickable(true);
          }
        },
        {
          text: 'Yes',
          handler: () => {
            this.map.setClickable(true);
            this
              .uberApi
              .requestRide(this.selectedProduct.product_id,
               fareInfo.fare.fare_id, this.fromGeo.latitude,
```

```
                    this.toGeo.latitude, this.fromGeo.longitude,
                    this.toGeo.longitude)
                .subscribe((rideInfo) => {
                    this.uberApi.hideLoader();
                    // console.log('rideInfo', rideInfo.json());
                    // Since we are making requests to the sandbox url
                    // the request will always be in processing.
                    // Once the request has been submitted, we need to
                    // keep polling the getCurrentRides() API
                    // to get the ride information
                    // WE ARE NOT GOING TO DO THAT!
                    this.isRideinProgress = true;
                    this.currentRideInfo = rideInfo.json();
                });
            }
        }
    ]
  });
  confirm.present();
}
```

processRideFares() takes the fare information as input and presents the fare to the user. If the user is okay with the fare and time estimate, we place a request to Uber to book a ride using requestRide().

And finally, if the user wants to cancel the current ride, we provide cancelRide():

```
// snipp
  private cancelRide() {
    this
      .uberApi
      .cancelCurrentRide()
      .subscribe((cancelInfo) => {
        this.uberApi.hideLoader();
        this.isRideinProgress = false;
        this.currentRideInfo = undefined;
      });
  }
```

This would be a call to cancelCurrentRide().

Now that we are done with the required logic for BookRidePage, we will create AutoCompletePage. Run the following:

```
ionic generate page autoComplete
```

Once this is done, we need to add `AutoCompletePage` to `riderr/src/app/app.module.ts`:

```
import { AutoCompletePage } from '../pages/auto-complete/auto-complete';
```

Add the `AutoCompletePage` reference to the `declarations` and `entryComponents` properties of `@NgModule()`.

The `AutoCompletePage` class will consist of the logic needed to work with the Google Places Service to search for a place. First, we will work with `auto-complete.html`. Open `riderr/src/pages/auto-complete/auto-complete.html` and update it as shown:

```html
<ion-header>
    <ion-toolbar>
        <ion-title>Enter address</ion-title>
        <ion-searchbar id="q" [(ngModel)]="autocomplete.query"
[showCancelButton]="true" (ionInput)="updateSearch()"
(ionCancel)="dismiss()"></ion-searchbar>
    </ion-toolbar>
</ion-header>
<ion-content>
    <ion-list>
        <!-- (click) is buggy at times, hmmm? -->
        <ion-item *ngFor="let item of autocompleteItems" tappable
(click)="chooseItem(item)">
            {{ item.description }}
        </ion-item>
    </ion-list>
</ion-content>
```

We have a search bar and an `ion-list` to display the search results. Next, we will work on `auto-complete.ts`. Open `riderr/src/pages/auto-complete/auto-complete.ts` and update it as shown:

```
import { Component, NgZone } from '@angular/core';
import { ViewController } from 'ionic-angular';

@Component({
  templateUrl: 'auto-complete.html'
})

// http://stackoverflow.com/a/40854384/1015046
export class AutocompletePage {
  autocompleteItems;
  autocomplete;
  ctr: HTMLElement = document.getElementById("q");
  service = new google.maps.places.AutocompleteService();
```

```
geocoder = new google.maps.Geocoder();

constructor(public viewCtrl: ViewController, private zone: NgZone) {
  this.autocompleteItems = [];
  this.autocomplete = {
    query: ''
  };
}

dismiss() {
  this.viewCtrl.dismiss();
}

chooseItem(item: any) {
  // we need the lat long
  // so we will make use of the
  // geocoder service
  this.geocoder.geocode({
    'placeId': item.place_id
  }, (responses) => {
    // send the place name
    // & latlng back
    this.viewCtrl.dismiss({
      description: item.description,
      latitude: responses[0].geometry.location.lat(),
      longitude: responses[0].geometry.location.lng()
    });
  });
}

updateSearch() {
  if (this.autocomplete.query == '') {
    this.autocompleteItems = [];
    return;
  }
  let that = this;
  this.service.getPlacePredictions({
    input: that.autocomplete.query,
    componentRestrictions: {
      country: 'IN'
    }
  }, (predictions, status) => {
    that.autocompleteItems = [];
    that.zone.run(function() {
      predictions = predictions || [];
      predictions.forEach(function(prediction) {
        that.autocompleteItems.push(prediction);
      });
```

```
        });
      });
    }
  }
```

Here, we are using `google.maps.places.AutocompleteService` to fetch the predictions as the user searches.

A very important point to note is that the places and Geocoder services are not available as an Ionic Native plugin. Hence, we will be using Google Maps JavaScript library to get access to the places and Geocoder services. For that, we will be installing typings and then Google Maps. We will be installing this at the end.

Once the user finds the place, they will tap on the location and this will trigger `chooseItem()`. Inside `chooseItem()`, we will take `place_id` and fetch the geo coordinates of the chosen location and pass it back to `modal.onDidDismiss()` inside `selectDestination()` in the `BookRidePage` class. Then the flow goes on as we have seen in the `BookRidePage` class.

Now, we will implement the `profile`, `history`, and `paymentMethods` endpoints. To generate the required pages, run the following commands:

```
ionic generate page profile
ionic generate page history
ionic generate page paymentMethods
```

Next, we will add the same to `riderr/src/app/app.module.ts`. The final version of the `app.module.ts` will be as follows:

```
import { NgModule, ErrorHandler } from '@angular/core';
import { IonicApp, IonicModule, IonicErrorHandler } from 'ionic-angular';
import { MyApp } from './app.component';
import { HomePage } from '../pages/home/home';
import { LoginPage } from '../pages/login/login';
import { BookRidePage } from '../pages/book-ride/book-ride';
import { AutocompletePage } from '../pages/auto-complete/auto-complete';
import { ProfilePage } from '../pages/profile/profile';
import { HistoryPage } from '../pages/history/history';
import { PaymentMethodsPage } from '../pages/payment-methods/payment-
methods';

import { UberAPI } from '../services/uber.service';
import { Storage } from '@ionic/storage';

import { StatusBar } from '@ionic-native/status-bar';
import { SplashScreen } from '@ionic-native/splash-screen';
```

```
import { Diagnostic } from '@ionic-native/diagnostic';

// export function provideStorage() {
//    return new Storage();
// }

@NgModule({
  declarations: [
    MyApp,
    HomePage,
    LoginPage,
    BookRidePage,
    AutocompletePage,
    ProfilePage,
    HistoryPage,
    PaymentMethodsPage
  ],
  imports: [
    IonicModule.forRoot(MyApp)
  ],
  bootstrap: [IonicApp],
  entryComponents: [
    MyApp,
    HomePage,
    LoginPage,
    BookRidePage,
    AutocompletePage,
    ProfilePage,
    HistoryPage,
    PaymentMethodsPage
  ],
  providers: [{ provide: ErrorHandler, useClass: IonicErrorHandler },
    UberAPI,
    // {provide: Storage, useFactory: provideStorage},
    Storage,
    StatusBar,
    SplashScreen,
    Diagnostic
  ]
})
export class AppModule { }
```

Now we are going to update the three pages we have scaffolded. Almost everything in these pages is quite self-explanatory.

The HTML in `riderr/src/pages/profile/profile.html` will be as follows:

```html
<ion-header>
    <ion-navbar>s
        <button ion-button menuToggle>
            <ion-icon name="menu"></ion-icon>
        </button>
        <ion-title>Riderr</ion-title>
    </ion-navbar>
</ion-header>
<ion-content padding>
    <h2 text-center>Your Profile</h2>
    <hr>
    <ion-list *ngIf="profile">
        <ion-item>
            <ion-avatar item-left>
                <img src="{{profile.picture}}">
            </ion-avatar>
            <h2>{{profile.first_name}} {{profile.last_name}}</h2>
            <h3>{{profile.email}}</h3>
            <p>{{profile.promo_code}}</p>
        </ion-item>
    </ion-list>
</ion-content>
```

The required logic will be in `riderr/src/pages/profile/profile.ts` as shown in the following code:

```typescript
import { Component } from '@angular/core';
import { UberAPI } from '../../services/uber.service';

@Component({
  selector: 'page-profile',
  templateUrl: 'profile.html'
})
export class ProfilePage {
  private profile;
  constructor(private uberApi: UberAPI) { }

  ngAfterViewInit() {
    this.uberApi.getMe().subscribe((data) => {
      // console.log(data.json());
      this.profile = data.json();
      // need a clean way to fix this!
      this.uberApi.hideLoader();
```

```
    }, (err) => {
      console.log(err);
      this.uberApi.hideLoader();
    });
  }
}
```

Next, we will work with `HistoryPage`. The HTML for `riderr/src/pages/history/history.html` will be as follows:

```
<ion-header>
    <ion-navbar>
        <button ion-button menuToggle>
            <ion-icon name="menu"></ion-icon>
        </button>
        <ion-title>Riderr</ion-title>
    </ion-navbar>
</ion-header>
<ion-content padding>
    <h2 text-center>Your Ride History</h2>
    <hr>
    <h3 text-center *ngIf="total">Showing last {{count}} of {{total}}
rides</h3>
    <ion-list>
        <ion-item *ngFor="let h of history">
            <h2>{{ h.start_city.display_name }}</h2>
            <h3>Completed at {{ h.end_time | date: 'hh:mm a'}}</h3>
            <p>Distance : {{ h.distance }} Miles</p>
        </ion-item>
    </ion-list>
</ion-content>
```

And the associated logic would be in `riderr/src/pages/history/history.ts` as shown:

```
import { Component } from '@angular/core';
import { UberAPI } from '../../services/uber.service';

@Component({
  selector: 'page-history',
  templateUrl: 'history.html'
})
export class HistoryPage {
  history: Array<any>;
  total: Number;
  count: Number;

  constructor(private uberApi: UberAPI) { }
```

```
ngAfterViewInit() {
  this.uberApi.getHistory().subscribe((data) => {
    // console.log(data.json());
    let d = data.json();
    this.history = d.history;
    this.total = d.count;
    this.count = d.history.length;

    // need a clean way to fix this!
    this.uberApi.hideLoader();
  }, (err) => {
    console.log(err);
    this.uberApi.hideLoader();
  });
}
}
```

Finally, we will implement the payment methods. The HTML for the same will be in `riderr/src/pages/payment-methods/payment-methods.html` as shown in the following code:

```
<ion-header>
    <ion-navbar>
        <button ion-button menuToggle>
            <ion-icon name="menu"></ion-icon>
        </button>
        <ion-title>Riderr</ion-title>
    </ion-navbar>
</ion-header>
<ion-content padding>
    <h2 text-center>Your Payment Methods</h2>
    <hr>
    <ion-list *ngIf="payment_methods">
        <ion-item *ngFor="let pm of payment_methods">
            <h2>{{ pm.type }}</h2>
            <h3>{{ pm.description }}</h3>
        </ion-item>
    </ion-list>
</ion-content>
```

And the required logic in `riderr/src/pages/payment-methods/payment-methods.ts` will be as follows:

```
import { Component } from '@angular/core';
import { UberAPI } from '../../services/uber.service';

@Component({
  selector: 'page-payment-methods',
```

```
    templateUrl: 'payment-methods.html'
})
export class PaymentMethodsPage {
  payment_methods;

  constructor(private uberApi: UberAPI) { }

  ngAfterViewInit() {
    this.uberApi.getPaymentMethods().subscribe((data) => {
      // console.log(data.json());
      this.payment_methods = data.json().payment_methods;
      // need a clean way to fix this!
      this.uberApi.hideLoader();
    }, (err) => {
      console.log(err);
      this.uberApi.hideLoader();
    });
  }
}
```

With this, we complete the required code. Next, we will install the required plugins and libraries.

Installing dependencies

Run the following commands to install the Cordova plugins needed for this app:

```
ionic plugin add cordova.plugins.diagnostic
ionic plugin add cordova-plugin-geolocation
ionic plugin add cordova-plugin-inappbrowser
ionic plugin add cordova-sqlite-storage
ionic plugin add cordova-custom-config
```

And their Ionic Native modules:

```
npm install --save @ionic-native/google-maps
npm install --save @ionic-native/Geolocation
npm install --save @ionic-native/diagnostic
npm install --save @ionic-native/in-app-browser
npm install --save @ionic/storage
```

Next, we will be installing the Cordova plugin for Google Maps. But before we install that, we need to get an API key. Use the **Get A Key** button at
https://developers.google.com/maps/documentation/android-api/signup to enable the Google Maps API for Android apps and get a key. Go to the following page for iOS:
https://developers.google.com/maps/documentation/ios-sdk/get-api-key.

Once you have the API key, run the following:

```
ionic plugin add cordova-plugin-googlemaps --variable API_KEY_FOR_ANDROID="
AIzaSyCZhTJB1kFAP70RuwDtt6uso9e3DCLdRWs" --variable
API_KEY_FOR_IOS="AIzaSyCZhTJB1kFAP70RuwDtt6uso9e3DCLdRWs"
```

Note: Please update the preceding command with your keys.

Next, for working with the Google Maps Places Service, we need to get an API key for accessing the Maps services via JavaScript. Navigate to `https://developers.google.com/maps/documentation/JavaScript/get-api-key` to get a key for JavaScript. Then open `riderr/src/index.html` and add the following reference in the header section of the document:

```
<script
src="http://maps.google.com/maps/api/js?v=3&libraries=places&key=AIzaSyDmFp
X80vy5p0YTuXGAgVJzWTkZfDqPl_s"></script>
```

Next, for the TypeScript Compiler not to complain about the use of the variable `google` in `riderr/src/pages/auto-complete/auto-complete.ts`, we need to add the required typings. Run the following:

```
npm install typings --global
```

Next, we run the following command:

```
typings install dt~google.maps --global --save
```

Open `riderr/tsconfig.json` and add `"typings/*.d.ts"` to the `"include"` array as shown in the following code:

```
{
  "compilerOptions": {
    "allowSyntheticDefaultImports": true,
    "declaration": false,
    "emitDecoratorMetadata": true,
    "experimentalDecorators": true,
    "lib": [
      "dom",
      "es2015"
    ],
    "module": "es2015",
    "moduleResolution": "node",
    "sourceMap": true,
    "target": "es5"
  },
  "include": [
```

```
    "src/**/*.ts",
    "typings/*.d.ts"
  ],
  "exclude": [
    "node_modules"
  ],
  "compileOnSave": false,
  "atom": {
    "rewriteTsconfig": false
  }
}
```

Refer to *How to install Typescript* typings for Google Maps:
`http://stackoverflow.com/a/40854384/1015046` for more information.

Finally, we need to request permission for Internet access and network access. Open
`riderr/config.xml` and update `<platform name="android"></ platform>` as
shown:

```
<platform name="android">
        <allow-intent href="market:*" />
        <config-file target="AndroidManifest.xml" parent="/*">
            <uses-permission android:name="android.permission.INTERNET"
            />
            <uses-permission
            android:name="android.permission.ACCESS_FINE_LOCATION" />
            <uses-permission
            android:name="android.permission.ACCESS_COARSE_LOCATION" />
        </config-file>
    </platform>
```

And then add `xmlns:android=http://schemas.android.com/apk/res/android` to
the widget tag present at the top of the page, as shown:

```
<widget id="app.example.riderr" version="0.0.1"
xmlns="http://www.w3.org/ns/widgets"
xmlns:cdv="http://cordova.apache.org/ns/1.0"
xmlns:android="http://schemas.android.com/apk/res/android">
```

This wraps up the *Installing dependencies* section.

Testing the app

Let's go ahead and test drive the app. First, we need to add the required platform. Run `ionic platform add android` or `ionic platform add ios`.

For testing the app, we need an emulator or an actual device.

Once the device/emulator is set up, we can run either the command `ionic run android` or `ionic run ios`.

The flow would be as follows:

First, the user launches the app. The login screen is presented, which is as follows:

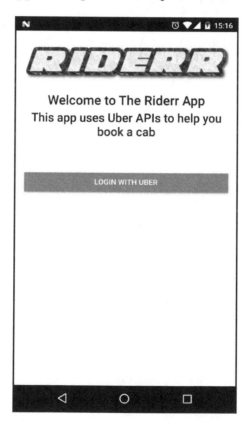

Once the user clicks on **LOGIN WITH UBER**, we redirect the user to the Uber Auth Screen, where the user will log in using their Uber Account:

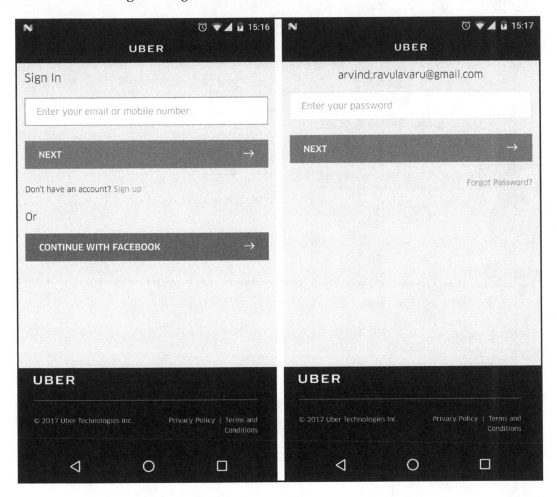

Once the authentication is successful, the consent screen will be shown with the list of permissions requested by the app:

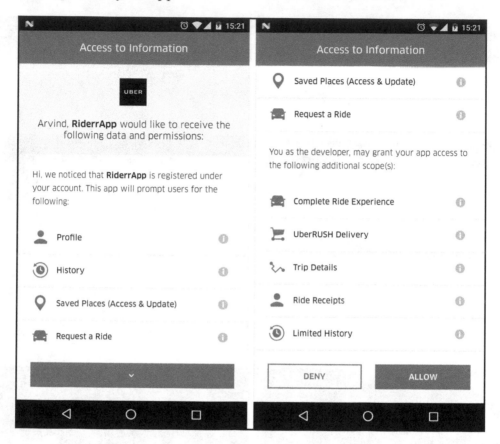

Once the user allows the app to access the data, we redirect the user to the home page.

On the home page, we provide the consent popup for accessing the user's location:

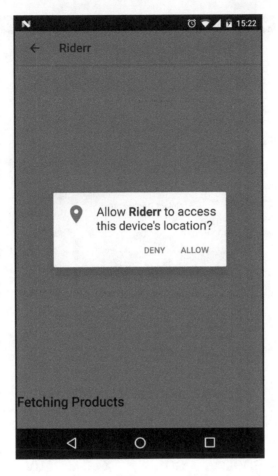

Once approved, we get the Geolocation of the user and, using that, the products.

The following is the screenshot of the completely loaded home screen:

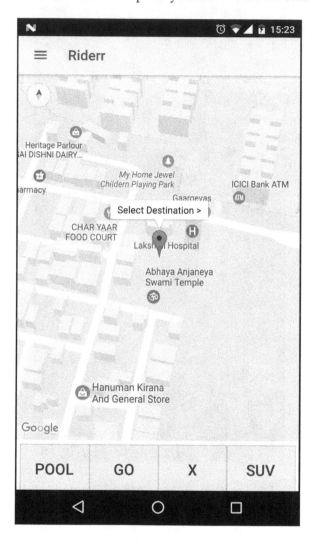

The **Menu** will be as follows:

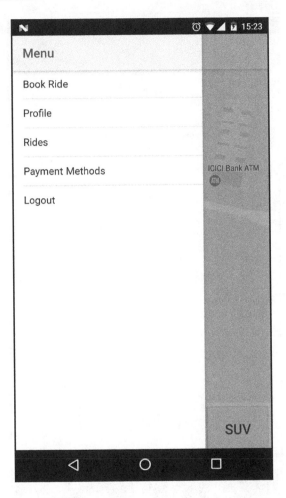

From here, the user can view their profile:

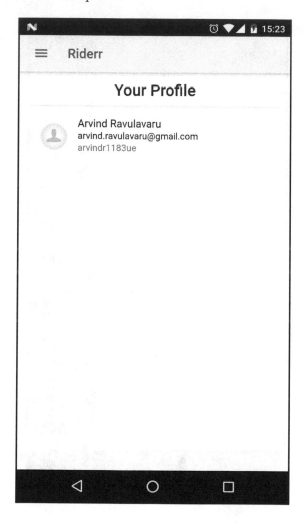

They can view their ride history:

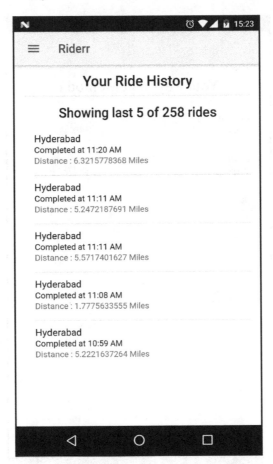

They can also review their payment methods:

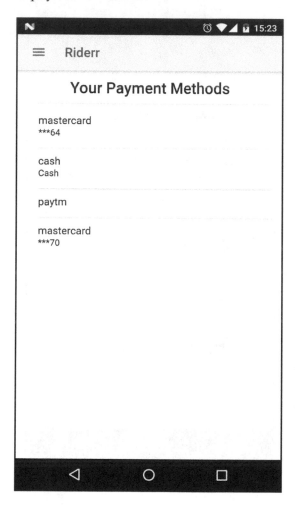

Before the user selects a destination, they need to pick a product:

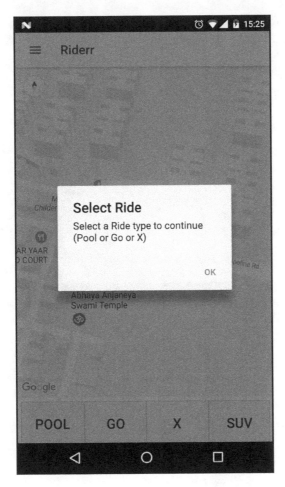

Once they have selected the product, they can choose a destination to ride to:

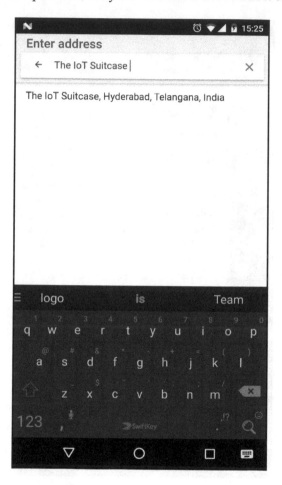

Now, we make the fare details and display the same:

If the user agrees, we book the ride and display the ride information:

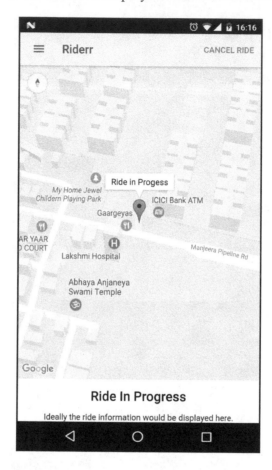

Do notice the **CANCEL RIDE** button at the top-right corner of the app. This will cancel the current ride.

Again, as a reminder, we are making calls to the Sandbox API URL. If you want to request an actual ride, update `UBERSANDBOXAPIURL` to `UBERAPIURL` in `riderr/src/services/uber.service.ts`.

Using the Uber (production) API, when we request a ride, we receive a processing response. We can keep polling a couple of times to fetch the current ride information. And this is what the response will look like if you make an actual ride request:

```
{
    "status": "accepted",
    "product_id": "18ba4578-b11b-49a6-a992-a132f540b027",
```

```
    "destination": {
        "latitude": 17.445949,
        "eta": 34,
        "longitude": 78.350058
    },
    "driver": {
        "phone_number": "+910000000000",
        "rating": 4.6,
        "picture_url":
        "https:\/\/d1w2poirtb3as9.cloudfront.net\
        /605de11c25139a1de469.jpeg",
        "name": "John Doe",
        "sms_number": null
    },
    "pickup": {
        "latitude": 17.4908514,
        "eta": 13,
        "longitude": 78.3375952
    },
    "request_id": "1beaae05-8d43-4711-951c-25dd5293c2f9",
    "location": {
        "latitude": 17.4875583,
        "bearing": 338,
        "longitude": 78.33165
    },
    "vehicle": {
        "make": "Maruti Suzuki",
        "picture_url": null,
        "model": "Swift Dzire",
        "license_plate": "XXXXXXXX"
    },
    "shared": false
}
```

You can build your interface accordingly.

Summary

In this chapter, we have gone through building an app with Ionic and integrating the same with Uber API as well as device features using Ionic Native. We have also used the Google Places Service as a raw JavaScript library and integrated it with our Ionic app using typings.

In the next chapter, we are going to look at migrating Ionic 1 apps to Ionic 2. This will be applicable if you are moving from Ionic 1 to Ionic 3 as well.

8
Ionic 2 Migration Guide

In this chapter, we are going to take a look at migrating an existing Ionic 1 app to Ionic 2/Ionic 3. We are first going to build a simple Todo app using Ionic 1 and then understand how we would go about migrating the same to Ionic 2:

- Why migration?
- Building a simple Ionic 1 Todo app
- Migration game plan
- Migrating the Ionic 1 Todo app to Ionic 2

This migration guide will still be valid if you would like to migrate from Ionic 1 to Ionic 3 as well. Refer to `Chapter 11`, *Ionic 3* to better understand the changes in Ionic 3.

Why migration?

So far, in this book, we have gone through the process of building apps with Ionic 2, without the knowledge of Ionic 1. But as far as the real world goes, there are a few thousand apps already deployed with Ionic 1. Those apps can take advantage of the improved features of Ionic 2 to make the app experience better.

Migrating code in the world of software is a daunting task. In our case, the migration is even more complex because we are not just upgrading the libraries of Ionic 1 to Ionic 2 but upgrading the language itself on which these are written for example, ES5 to ES6 and TypeScript.

The new ecosystem for JavaScript apps primarily revolves around ES6, TypeScript, and Web Components. Adapting to these to take advantage of the latest technologies is what Angular 2 has done. Ionic 2 has also done this.

IMHO, with so many changes, migrating a fully functioning app from Ionic 1 to Ionic 2 should be taken with a pinch of salt and needs to be done only if necessary.

If things work, why change?

When it comes to changing an app base from Ionic 1 to Ionic 2, some call it migration, but I call it rewriting.

Todo app - Ionic v1

In this section, we are going to build a Todo app using Ionic 1. The app we are going to build is going to have a piece of almost all the features of a typical Ionic app. We are going to have:

- Routing
- Persistence
- Local notifications
- REST API integration

The first page in the two-page Todo app will be a login page and on the second page, we work with Todos. We are going to use `LocalStorage` to save the authentication status as well as the Todos that we are going to create. We are also going to show local notifications when a user creates, updates, or deletes a todo. Showing local notifications is more along the lines of interfacing an Ionic app with device features. And finally a REST API request to `https://www.ipify.org/` to fetch the IP address of the device we are accessing this app from.

The final app is going to look like the following image:

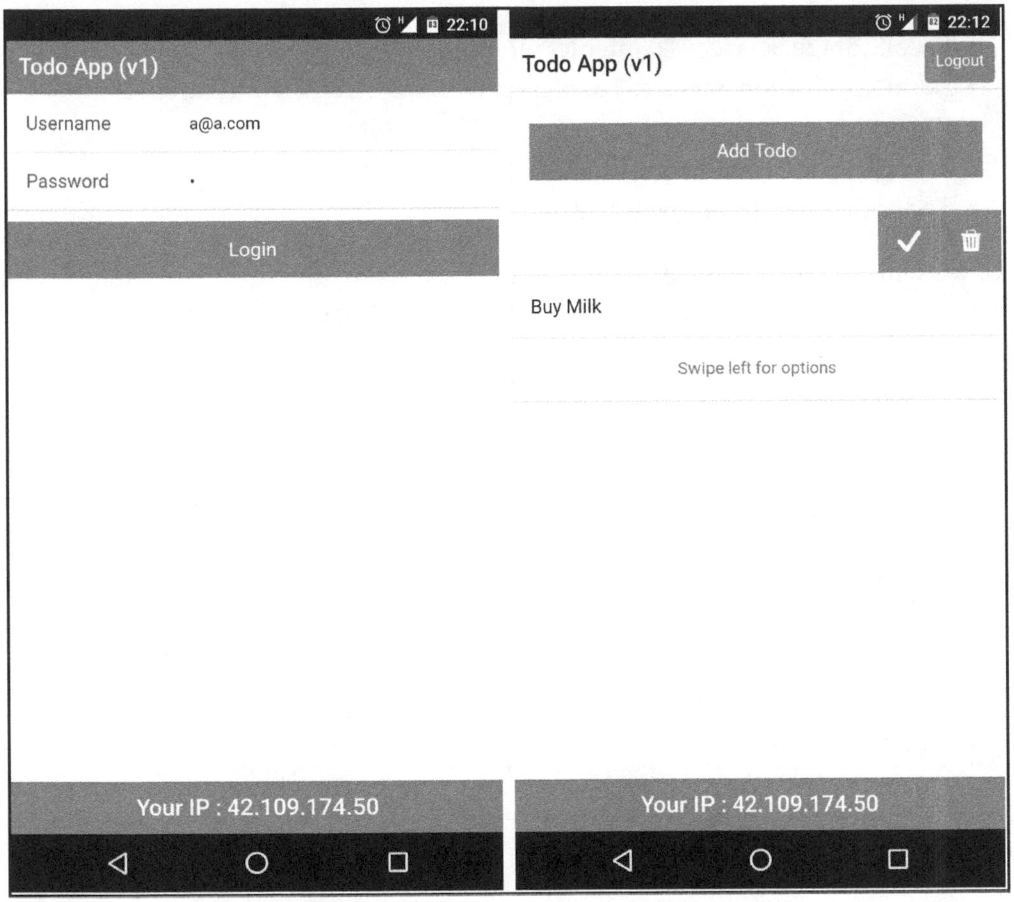

Building the app

Now that we have an idea as to what we are going to build, let us get started. Create a folder named chapter8 and open a new command prompt/terminal inside the chapter8 folder and run:

```
ionic start -a "TodoApp-v1" -i app.example.todoapp_v1 todoapp_v1   blank
```

We are scaffolding a blank project using Ionic v1. Do notice that we are not using the --v2 flag. Once the project is scaffolded, open it in your favorite text editor.

Before we start working on the two pages, we are going to create the required services. We are going to create five services:

- LocalStorage Service: To interact with LocalStorage
- LocalNotification Service: To interact with $cordovaLocalNotification
- IP Service: To interact with https://api.ipify.org
- Auth Service: To manage authentication
- Todos Service: To manage Todos

For that, we will create another file named services.js inside the www/js folder. Open todoapp_v1/www/js/services.js and add the following code:

```
angular.module('starter')
.service('LS', function($window) { // local storage
    this.set = function(key, value) {
        // http://stackoverflow.com/a/23656919/1015046
        $window.localStorage.setItem(key,
        $window.angular.toJson(value));
    }

    this.get = function(key) {
        return $window.JSON.parse($window.localStorage.getItem(key));
    }

    this.remove = function(key) {
        $window.localStorage.removeItem(key);
    }
})
```

The LS service exposes a wrapper to the HTML5 localStorage.

Next, add a wrapper for the local notification service in the same file, after the LS service:

```
// snipp
.service('LN', function($ionicPlatform, $cordovaLocalNotification) { //
local notifications
    var i = 1;
    this.show = function(text) {
        $ionicPlatform.ready(function() {
            var notifPromise = $cordovaLocalNotification.schedule({
                id: i++,
                title: 'Todo App',
                text: text
            })
            return notifPromise;
        });
```

```
        }
})
```

We will add the required dependencies from ngCordova at the end of writing the code.

Next, we will add the IP service to interact with https://api.ipify.org and get the IP address of the user. Append the following code:

```
// snipp
.service('IP', function ($http) {
    this.get = function(){
        return $http.get('https://api.ipify.org/?format=json');
    }
})
```

And finally, the two key services to manage authentication and todos. Add the following code:

```
// snipp
.service('AUTH', function(LS) {
    var LS_AUTH_KEY = 'auth';
    this.login = function(user) {
        if (user.email === 'a@a.com', user.password === 'a') {
            LS.set(LS_AUTH_KEY, true);
            return true;
        } else {
            return false;
        }
    }

    this.isAuthenticated = function() {
        return !!LS.get(LS_AUTH_KEY);
    }

    this.logout = function() {
        LS.remove(LS_AUTH_KEY);
    }

})

.service('TODOS', function(LS) {
    var LS_TODOS_KEY = 'todos';

    this.set = function(todos) {
        LS.set(LS_TODOS_KEY, todos);
    }

    this.get = function() {
```

```
        return LS.get(LS_TODOS_KEY) || [];
    }
});
```

With this, we are done with the required services.

Since this is going to be a two-page app, we will be working with the State router to define and manage routes. Open `todoapp_v1/www/js/app.js` and add the following `config` section under the `run` method:

```
.config(function($stateProvider, $urlRouterProvider) {
    $stateProvider
        .state('login', {
            url: '/login',
            templateUrl: 'templates/login.html',
            controller: 'LoginCtrl'
        })
        .state('home', {
            url: '/home',
            templateUrl: 'templates/home.html',
            controller: 'HomeCtrl'
        });
    // if none of the above states are matched, use this as the fallback
    $urlRouterProvider.otherwise('/login');
});
```

In the preceding snippet we have defined two routes - Login and Home. Now we need to create the required templates and controllers.

Create a new file named `controllers.js` inside `www/js` folder. Open `todoapp_v1/www/js/controllers.js` and the `LoginCtrl` as shown in the following code:

```
angular.module('starter')

.controller('LoginCtrl', function($scope, AUTH, $state, $ionicHistory,
$ionicPopup) {

    // check Auth before proceeding
    if (AUTH.isAuthenticated()) {
        $state.go('home');
    }

    // hardcode the test user
    $scope.user = {
        email: 'a@a.com',
        password: 'a'
```

```
    }

    $scope.login = function() {
        if (AUTH.login($scope.user)) {
            // remove all views in stack
            // this way when the user clicks on the
            // back button on the home page
            // we do not show the login screen again
            $ionicHistory.clearHistory();
            $state.go('home');
        } else {
            $ionicPopup.alert({
                title: 'LOGIN FAILED',
                template: 'Either the email or password is invalid.'
            });
        };
    }
})
```

Here we are checking if the user is already authenticated, if yes, we redirect the user to the home page. The login() takes the user's credentials and validates them with AUTH.login(). If the authentication fails, we show an alert using $ionicPopup service.

Next, we will add the HomeCtrl as shown in the following code::

```
// snipp

.controller('HomeCtrl', function($scope, $state, AUTH, TODOS,
$ionicHistory, $ionicPopup, $ionicListDelegate, LN) {

    $scope.todo = {};
    // check Auth before proceeding
    if (!AUTH.isAuthenticated()) {
        $state.go('login');
    }

    // fetch todos on load
    $scope.todos = TODOS.get();

    $scope.add = function() {
        //reset
        $scope.todo.text = '';
        var addTodoPopup = $ionicPopup.show({
            template: '<input type="text" ng-model="todo.text">',
            title: 'Add Todo',
            subTitle: 'Enter a Todo To Do',
            scope: $scope,
            buttons: [
```

```
                    { text: 'Cancel' }, {
                        text: '<b>Save</b>',
                        type: 'button-positive',
                        onTap: function(e) {
                            // validation
                            if (!$scope.todo.text) {
                                e.preventDefault();
                            } else {
                                return $scope.todo.text;
                            }
                        }
                    }
                ]
            });

            addTodoPopup.then(function(text) {
                if (text) {
                    var todo = {
                        text: text,
                        isCompleted: false
                    };

                    $scope.todos.push(todo);
                    // save it to LS
                    TODOS.set($scope.todos);
                    LN.show('Todo Created');
                }
            });
        }

        $scope.update = function(todo) {
            todo.isCompleted = !todo.isCompleted;
            $ionicListDelegate.closeOptionButtons();
            // update LS
            TODOS.set($scope.todos);
            LN.show('Todo Updated');
        }

        $scope.delete = function($index, todo) {

            var deleteConfirmPopup = $ionicPopup.confirm({
                title: 'Delete Todo',
                template: 'Are you sure you want to delete "' + todo.text +
                '"? '
            });

            deleteConfirmPopup.then(function(res) {
                if (res) {
```

```
                  $scope.todos.splice($index, 1);
                  // update LS
                  TODOS.set($scope.todos);
                  LN.show('Todo Deleted');
              }
          });
      }

      $scope.logout = function() {
          AUTH.logout();
          $ionicHistory.clearHistory();
          $state.go('login');
      }
  });
```

We start off by checking authentication. Next, we fetch all the todos. We have defined four methods on `HomeCtrl` scope: `add()`, `update()`, `delete()`, and `logout()`.

Add method is used to add a new todo. We show a popup using `$ionicPopup` service, where the user enters the Todo text. Once the todo is added, we push a local notification using the `LN` service.

Update method updates the todo's `isCompleted` property in the local storage and pushes a local notification indicating the same.

Delete method shows a confirm box asking the user to confirm the deletion activity. If the user confirms the deletion, we remove the todo from the collection and persist the collection back to the local storage. To complete the deletion process, we push a local notification indicating that the todo is deleted.

And finally the logout method clears the authentication status and redirects the user back to the login page.

Now that we are done with the controllers, we will work on the required templates. Create a new folder named `templates` inside the `www` folder. Inside the templates folder, create a file named `login.html`. Open `todoapp_v1/www/templates/login.html` and update it as shown in the following code::

```html
<ion-view view->
    <ion-content>
        <div class="list">
            <label class="item item-input">
                <span class="input-label">Username</span>
                <input type="email" ng-model="user.email"
                placeholder="Enter your email">
            </label>
```

```
            <label class="item item-input">
                <span class="input-label">Password</span>
                <input type="password" ng-model="user.password"
                placeholder="Enter your password">
            </label>
            <button ng-click="login()" class="button button-positive
            button-full" ng-disabled="!user.email || !user.password">
                Login
            </button>
        </div>
    </ion-content>
    <ion-footer-bar align- class="bar-positive">
        <h1 class="title">Your IP : {{ip}}</h1>
    </ion-footer-bar>
</ion-view>
```

We have a simple login form. In the footer, we will be displaying the IP address of the user.
To get the IP address of the user, we are going to update the `run` method in
`todoapp_v1/www/js/app.js` as shown in the following code:

```
// snipp
.run(function($ionicPlatform, IP, $rootScope) {
    $ionicPlatform.ready(function() {
        if (window.cordova && window.cordova.plugins.Keyboard) {
            cordova.plugins.Keyboard.hideKeyboardAccessoryBar(true);
            cordova.plugins.Keyboard.disableScroll(true);
        }
        if (window.StatusBar) {
            StatusBar.styleDefault();
        }

        IP.get().then(function(resp) {
            // console.log(resp.data);
            $rootScope.ip = resp.data.ip;
        });
    });
})
// snipp
```

We are storing the IP address on the root scope.

Next, create a new file named `home.html` inside the `www/templates` folder. Update
`todoapp_v1/www/templates/home.html` as shown shown in the following code:

```
<ion-view view->
    <ion-nav-bar class="bar-default">
        <ion-nav-buttons side="right">
            <button class="button button-assertive" ng-click="
```

```
                logout()">
                    Logout
                </button>
            </ion-nav-buttons>
        </ion-nav-bar>
        <ion-content>
            <ion-list can-swipe="true">
                <ion-item>
                    <button class="button button-full button-positive" ng-
                    click="add()">
                        Add Todo
                    </button>
                </ion-item>
                <ion-item ng-repeat="todo in todos">
                    <h2 ng-class="{ 'strike' : todo.isCompleted}">
                    {{todo.text}}</h2>
                    <ion-option-button class="button-assertive icon ion-
                    trash-a" ng-click="delete($index, todo)">
                    </ion-option-button>
                    <ion-option-button class="button-positive icon" ng-
                    class="{'ion-checkmark-round' :
                    !todo.isCompleted, 'ion-close-round' :
                    todo.isCompleted}" ng-click="update(todo)">
                    </ion-option-button>
                </ion-item>
                <ion-item ng-if="todos.length > 0">
                    <p class="text-center">Swipe left for options</p>
                </ion-item>
                <ion-item ng-if="todos.length === 0">
                    <h2 class="text-center">No Todos</h2>
                </ion-item>
            </ion-list>
        </ion-content>
        <ion-footer-bar align- class="bar-positive">
            <h1 class="title">Your IP : {{ip}}</h1>
        </ion-footer-bar>
    </ion-view>
```

When a user marks a `todo` as completed, for visual effect, we are adding a class named
`strike`. Open `todoapp_v1/www/css/style.css` and update it as shown in the following
code:

```
.strike{
  text-decoration: line-through;
  color: #999;
}
```

With this, we are done with implementing the required code. Now, we are going to add the required dependencies and update `www/index.html`.

First, we are going to add `ngCordova` (`http://ngcordova.com/`) support to our project. Run the following:

```
bower install ngCordova --save
```

Next, the local notification plugin:
(`http://ngcordova.com/docs/plugins/localNotification/`) cordova plugin add: `https://github.com/katzer/cordova-plugin-local-notifications.git`.

Now, we will update `www/index.html` to add the `ngCordova` dependency. Add the following:

```
<script src="lib/ngCordova/dist/ng-cordova.js"></script> before <script
src="cordova.js"></script>.
```

Next, add references to `services.js` and `controllers.js`:

```
<script src="js/services.js"></script>
<script src="js/controllers.js"></script>
```

After `app.js` has been included. Next, will update the body section as shown in the following code:

```
<ion-pane>
        <ion-nav-bar class="bar-positive">
        </ion-nav-bar>
        <ion-nav-view></ion-nav-view>
</ion-pane>
```

We have added `<ion-nav-view></ion-nav-view>` to support routing.

Now, open `todoapp_v1/www/js/app.js` and update the starter module definition to:
`angular.module('starter', ['ionic', 'ngCordova'])`

That is it! Now all we need to do is add a platform and start testing the **Todo** app built with Ionic v1:

```
ionic platform add android or ionic platform add ios
```

And then run the following:

```
ionic run android or ionic run ios
```

And we should see the **Login** page come up:

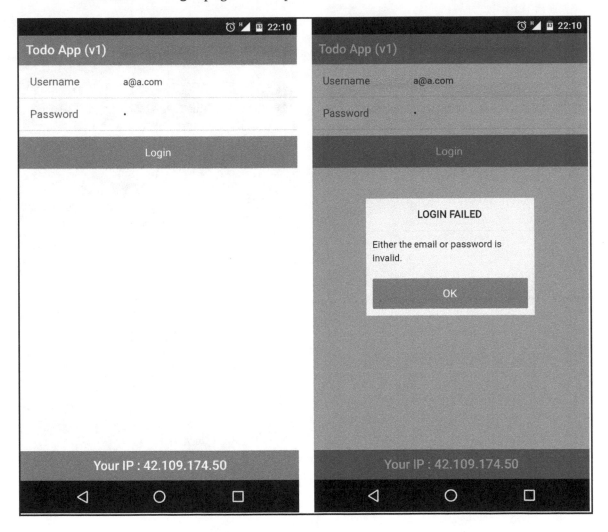

Once successfully logged in, we should be able to add a new todo:

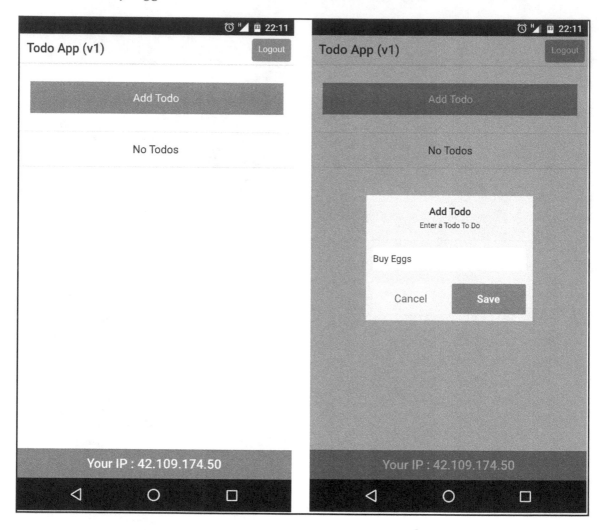

We can update the todo or delete the todo:

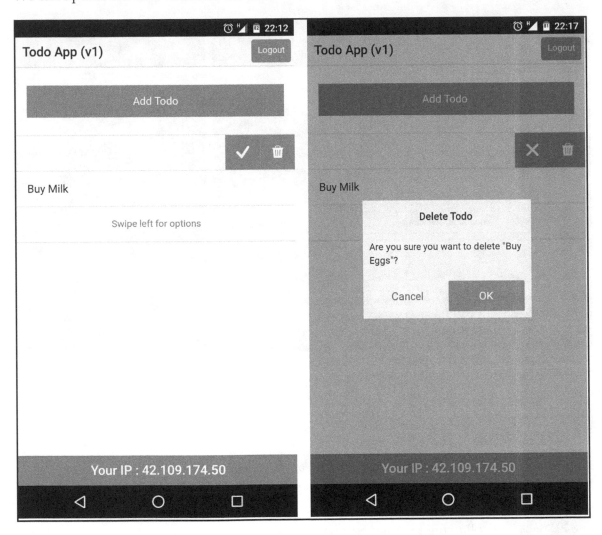

When a todo is added, updated, or deleted, we push a local notification:

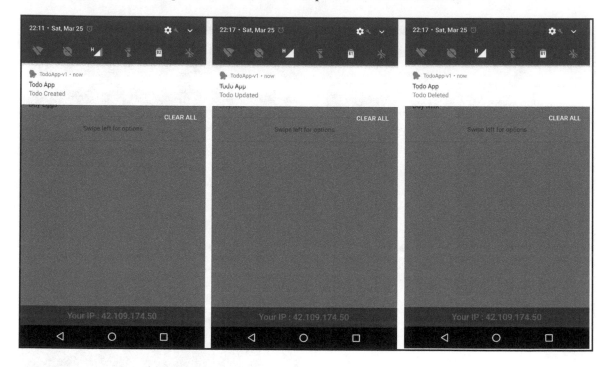

With this, we complete building an Ionic 1 Todo app.

Migration plan

Now that we are done with our Ionic v1 Todo app, we will be looking at migrating the same to Ionic 2.

Note: If you were planning to migrate from Ionic 1 to Ionic 3, you would be following a similar approach.

The plan is simple; we are going to scaffold a new blank template using the `--v2` flag and start putting stuff together. The following table would be a good starting point:

Component	Ionic 1	Ionic 2
Ionic starter template	Blank	Blank
Bootstrap application	ng-app	`NgModule`
Navigation	State router	`NavController`
Components	Templates and controllers	`@Component`
Services/factory	Service provider	`@Injectable Provider`
Persistence	Local storage	Storage API
Device interaction	`NgCordova`	Ionic Native
Local notifications	`$cordovaLocalNotification` service	LocalNotifications class

Now that we are aware of the high level mapping, we will start by scaffolding a new blank template in v2.

Inside the `chapter8` folder, open a new command prompt/terminal and run:

```
ionic start -a "TodoApp-v2" -i app.example.todoapp_v2 todoapp_v2  blank --
v2
```

Once the scaffolding is completed, `cd` into the `todoapp_v2` folder. We will be generating the required components and providers. Run the following:

```
ionic generate page login
```

This will generate the login page. Next, the three providers:

```
ionic generate provider auth
ionic generate provider todos
ionic generate provider IP
```

Since we are using the Storage API from Ionic 2, we are not going to create a separate provider for that.

Now that we have the required pages and providers, we will bootstrap the app.

Open `todoapp_v2/src/app/app.module.ts` and the required imports:

```
// snipp
import { LoginPage } from '../pages/login/login';

import { Auth } from '../providers/auth';
import { Todos } from '../providers/todos';
import { IP } from '../providers/ip';

import { IonicStorageModule } from '@ionic/storage';
import { LocalNotifications } from '@ionic-native/local-notifications';
```

Next, we will update the `@NgModule` as shown in the following code:

```
@NgModule({
  declarations: [
    MyApp,
    HomePage,
    LoginPage
  ],
  imports: [
    IonicModule.forRoot(MyApp),
    IonicStorageModule.forRoot()
  ],
  bootstrap: [IonicApp],
  entryComponents: [
    MyApp,
    HomePage,
    LoginPage
  ],
  providers: [
    StatusBar,
    SplashScreen,
    {provide: ErrorHandler, useClass: IonicErrorHandler},
    Auth,
    Todos,
    IP,
    LocalNotifications
  ]
})
```

As we did with the Ionic 1 app, we will install the required dependencies at the end.

Open `todoapp_v2/src/app/app.component.ts` and update the `rootPage` to `LoginPage`. We would update the `import { HomePage }` from `'../pages/home/home';` to `import { LoginPage }` from `'../pages/login/login';` and `rootPage = HomePage;` to `rootPage = LoginPage;`

Now, we will update the providers. Open `todoapp_v2/src/providers/ip.ts` and update it as shown in the following code:

```
import { Injectable } from '@angular/core';
import { Http, Response } from '@angular/http';
import { Observable } from 'rxjs/Observable';

@Injectable()
export class IP {
  constructor(private http: Http) {}

  get() : Observable <Response>{
    return this.http.get('https://api.ipify.org/?format=json');
  }
}
```

Next, open `todoapp_v2/src/providers/auth.ts`. Update it as shown as following:

```
import { Injectable } from '@angular/core';
import { Storage } from '@ionic/storage';

@Injectable()
export class Todos {
  private LS_TODOS_KEY = 'todos';

  constructor(private storage: Storage) { }

  set(todos): void {
    this.storage.set(this.LS_TODOS_KEY, todos);
  }

  get(): Promise<any> {
    return this.storage.get(this.LS_TODOS_KEY);
  }
}
```

And finally, open `todoapp_v2/src/providers/auth.ts` and update it as following:

```
import { Injectable } from '@angular/core';
import { Storage } from '@ionic/storage';

@Injectable()
export class Auth {
  private LS_AUTH_KEY = 'auth';

  constructor(private storage: Storage) { }

  login(user: any): Boolean {
```

```
      if (user.email === 'a@a.com', user.password === 'a') {
        this.storage.set(this.LS_AUTH_KEY, true)
        return true;
      } else {
        return false;
      }
    }

    isAuthenticated(): Promise<Storage> {
      return this.storage.get(this.LS_AUTH_KEY);
    }

    logout(): void {
      this.storage.set(this.LS_AUTH_KEY, undefined);
    }
  }
```

The preceding three providers are quite simple. They replicate the same logic as shown in Ionic 1, except these are written in TypeScript, following Angular 2 structure.

Now, we are going to work on the pages. First is the login page. Open `todoapp_v2/src/pages/login/login.ts` and update it as in the following code:

```
import { Component } from '@angular/core';
import { NavController, AlertController } from 'ionic-angular';
import { HomePage } from '../home/home';
import { Auth } from '../../providers/auth';
import { IP } from '../../providers/ip';

@Component({
  selector: 'page-login',
  templateUrl: 'login.html'
})
export class LoginPage {
  userIp = '';
  user = {
    email: 'a@a.com',
    password: 'a'
  }

  constructor(
    public navCtrl: NavController,
    public alertCtrl: AlertController,
    private auth: Auth,
    private ip: IP) {

    // check if the user is already
    // authenticated
```

```
auth.isAuthenticated().then((isAuth) => {
  if (isAuth) {
    navCtrl.setRoot(HomePage);
  }
});

// Get the user's IP
ip.get().subscribe((data) => {
  this.userIp = data.json().ip;
});
}

login() {
  if (this.auth.login(this.user)) {
    this.navCtrl.setRoot(HomePage);
  } else {
    let alert = this.alertCtrl.create({
      title: 'LOGIN FAILED',
      subTitle: 'Either the email or password is invalid.',
      buttons: ['OK']
    });
    alert.present();
  }
}
}
```

The logic in this file is quite similar to the one from `LoginCtrl` in Ionic 1 app. Next we will update `todoapp_v2/src/pages/login/login.html` as shown in the following code:

```html
<ion-header class="positive">
    <ion-navbar>
        <ion-title>Todo App (v2)</ion-title>
    </ion-navbar>
</ion-header>
<ion-content>
    <ion-list>
        <ion-item>
            <ion-label fixed>Username</ion-label>
            <ion-input type="email" placeholder="Enter your email"
            [(ngModel)]="user.email"></ion-input>
        </ion-item>
        <ion-item>
            <ion-label fixed>Password</ion-label>
            <ion-input type="password" placeholder="Enter your
            password" [(ngModel)]="user.password"></ion-input>
        </ion-item>
    </ion-list>
    <button ion-button full (click)="login()" [disabled]="!user.email ||
```

```
!user.password">Login</button>
</ion-content>
<ion-footer>
  <h3>Your IP : {{userIp}}</h3>
</ion-footer>
```

The page structure is exactly the same as Ionic 1 except for the way in which we interact with the components; `[(ngModel)]` syntax for two-way data binding `(ng-model)` and `(click)` syntax for event handling on the button `(ng-click)`.

Do notice the class positive on `ion-header`. We will use this to give almost the same look and feel for the page as we did for the Ionic 1 app.

Now we are going to work on `todoapp_v2/src/pages/home/home.ts`. Update `todoapp_v2/src/pages/home/home.ts` as shown in the following code:

```
import { Component } from '@angular/core';
import { LocalNotifications } from '@ionic-native/local-notifications';
import { NavController, AlertController } from 'ionic-angular';
import { LoginPage } from '../login/login';
import { Auth } from '../../providers/auth';
import { IP } from '../../providers/ip';
import { Todos } from '../../providers/todos';

@Component({
  selector: 'page-home',
  templateUrl: 'home.html'
})
export class HomePage {
  private i = 1; // ID for notifications
  userIp = '';
  userTodos = [];

  constructor(
    public navCtrl: NavController,
    public alertCtrl: AlertController,
    private localNotifications: LocalNotifications,
    private auth: Auth,
    private ip: IP,
    private todos: Todos) {

    // check if the user is authenticated
    auth.isAuthenticated().then((isAuth) => {
      if (!isAuth) {
        navCtrl.setRoot(LoginPage);
      }
    });
```

```
  // fetch todos on load
  this.todos.get().then((_todos) => {
    this.userTodos = _todos || [];
  });

  // Get the user's IP
  ip.get().subscribe((data) => {
    this.userIp = data.json().ip;
  });
}

add() {
  let addTodoPopup = this.alertCtrl.create({
    title: 'Add Todo',
    inputs: [
      {
        name: 'text',
        placeholder: 'Enter a Todo To Do'
      }
    ],
    buttons: [
      {
        text: 'Cancel',
        role: 'cancel',
        handler: (data) => {
          // console.log('Cancel clicked');
        }
      },
      {
        text: 'Save',
        handler: (data) => {
          if (data.text) {
            let todo = {
              text: data.text,
              isCompleted: false
            };
            this.userTodos.push(todo);
            // store the todos
            this.todos.set(this.userTodos);
            this.notify('Todo Created');

          } else {
            return false;
          }
        }
      }

    ]
```

```
    });
    addTodoPopup.present();
  }

  update(todo, slidingItem) {
    todo.isCompleted = !todo.isCompleted;
    // store the todos
    this.todos.set(this.userTodos);
    slidingItem.close();
    this.notify('Todo Updated');
  }

  delete(todo, index) {
    let alert = this.alertCtrl.create({
      title: 'Delete Todo',
      message: 'Are you sure you want to delete "' + todo.text + '"? ',
      buttons: [
        {
          text: 'No',
          role: 'cancel',
          handler: () => {
            // console.log('Cancel clicked');
          }
        },
        {
          text: 'Yes',
          handler: () => {
            this.userTodos.splice(index, 1);
            this.todos.set(this.userTodos);
            this.notify('Todo Deleted');
          }
        }
      ]
    });
    alert.present();

  }

  logout() {
    this.auth.logout();
    this.navCtrl.setRoot(LoginPage);
  }

  private notify(text) {
    this.localNotifications.schedule({
      id: this.i++,
      title: 'Todo App',
      text: text,
```

```
        });
    }
}
```

The same logic of `HomeCtrl` is replicated here. The only key difference is that `notify()` is used as a wrapper to present Local Notifications, unlike in Ionic 1 app, where we had a service for the same.

The updated `todoapp_v2/src/pages/home/home.html` would be as follows:

```html
<ion-header>
    <ion-navbar>
        <ion-title>Todo App (v2)</ion-title>
        <ion-buttons end>
            <button ion-button color="danger" (click)="logout()">
                Logout
            </button>
        </ion-buttons>
    </ion-navbar>
</ion-header>
<ion-content>
    <button ion-button full (click)="add()">
        Add Todo
    </button>
    <ion-list can-swipe="true">
        <ion-item-sliding *ngFor="let todo of userTodos" #slidingItem>
            <ion-item [class.strike]="todo.isCompleted">
                {{todo.text}}
            </ion-item>
            <ion-item-options side="right">
                <button ion-button icon-only (click)="update(todo,
                slidingItem)">
                    <ion-icon [name]="todo.isCompleted ? 'close' :
                    'checkmark'"></ion-icon>
                </button>
                <button ion-button icon-only color="danger"
                (click)="delete(todo, index)">
                    <ion-icon name="trash"></ion-icon>
                </button>
            </ion-item-options>
        </ion-item-sliding>
        <ion-item *ngIf="userTodos.length > 0">
            <p text-center>Swipe left for options</p>
        </ion-item>
        <ion-item *ngIf="userTodos.length === 0">
            <h2 class="text-center">No Todos</h2>
        </ion-item>
    </ion-list>
```

```
</ion-content>
<ion-footer>
    <h3>Your IP : {{userIp}}</h3>
</ion-footer>
```

Finally, the styles. Open `todoapp_v2/src/app/app.scss` and add the following CSS rules:

```scss
ion-header.positive ion-navbar .toolbar-background,
ion-footer,
{
    background-color: #387ef5;
}

ion-header.positive .toolbar-title,
ion-footer {
    color: #fff;
}

.toolbar-title,
ion-footer {
    text-align: center;
}

ion-navbar button[color=danger]{
    background: #f53d3d;
    color: #fff;
    border-radius: 4px
}

.strike {
    text-decoration: line-through;
    color:#999;
}
```

This wraps our coding part. Now, we will install the required dependencies. First storage-related dependencies, run the following:

```
ionic plugin add cordova-sqlite-storage -save
npm install --save @ionic/storage
```

Next, local notification dependencies:

```
ionic plugin add de.appplant.cordova.plugin.local-notification
npm install --save @ionic-native/local-notifications
```

This should take care of the required dependencies.

Now, we will add a platform and test the app:

```
ionic platform add android or ionic platform add ios
```

And then run the following:

```
ionic run android or ionic run ios
```

And you should see the Login page come up:

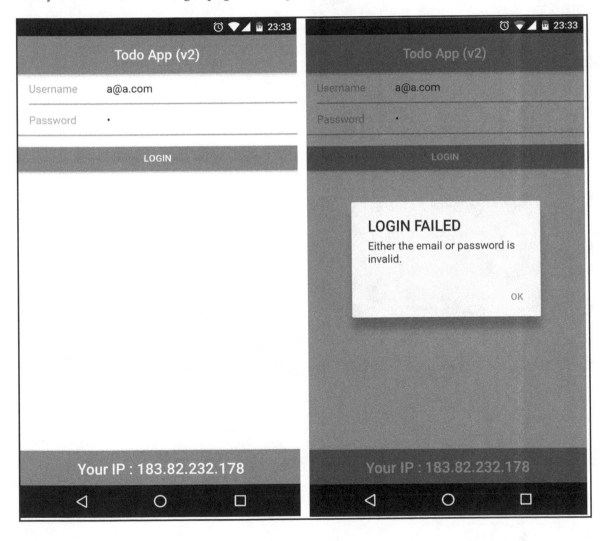

The home page that manages Todos:

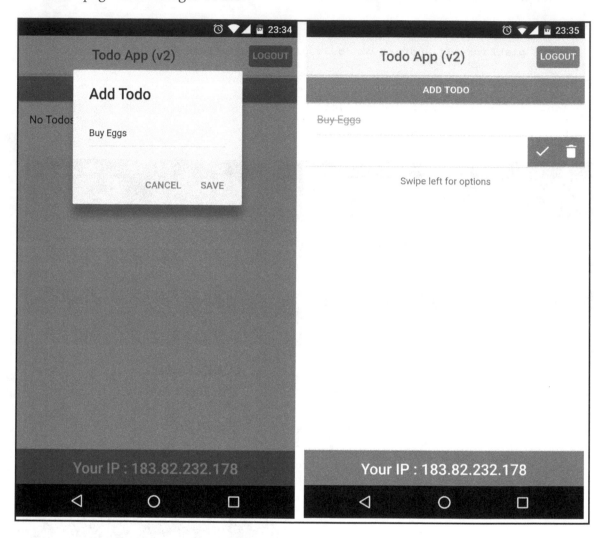

Finally, the notifications that get pushed:

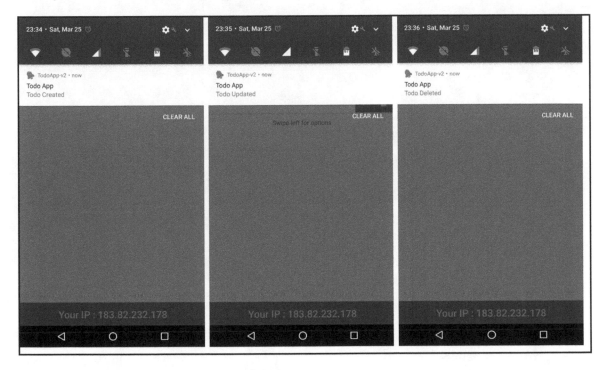

With this, we have completed the migration of our Ionic 1 Todo App to Ionic 2. Hopefully, this example has given some idea on how to approach the migration of Ionic 1 apps to Ionic 2 as well as Ionic 3.

Summary

In this chapter, we have gone through the process of building a simple Ionic 1 Todo App. Next, we prepared a rough migration plan and followed the same to migrate the Ionic 1 Todo app to Ionic 2. We have seen some key differences between the Ionic 1 and Ionic 2 app, when it comes to migration and taking advantage of the latest features such as Ionic Native and Storage API.

Do check out Chapter 11, *Ionic 3* to see the difference between Ionic 2 and Ionic 3.

In the next chapter, we will be testing the Ionic 2 Todo App that we have migrated.

9
Testing an Ionic 2 App

In this chapter, we are going to look at testing a Mobile Hybrid app built using Cordova (and Ionic 2). Testing can be done in multiple layers, the first being unit testing, followed by end-to-end testing, and finally deploying the app on to an actual device and executing tests. In this chapter, we are going to take the Ionic 2 Todo app we have built in Chapter 8, *Ionic 2 Migration Guide* and execute the following tests on it:

- Unit testing
- End-to-end testing
- Monkey OR Fuzz testing with AWS Device Farm
- Testing with AWS Device Farm

Testing methodologies

In the world of app development, there are two ways in which testing comes into the app development life cycle. One is the more traditional way where the development happens first and then test runs are designed and executed based on the requirements. The other and more effective way is to adopt **Test Driven Development** (TDD). Over a period of time, TDD has proven to produce a more bug-free way of developing apps. You can read more about TDD here: http://agiledata.org/essays/tdd.html.

The by-product of TDD is **Behavioural Driven Testing** (BDT). BDT revolves more around behavior testing than requirement testing. A good combination of unit testing and automation testing with BDT would yield an excellent product with minimal bugs. Since BDT involves more user-centric testing, one can easily discover issues that the end user might encounter during the testing phase itself.

In this chapter, we are going to follow the more traditional process of testing an app, which is after it is built. We are going to implement unit testing, end-to-end testing, and then we will upload the app to AWS Device Farm and perform monkey testing.

Setting up the unit testing environment

The app scaffolded by Ionic CLI does not include any test setup as of the day of writing this chapter. So, we need to add the required testing setup ourselves.

Setting up the project

To start with, we will create a new folder named chapter9 and copy the todoapp_v2 from chapter8 folder to the chapter9 folder.

Install the dependencies if they are missing by running npm install from the root of the chapter9/todoapp_v2 folder.

Run ionic serve and see if the app is working as expected. When you create, update, and delete a todo, you may see a warning in the console mentioning that the Cordova environment is not present. This is because we are using the local notification plugin inside the browser.

The environment setup we are going to do for unit testing our Todo app is going to be based on the article: *Ionic 2 Unit Testing Setup: The Best Way* (http://www.roblouie.com/article/376/ionic-2-set-up-unit-testing-the-best-way/).

To get started we are going to install Karma and Jasmine:

- **Karma**: Karma is a JavaScript test runner that runs on Node.js. Quoting from Karma's documentation, *Karma is essentially a tool which spawns a web server that executes source code against test code for each of the browsers connected. The results of each test against each browser are examined and displayed via the command line to the developer such that they can see which browsers and tests passed or failed.*

  We are going to use Karma to execute the test cases we are going to write:

- **Jasmine**: Jasmine is a behavior-driven development framework for testing JavaScript code. It does not depend on any other JavaScript frameworks. It does not require a DOM. And it has a clean, obvious syntax so that we can easily write tests.

We are going to use Jasmine to define our tests and write assertions. We would generally start off a test by writing a describe block. And then we start defining our test cases using the `it` construct.

For example:

```
describe('Component: MyApp Component', () => {
  it('should be created', () => {
     // assertions go here
  });
});
```

Assertions are simple comparison statements that validate the actual result and expected result:

```
expect(1 + 1).toBe(2);
expect(!!true).toBeTruthy();
```

And so on.

Now that we have a basic understanding of Karma and Jasmine, we will install the required dependencies.

 During the installation, if you see any errors, please update to the latest version of Node.js.

To install Karma run the following command:

```
npm install -g karma-cli
```

Next, install Jasmine and the related dependencies:

```
npm install --save-dev @types/jasmine@2.5.41 @types/node html-loader
jasmine karma karma-webpack ts-loader karma-sourcemap-loader karma-jasmine
karma-jasmine-html-reporter angular2-template-loader karma-chrome-launcher
null-loader karma-htmlfile-reporter
```

Once this is done, we will add the required configuration files.

Create a new folder named `test-config` at the root of the `todoapp_v2` folder. Inside the `test-config` folder, create a file named `webpack.test.js`. Update `todoapp_v2/test-config/webpack.test.js` with the following code:

```
var webpack = require('webpack');
var path = require('path');

module.exports = {
    devtool: 'inline-source-map',
    resolve: {
        extensions: ['.ts', '.js']
    },
    module: {
        rules: [{
            test: /.ts$/,
            loaders: [{
                loader: 'ts-loader'
            }, 'angular2-template-loader']
        }, {
            test: /.html$/,
            loader: 'html-loader'
        }, {
            test: /.(png|jpe?g|gif|svg|woff|woff2|ttf|eot|ico)$/,
            loader: 'null-loader'
        }]
    },
    plugins: [
        new webpack.ContextReplacementPlugin(
            // The (|/) piece accounts for
            path separators in *nix and Windows
            /angular(|/)core(|/)
            (esm(|/)src|src)(|/)linker/,
            root('./src'), // location of your src
            {} // a map of your routes
        )
    ]
};


function root(localPath) {
    return path.resolve(__dirname, localPath);
}
```

Next, create another file named `karma-test-shim.js` inside the `test-config` folder. Update `todoapp_v2/test-config/karma-test-shim.js` with the following code:

```
Error.stackTraceLimit = Infinity;
```

```
require('core-js/es6');
require('core-js/es7/reflect');

require('zone.js/dist/zone');
require('zone.js/dist/long-stack-trace-zone');
require('zone.js/dist/proxy');
require('zone.js/dist/sync-test');
require('zone.js/dist/jasmine-patch');
require('zone.js/dist/async-test');
require('zone.js/dist/fake-async-test');

var appContext = require.context('../src', true, /.spec.ts/);

appContext.keys().forEach(appContext);

var testing = require('@angular/core/testing');
var browser = require('@angular/platform-browser-dynamic/testing');

testing.TestBed.initTestEnvironment(browser.BrowserDynamicTestingModule,
browser.platformBrowserDynamicTesting());
```

Finally, create a file named `karma.conf.js` inside the `test-config` folder. Update `todoapp_v2/test-config/karma.conf.js` with the following code:

```
var webpackConfig = require('./webpack.test.js');
module.exports = function(config) {
    var _config = {
        basePath: '',
        frameworks: ['jasmine'],
        files: [
            { pattern: './karma-test-shim.js', watched: true }
        ],
        preprocessors: {
            './karma-test-shim.js': ['webpack', 'sourcemap']
        },
        webpack: webpackConfig,
        webpackMiddleware: {
            stats: 'errors-only'
        },
        webpackServer: {
            noInfo: true
        },
        reporters: ['html', 'dots'],
        htmlReporter: {
            outputFile: './unit-test-report.html',
            pageTitle: 'Todo App Unit Tests',
            subPageTitle: 'Todo App Unit Tests Report',
            groupSuites: true,
```

```
        useCompactStyle: true,
        useLegacyStyle: true
    },
    port: 9876,
    colors: true,
    logLevel: config.LOG_INFO,
    autoWatch: true,
    browsers: ['Chrome'],
    singleRun: true
};
config.set(_config);
};
```

With this we finish the basic configuration needed to run unit tests.

The article mentioned earlier itself has the required information about the three configuration files we have added. For more information, refer to: `https://angular.io/docs/ts/latest/guide/webpack.html#!#test-configuration`.

Writing unit tests

Now that we have the required setup, we are going to start writing the unit tests. Unit tests are written in a file next to the source file with `.spec` added to the filename. For example, if we are writing test cases for `app.component.ts`, we would create a file named `app.component.spec.ts` in the same folder and write the required test cases.

Refer to `https://angular.io/docs/ts/latest/guide/testing.html#!#q-spec-file-location` and `https://angular.io/docs/ts/latest/guide/style-guide.html#!#02-10` for more information.

First, we would start off by writing tests for the app component. We are going to test the following cases:

- If the component has been created.
- If `rootPage` is set as `LoginPage`.

Now, create a file named `app.component.spec.ts` inside the `todoapp_v2/src/app` folder. Update `todoapp_v2/src/app/app.component.spec.ts` with the following code:

```
import { async, TestBed } from '@angular/core/testing';
import { IonicModule } from 'ionic-angular';
import { StatusBar } from '@ionic-native/status-bar';
import { SplashScreen } from '@ionic-native/splash-screen';
```

```
import { MyApp } from './app.component';
import { LoginPage } from '../pages/login/login';

describe('Component: MyApp Component', () => {
  let fixture;
  let component;

  beforeEach(async(() => {
    TestBed.configureTestingModule({
      declarations: [MyApp],
      imports: [
        IonicModule.forRoot(MyApp)
      ],
      providers: [
        StatusBar,
        SplashScreen
      ]
    })
  }));

  beforeEach(() => {
    fixture = TestBed.createComponent(MyApp);
    component = fixture.componentInstance;
  });

  it('should be created', () => {
    expect(component instanceof MyApp).toBe(true);
  });

  it('should set the rootPage as LoginPage', () => {
    expect(component.rootPage).toBe(LoginPage);
  });

});
```

There is quite a lot going on. First, we have imported the required dependencies. Next, we have added the describe block. Inside the describe block, we have added beforeEach(). beforeEach() runs before each test gets executed. In the first beforeEach(), we are defining the TestBed. In the second beforeEach(), we are creating the required component and getting its instance.

TestBed configures and initializes the environment for unit tests. To know in-depth on how testing is set up and performed in Angular 2, check out: *Testing Angular 2, Julie Ralph* available at: https://www.youtube.com/watch?v=f493Xf0F2yU.

Once the TestBed is defined and the components have been initialized, we write our test cases.

Note: we have wrapped the callback function of `beforeEach()` with `async`. `async` does not let the next test start till all the pending tasking are completed. To know when to use `async` while testing, refer to *Angular 2 Testing -- Async function call --when to use*: `http://stackoverflow.com/a/40127164/1015046`.

Next, we are going to test the login page.

Create a filename `login.spec.ts` inside the `todoapp_v2/src/pages/login` folder. We are going to test the following:

- That the component has been created
- That the `userIp` variable is initialized to an empty string
- That the user object contains an e-mail with the value `a@a.com`
- That the user object contains a password with the value `a`

Update `todoapp_v2/src/pages/login/login.spec.ts` with the following code:

```
import { async, TestBed } from '@angular/core/testing';
import { IonicModule, NavController, AlertController } from 'ionic-
angular';
import { IonicStorageModule } from '@ionic/storage';
import { MyApp } from '../../app/app.component';
import { LoginPage } from './login';
import { Auth } from '../../providers/auth';
import { IP } from '../../providers/ip';

describe('Component: Login Component', () => {
  let fixture;
  let component;

  beforeEach(async(() => {
    TestBed.configureTestingModule({
      declarations: [
        MyApp,
        LoginPage
      ],
      imports: [
        IonicModule.forRoot(MyApp),
        IonicStorageModule.forRoot()
      ],
      providers: [
        Auth,
        IP,
        NavController,
        AlertController
      ]
```

```
      })
  }));

  beforeEach(() => {
    fixture = TestBed.createComponent(LoginPage);
    component = fixture.componentInstance;
  });

  it('should be created', () => {
    expect(component instanceof LoginPage).toBe(true);
  });

  it('should initialize `userIp` to '''', () => {
    expect(component.userIp).toBe('');
  });

  it('should initialize `user`', () => {
    expect(component.user.email).toBe('a@a.com');
    expect(component.user.password).toBe('a');
  });

});
```

The preceding code is quite self-explanatory.

Next, we move on to the home page component. Create a file named `home.spec.ts` inside the `todoapp_v2/src/pages/home` folder. In this component, we are going to test the following:

- That the component has been created
- That the `userIp` variable is initialized to an empty string
- That the `userTodos` variable is initialized to an empty array
- When a local notification is fired (this is how we do unit testing on Ionic Native plugins)

Update `todoapp_v2/src/pages/home/home.spec.ts` with the following code:

```
import { async, TestBed } from '@angular/core/testing';
import { IonicModule, NavController, AlertController } from 'ionic-angular';
import { MyApp } from '../../app/app.component';
import { HomePage } from './home';
import { LoginPage } from '../login/login';
import { IonicStorageModule } from '@ionic/storage';
import { LocalNotifications } from '@ionic-native/local-notifications';
import { LocalNotificationsMocks } from
```

```
'../../mocks/localNotificationMocks';
import { Auth } from '../../providers/auth';
import { IP } from '../../providers/ip';
import { Todos } from '../../providers/todos';

describe('Component: Home Component', () => {
  let fixture;
  let component;
  let localNotif;

  beforeEach(async(() => {
    TestBed.configureTestingModule({
      declarations: [
        MyApp,
        HomePage,
        LoginPage
      ],
      imports: [
        IonicModule.forRoot(MyApp),
        IonicStorageModule.forRoot()
      ],
      providers: [
        Auth,
        Todos,
        IP,
        { provide: LocalNotifications, useClass:
          LocalNotificationsMocks },
        NavController,
        AlertController
      ]
    })
  }));

  beforeEach(() => {
    fixture = TestBed.createComponent(HomePage);
    component = fixture.componentInstance;
    localNotif = new LocalNotificationsMocks();
  });

  it('should be created', () => {
    expect(component instanceof HomePage).toBe(true);
  });

  it('should initialize `userIp` to ''', () => {
    expect(component.userIp).toBe('');
  });

  it('should initialize `userTodos`', () => {
```

```
      expect(component.userTodos.length).toBe(0);
   });

   // this is how we mock and test
   // ionic-native plugins
   it('should return null when a new notification is scheduled', () => {
      expect(component.notify()).toBe(localNotif.schedule());
   });
});
```

The key thing to notice from the preceding code is the provider's property passed to `TestBed.configureTestingModule()`. Since we are running the tests inside a simulated environment, where there is no Cordova, we need to simulate or mock the `LocalNotifications` service.

The way we do that is to create another class named `LocalNotificationsMocks` and use it when `LocalNotifications` is called. In `LocalNotificationsMocks`, we implement dummy methods that return predefined values to mock the service.

So, we are going to create a mock service for `LocalNotifications`. Inside the `src` folder, create a folder named mocks. Inside the `mocks` folder, create a file named `localNotificationMocks.ts`. Update `todoapp_v2/src/mocks/localNotificationMocks.ts` with the following code:

```
export class LocalNotificationsMocks {
   public schedule(config: any): void {
      // https://github.com/driftyco/ionic-
      native/blob/5aa484c024d7cac3b6628c5dd8694395e8a29ed4/src/%40ionic-
      native/plugins/local-notifications/index.ts#L160
      return;
   }
}
```

We are overriding the `schedule()` to return void based on the original definition.

With this we are done with testing components. Next, we are going to test the providers.

Create a file named `ip.spec.ts` inside the `todoapp_v2/src/providers` folder. In this provider, we are going to mock an HTTP request and compare the output of the mock response with a hardcoded response. The cases we are going to test are:

- The provider is constructed
- We get an IP address from the mock backend service

Open `todoapp_v2/src/providers/ip.spec.ts` and update it with the following code:

```
import { async, TestBed, inject } from '@angular/core/testing';
import { IP } from './ip';
import { Headers, Http, HttpModule, BaseRequestOptions, XHRBackend,
Response, ResponseOptions } from '@angular/http';
import { MockBackend, MockConnection } from '@angular/http/testing';

//
https://kendaleiv.com/angular-2-mockbackend-service-testing-template-using-
testbed/
describe('Service: IPService', () => {
  let service;
  let http;

  const mockResponse = {
    ip: '11:22:33:44'
  };

  beforeEach(async(() => {
    TestBed.configureTestingModule({
      imports: [
        HttpModule
      ],
      providers: [
        MockBackend,
        BaseRequestOptions,
        {
          provide: Http,
          useFactory: (backend, options) => new Http(backend, options),
          deps: [MockBackend, BaseRequestOptions]
        },
        IP
      ]
    })
  }));

  it('should construct', async(inject(
    [IP, MockBackend], (ipService, mockBackend) => {
      expect(ipService).toBeDefined();
    })));

  it('should get IP equal to `11:22:33:44`', async(inject(
    [IP, MockBackend], (ipService, mockBackend) => {

      mockBackend.connections.subscribe(conn => {
        conn.mockRespond(new Response(new ResponseOptions({ body:
JSON.stringify(mockResponse) })));
```

```
      });

      const result = ipService.get();

      result.subscribe((res) => {
        expect(res.json()).toEqual({
          ip: '11:22:33:44'
        });
      });
    })));
});
```

Do notice the provider for HTTP. We have wired it to `MockBackend` and are returning a `mockResponse` when a request is made.

Next comes the Auth provider. Create a file named `auth.spec.ts` inside the `todoapp_v2/src/providers` folder. We are going to test the following in this provider:

- That the provider is constructed
- That there is a successful login with valid credentials
- That there is a successful failure with invalid credentials
- The value of `isAuthenticated()`
- The value of `authStatus` on `logout()`

Open `todoapp_v2/src/providers/auth.spec.ts` and update it with the following code:

```
import { async, TestBed, inject } from '@angular/core/testing';
import { Auth } from './auth';
import { IonicStorageModule } from '@ionic/storage';
import { StorageMocks } from '../mocks/storageMocks';

let validUser = {
  email: 'a@a.com',
  password: 'a'
}

let inValidUser = {
  email: 'a@a.com',
  password: 'b'
}

describe('Service: AuthService', () => {
  beforeEach(async(() => {
    TestBed.configureTestingModule({
      imports: [
```

```
        IonicStorageModule.forRoot()
      ],
      providers: [
        Auth,
        { provide: IonicStorageModule, useClass: StorageMocks },
      ]
    });

}));

it('should construct', async(inject(
  [Auth, IonicStorageModule], (authService, ionicStorageModule) => {
    expect(authService).toBeDefined();
  })));

it('should login user with valid credentials', async(inject(
  [Auth, IonicStorageModule], (authService, ionicStorageModule) => {
    expect(authService.login(validUser)).toBeTruthy();
  })));

it('should not login user with invalid credentials', async(inject(
  [Auth, IonicStorageModule], (authService, ionicStorageModule) => {
    expect(authService.login(inValidUser)).toBeFalsy();
  })));

it('should return the auth status as true', async(inject(
  [Auth, IonicStorageModule], (authService, ionicStorageModule) => {
    // log the user in!
    authService.login(validUser);
    let result = authService.isAuthenticated();

    result.then((status) => {
      expect(status).toBeTruthy();
    })
  })));


it('should set auth to falsy on logout', async(inject(
  [Auth, IonicStorageModule], (authService, ionicStorageModule) => {
    // log the user in!
    let authStatus = authService.login(validUser);
    // check if login is successful
    expect(authStatus).toBeTruthy();

    // trigger logout
    let result = authService.logout();
    result.then((status) => {
      expect(status).toBeFalsy();
```

```
      });
    })));

  });
```

To execute the preceding test cases successfully, we need to mock the
`IonicStorageModule`. Create a new file named `storageMocks.ts` inside the
`todoapp_v2/src/mocks` folder. Update
`todoapp_v2/src/mocks/storageMocks.ts` with the following code:

```
export class StorageMocks {
  // mock store
  store = {};

  public get(key) {
    return new Promise((resolve, reject) => {
      resolve(this.store[key]);
    });
  }

  public set(key, value){
    return new Promise((resolve, reject) => {
      this.store[key] = value;
      resolve(this.store[key]);
    });
  }
}
```

Here we are overriding the behavior of the `IonicStorageModule` using an in-memory
object.

The last provider that we are going to test is Todos. Create a file named `todos.spec.ts`
inside the `todoapp_v2/src/providers` folder. We are going to test the following:

- That the provider is constructed
- That Todos has an initial length of 0
- Saving a todo
- Updating a todo
- Deleting a todo

Open `todoapp_v2/src/providers/todos.spec.ts` and update it as follows:

```
import { async, TestBed, inject } from '@angular/core/testing';
import { Todos } from './todos';
import { IonicStorageModule } from '@ionic/storage';
```

```
import { StorageMocks } from '../mocks/storageMocks';

let todos = [{
  text: 'Buy Eggs',
  isCompleted: false
}];

describe('Service: TodoService', () => {
  beforeEach(async(() => {
    TestBed.configureTestingModule({
      imports: [
        IonicStorageModule.forRoot()
      ],
      providers: [
        Todos,
        { provide: IonicStorageModule, useClass: StorageMocks },
      ]
    });

  }));

  it('should construct', async(inject(
    [Todos, IonicStorageModule], (todoService, ionicStorageModule) => {
      expect(todoService).toBeDefined();
    })));

  it('should fetch 0 todos initally', async(inject(
    [Todos, IonicStorageModule], (todoService, ionicStorageModule) => {
      let result = todoService.get();
      result.then((todos) => {
        expect(todos).toBeFalsy();
      });
    })));

  it('should save a todo', async(inject(
    [Todos, IonicStorageModule], (todoService, ionicStorageModule) => {
      let result = todoService.set(todos);
      result.then((_todos) => {
        expect(_todos).toEqual(todos);
        expect(_todos.length).toEqual(1);
      });
    })));

  it('should update a todo', async(inject(
    [Todos, IonicStorageModule], (todoService, ionicStorageModule) => {
      let todo = todos[0];
      todo.isCompleted = true;
      todos[0] = todo;
```

```
      let result = todoService.set(todos);
      result.then((_todos) => {
        expect(_todos[0].isCompleted).toBeTruthy();
      });
    })));

  it('should delete a todo', async(inject(
    [Todos, IonicStorageModule], (todoService, ionicStorageModule) => {
      todos.splice(0, 1);
      let result = todoService.set(todos);
      result.then((_todos) -> {
        expect(_todos.length).toEqual(0);
      });
    })));

});
```

Do notice the `StorageMocks` setup in the provider. With this, we are done writing the test cases. The next step is execution.

Executing unit tests

To start the execution process, we will add a script to the `package.json` file, so we can run tests easily by executing `npm test` from the command prompt/terminal.

Open `package.json` and add the following line to the scripts section:

```
"test": "karma start --reporters html ./test-config/karma.conf.js"
```

Now run the following command:

```
npm test
```

And you should see a browser launch and our test case execute. The command prompt/terminal log should look something like this:

```
todoapp_v2 npm test

> ionic-hello-world@ test /chapter9/todoapp_v2
> karma start --reporters html ./test-config/karma.conf.js


webpack: Compiled successfully.
webpack: Compiling...
ts-loader: Using typescript@2.0.9 and
    /chapter9/todoapp_v2/tsconfig.json
```

```
webpack: Compiled successfully.
26 03 2017 23:26:55.201:INFO [karma]: Karma v1.5.0 server started
    at http://0.0.0.0:9876/
26 03 2017 23:26:55.204:INFO [launcher]: Launching browser Chrome
    with unlimited concurrency
26 03 2017 23:26:55.263:INFO [launcher]: Starting browser Chrome
26 03 2017 23:26:57.491:INFO [Chrome 56.0.2924 (Mac OS X 10.12.1)]:
    Connected on socket DHM_DNgQakmVtg7RAAAA with id 44904930
```

And you should also see a file named `unit-test-report.html` created inside the `test-config` folder. If you launch this file in the browser, you should see the following:

Todo App Unit Tests
Todo App Unit Tests Report

Browser: Chrome 56.0.2924 (Mac OS X 10.12.1)

Timestamp: 3/26/2017, 11:26:58 PM

21 tests / 0 errors / 0 failures / 0 skipped / runtime: 4.348s

Status	Spec	Suite / Results
Passed in 0.947s	should be created	Component: MyApp Component
Passed in 0.494s	should set the rootPage as LoginPage	Component: MyApp Component
Passed in 0.43s	should be created	Component: Home Component
Passed in 0.412s	should initialize `userIp` to ``	Component: Home Component
Passed in 0.409s	should initialize `userTodos`	Component: Home Component
Passed in 0.38s	should return null when a new notification is scheduled	Component: Home Component
Passed in 0.358s	should be created	Component: Login Component
Passed in 0.339s	should initialize `userIp` to ``	Component: Login Component
Passed in 0.364s	should initialize `user`	Component: Login Component
Passed in 0.035s	should construct	Service: AuthService
Passed in 0.023s	should login user with valid credentials	Service: AuthService
Passed in 0.011s	should not login user with invalid credentials	Service: AuthService
Passed in 0.014s	should return the auth status as true	Service: AuthService
Passed in 0.011s	should set auth to falsy on logout	Service: AuthService
Passed in 0.014s	should construct	Service: IPService
Passed in 0.026s	should get IP equal to `11:22:33:44`	Service: IPService
Passed in 0.021s	should construct	Service: TodoService
Passed in 0.017s	should fetch 0 todos initally	Service: TodoService
Passed in 0.011s	should save a todo	Service: TodoService
Passed in 0.015s	should update a todo	Service: TodoService
Passed in 0.017s	should delete a todo	Service: TodoService

The preceding table summarizes the tests that were executed.

driftyco/ionic-unit-testing-example

Three days before writing this chapter, the Ionic team released a blog post indicating that they are going to support unit and end-to-end testing and this will be a part of the Ionic scaffolded project itself. More information can be found here:
`http://blog.ionic.io/basic-unit-testing-in-ionic/`.

This project is based on a couple of very valuable contributors in the Ionic 2 testing space as mentioned in the blog post. As of today, the *driftyco/ionic-unit-testing-example* (`https://github.com/driftyco/ionic-unit-testing-example`) repo does not have the complete implementation and supports only unit tests.

But by the time the book is out, they would have launched it. The setup inside `driftyco/ionic-unit-testing-example` should still be along the same lines we have followed here. I have brought this to your notice so you can follow the project.

E2E testing

In unit testing, we have tested units of code. In end-to-end testing, we are going to test a complete feature such as login or logout, or fetch IP address, and so on. Here we are going to look at the app as a whole instead of just one piece of functionality. Some people refer to this as integration testing as well.

We are going to use Protractor to help us with the execution of E2E tests. We are still going to use Jasmine to describe our tests, only the test runner changes from Karma to Protractor.

Quoting from `http://www.protractortest.org`:

> *"Protractor is an end-to-end test framework for Angular apps. Protractor runs tests against your app running in a real browser, interacting with it as a user would."*

YouTube has quite a lot of videos which explain Protractor and Selenium in depth as well as various APIs of Protractor that can be used for testing, in case you want more information on Protractor.

The testing we are going to do is as follows:

- Login to the app
- Validate login
- Logout of the app
- Validate logout

Setting up the project

I am going to follow the article named E2E (End-to-End) Testing in *Ionic 2 - An Introduction* (`https://www.joshmorony.com/e2e-end-to-end-testing-in-ionic-2-an-introduction/`) to set up the E2E environment.

We will be using the same example on which we have implemented the unit tests.

First install protractor by running the following command:

```
npm install protractor --save-dev
```

Next, install the `webdriver-manager` and update it:

```
npm install -g webdriver-manager
webdriver-manager update
```

Now, we will install the dependencies for Protractor by running the following command:

```
npm install jasmine-spec-reporter ts-node connect @types/jasmine@2.5.41
@types/node --save-dev
```

Do notice the version of Jasmine types. It is hardcoded to `2.5.41`. At the time of writing, there are some conflicts between the TypeScript version of Jasmine types and the Ionic 2 project. If you are using Ionic 3.0, this should have been fixed.

Next, at the root of the `todoapp_v2` project folder, create a file named `protractor.conf.js`. Update `todoapp_v2/protractor.conf.js` with the following code:

```
var SpecReporter = require('jasmine-spec-reporter').SpecReporter;

exports.config = {
    allScriptsTimeout: 11000,
    directConnect: true,
    capabilities: {
        'browserName': 'chrome'
    },
    framework: 'jasmine',
    jasmineNodeOpts: {
        showColors: true,
        defaultTimeoutInterval: 30000,
        print: function() {}
    },
    specs: ['./e2e/**/*.e2e-spec.ts'],
    baseUrl: 'http://localhost:8100',
    useAllAngular2AppRoots: true,
```

```
    beforeLaunch: function() {

        require('ts-node').register({
            project: 'e2e'
        });

        require('connect')().use(require('serve-static')
        ('www')).listen(8100);

    },
    onPrepare: function() {
        jasmine.getEnv().addReporter(new SpecReporter());
    }
}
```

This file defines the launch properties of Protractor and Selenium.

Next, we are going to create a folder named e2e at the root of todoapp_v2 folder. Inside the todoapp_v2/e2e folder, create a file named tsconfig.json. Update todoapp_v2/e2e/tsconfig.json with the following code:

```
{
  "compilerOptions": {
    "sourceMap": true,
    "declaration": false,
    "moduleResolution": "node",
    "emitDecoratorMetadata": true,
    "experimentalDecorators": true,
    "lib": [
      "es2016"
    ],
    "outDir": "../dist/out-tsc-e2e",
    "module": "commonjs",
    "target": "es6",
    "types":[
      "jasmine",
      "node"
    ]
  }
}
```

This completes our setup for end-to-end testing. Now, we will start writing the tests.

Writing E2E tests

Now that we have the required setup, we will start writing the tests. Create a new file named `test.e2e-spec.ts` inside the `todoapp_v2/e2e`folder.

As mentioned earlier, we are going to perform a simple test -- login to the app, validating login, logging out of the app, and validating logout. The required tests should look like this:

```
import { browser, element, by, ElementFinder } from 'protractor';

//
https://www.joshmorony.com/e2e-end-to-end-testing-in-ionic-2-an-introductio
n/
describe('Check Navigation : ', () => {

  beforeEach(() => {
    browser.get('');
  });

  it('should have `Todo App (v2)` as the title text on the Login Page',
  () => {
      expect(element(by.css('.toolbar-title'))
        .getAttribute('innerText'))
        .toContain('Todo App (v2)');

  });

  it('should be able to login with prefilled credentials', () => {
    element(by.css('.scroll-content > button')).click().then(() => {
      // Wait for the page transition
      browser.driver.sleep(3000);

      // check if we have really redirected
      expect(element(by.css('.scroll-content > button'))
        .getAttribute('innerText'))
        .toContain('ADD TODO');

      expect(element(by.css('h2.text-center'))
        .getAttribute('innerText'))
        .toContain('No Todos');

      expect(element(by.css('ion-footer > h3'))
        .getAttribute('innerText'))
        .toContain('Your IP : 183.82.232.178');

    });
```

```
  });

  it('should be able to logout', () => {
    element(by.css('ion-buttons > button')).click().then(() => {

      // Wait for the page transition
      browser.driver.sleep(3000);

      // check if we have really redirected
      expect(element(by.css('.toolbar-title'))
        .getAttribute('innerText'))
        .toContain('Todo App (v2)');
    });
  });

});
```

The preceding code is a self-explanatory. Do notice that I have hardcoded my IP address to validate the same while testing. Do update the IP address before you start executing the E2E tests.

Executing E2E tests

Now that we have completed writing the tests, we will execute the same. Open a command prompt/terminal at the root of the project and run the following command:

```
protractor
```

You may face an error, which looks something like:

```
// snipp
Error message: Could not find update-config.json. Run 'webdriver-
manager update' to download binaries.
// snipp
```

If so, run the following command:

```
./node_modules/protractor/bin/webdriver-manager update
```

And after that run `protractor` or `./node_modules/.bin/protractor`.

And you should see a browser launch and the app being navigated. If everything goes well, you should see the following output in the command prompt/terminal:

```
→   todoapp_v2 ./node_modules/.bin/protractor
[00:37:27] I/launcher - Running 1 instances of WebDriver
[00:37:27] I/direct - Using ChromeDriver directly...
Spec started

  Check Navigation :
√ should have `Todo App (v2)` as the title text on the Login Page
√ should be able to login with prefilled credentials
√ should be able to logout

Executed 3 of 3 specs SUCCESS in 11 secs.
[00:37:40] I/launcher - 0 instance(s) of WebDriver still running
[00:37:40] I/launcher - chrome #01 passed
```

With this we complete the two major types of testing on an Ionic app.

The final test we are going to do is using AWS Device Farm.

Note: While testing Cordova features, you can always mock them like we have seen earlier. Instead of updating the test bed, we will update the `app.module.ts` directly before executing the E2E tests. But do remember to change it back once the testing is completed.

Code coverage

Checking code coverage is a very important activity while testing. Code coverage helps us understand how much code written by us is tested. You can refer to the *karma-coverage* (`https://github.com/karma-runner/karma-coverage`) module and the *remap-istanbul* (`https://github.com/SitePen/remap-istanbul`) module to implement code coverage.

You can also refer to *How to Add a Test Coverage Report to an Angular 2 Project*: `https://www.angularonrails.com/add-test-coverage-report-angular-2-project/` for further reference.

AWS Device Farm

Now that we have unit tested as well as end-to-end tested our app, we will deploy the app on to an actual device and test it.

To start testing on actual devices, we need to borrow or purchase them, which may not seem practical for an one-off app. That is where the concept of device farms comes into the picture. Device farms are collections of various devices that can be accessed through a web interface. These devices can be accessed and tested over the web in a similar way how one would do testing on an actual device.

There are many providers out there who offer pay-as-you-go device farms. After a lot of hits and misses with many device farms, I kind of grew a liking towards AWS Device Farm. It is simple, easy to use, and quite verbose with the error logging, screenshots, and videos. The latter really helps you in identifying an issue that your end user or a bug crash reporter reported on a specific device.

As of the day of writing this chapter, AWS charges $0.17/device minute with the first 250 minutes free. Or if you are a heavy user, you can subscribe for an unlimited testing plan based on your usage as well. This starts from $250 a month.

In this topic, using AWS Device Farm, we are going to upload the APK of our Todo app that we have migrated in Chapter 8, *Ionic 2 Migration Guide*, and execute two tests:

- Monkey testing the app to see if the app crashes
- Manually testing the app on an actual device

Setting up AWS Device Farm

Before we get started with testing on actual devices, we will set up a new AWS account, if you don't have one. You can navigate to https://aws.amazon.com/ to sign up and sign in.

Once you are inside the AWS console, select **Device Farm** from the **Services** option in the header of the page. Device Farm is AWS region agonistic. You need not be in a specific region to access it.

Once you are at the home page of AWS Device Farm, you should see a screen like this:

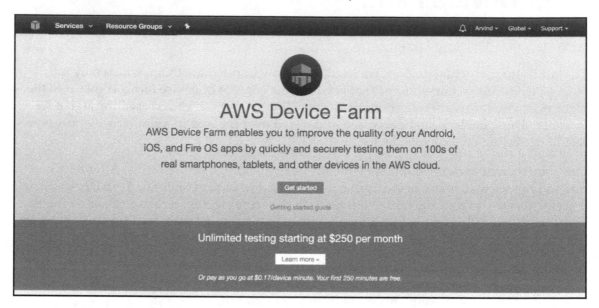

Click on **Get started**. This will prompt us to enter a project name. A project in Device Farm is a logic grouping of types of tests that we would execute, types of devices we want to test, or versions of our app.

I am going to name my project as `Todo App v1`. When I have another release I am going to name it as `Todo App v2`:

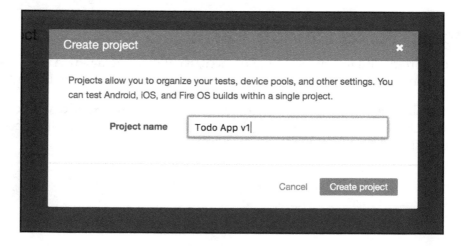

Note: Here v1 refers to the v1 release of our Todo app and not the Todo app built with Ionic v1.

Click on **Create project** and you should land on the project home page.

Setting up Todo app

Now that we are ready to test our app, let us go ahead and build it. Navigate to the todoapp_v2 folder and open a new command prompt/terminal. Run ionic platform add android or ionic platform add ios and then build the app:

```
ionic build
```

For this example, I am going to build for Android and use the APK for device testing. Once the build is completed, navigate to the todoapp_v2/platforms/android/build/outputs/apk folder and you should find a file named android-debug.apk. We are going to upload this APK file for testing.

The process for iOS testing is also similar, except we upload an IPA file.

Monkey testing the Todo app

Monkey testing or fuzz testing is an automated testing technique where a test executer will enter random inputs, executing random clicks at random parts of the app or page to see if the app crashes. To know more about monkey testing, refer to: https://en.wikipedia.org/wiki/Monkey_testing.

Device Farm offers this as a good starting point for testing an app on a device.

Once we are on the project home page, we should see two tabs: **Automated tests** and **Remote access**:

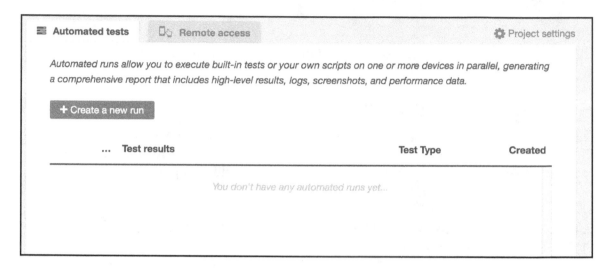

On the **Automated tests** tab, click on **Create a new run**. In the **Choose your application** section, select your choice, as shown in the following screenshot:

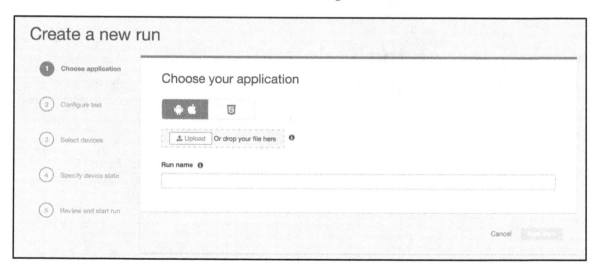

Next upload the APK or IPA file. Once the app is successfully uploaded, we should see something like this:

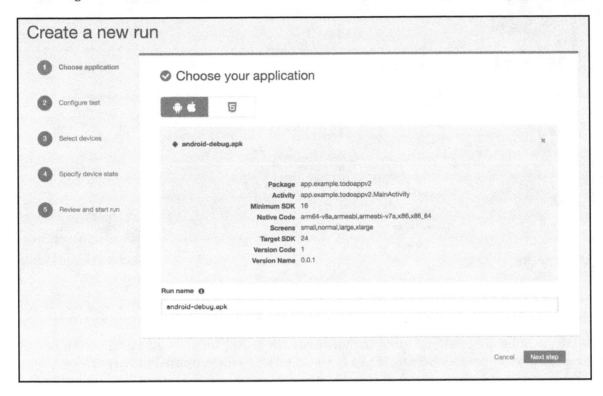

Click **Next step**.

In the configure test section, select **Built-in: Fuzz** as shown in the following screenshot:

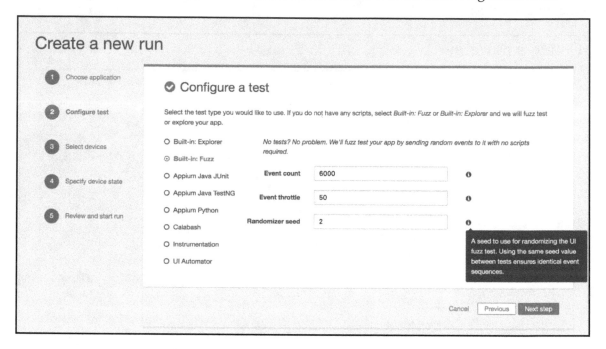

There are other automation testing frameworks such as Appium or Calabash that can be used to build automation testing suites as well. Device Farm supports those as well.

Click **Next step**.

This is where we select the targeted devices. By default, AWS Device Farm picks **Top Devices**. We can either go with this or build our own device pool:

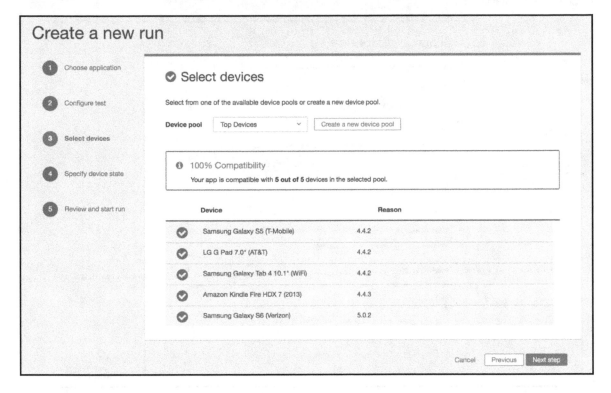

For this example, I am going to go with the **Top Devices** selection.

Click **Next step** to move to the **Specify device state** section. Here, we can override device features if needed:

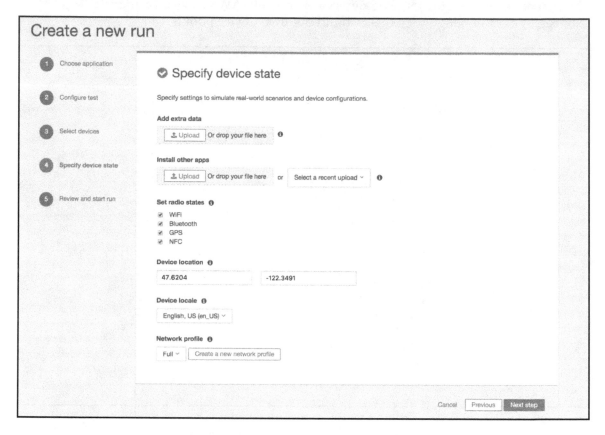

We are going to leave this as is.

Click **Next step** and here we set the estimates for our test. I have selected 5 minutes per device as shown:

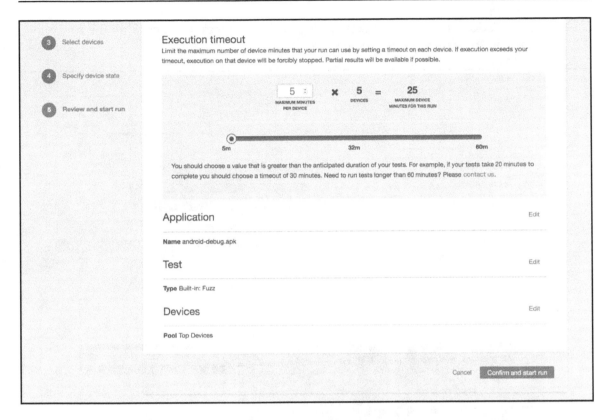

Click **Confirm and start run** to kick off the monkey testing. This will take approximately 25 minutes to complete. You can go for a run or get a coffee or do some yoga, basically you need to kill 25 minutes.

Now that the tests are completed, you should see a screen like this:

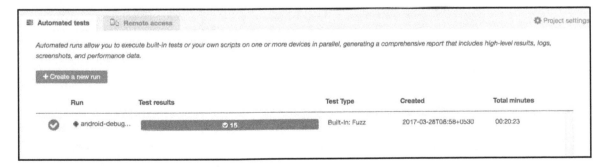

Looks like the Todo app passed monkey testing on five devices. If we click on the row, we should see the in-depth analysis of the results:

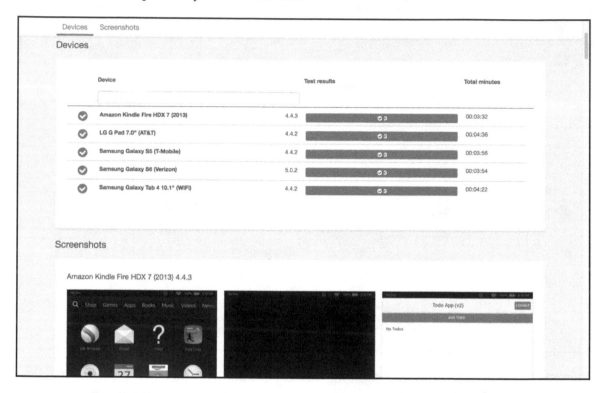

As you can see from the preceding steps, we have the results per device and screenshots of all the devices. To get deeper insights, we will click on a device:

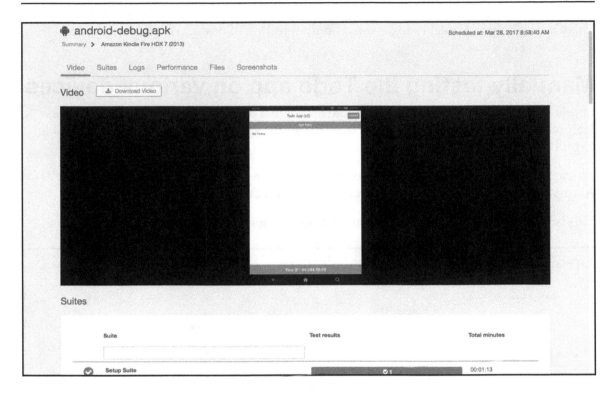

As you can see from the preceding image, we can view the test execution video, logs, performance, and screenshots as well:

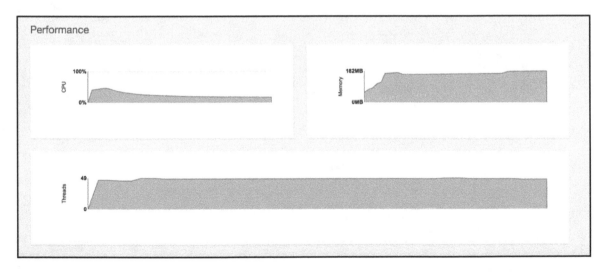

An overview of the performance would be as shown in the preceding screenshot.

This kind of helps us quickly to do some random testing of our app on various devices.

Manually testing the Todo app on various devices

In this section, we are going to gain remote access to a device and test our app on it. This feature is very helpful when a user reports a bug on a specific device that you are not able to replicate on other devices.

To start the manual testing, navigate to the project home page and click on the **Remote Access** tab. And then click on the **Start a new session** button.

This will redirect to another page, where we need to select a device as shown:

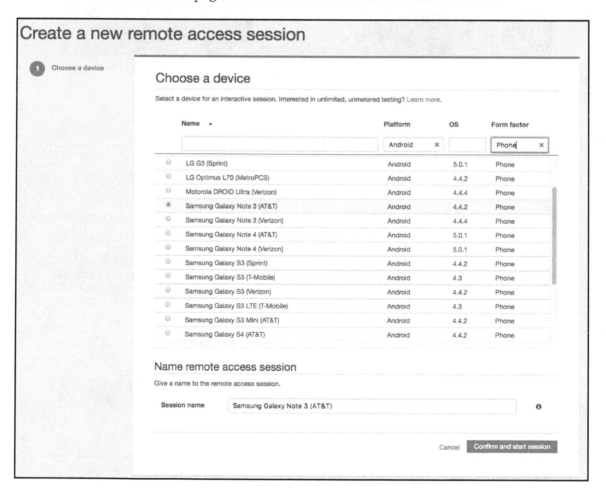

I have picked an Android device and initiated a new session by clicking on **Confirm and start session**. This will kick off a new session:

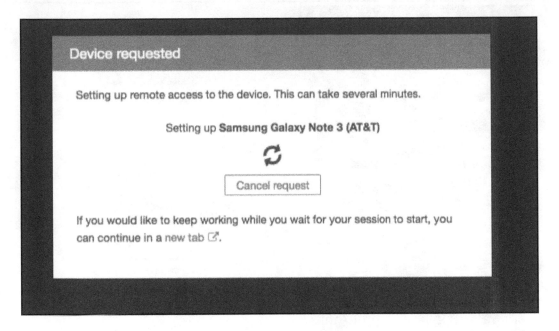

Once a device is made available, we should see something like this:

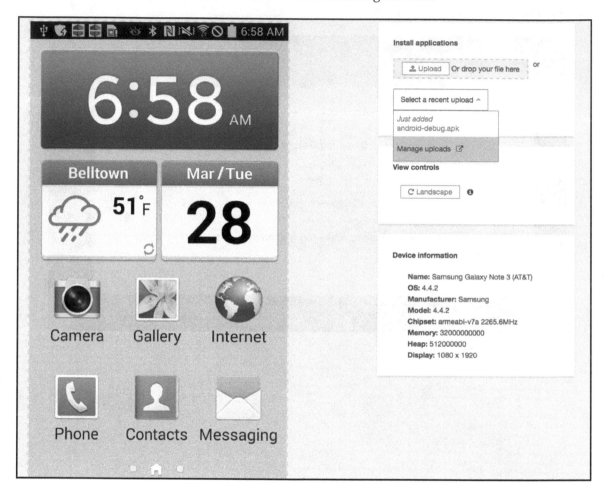

By default, the APK we have recently uploaded will be installed on this device. Otherwise you can use **Install applications** in the top right to install a specific app as shown in the preceding screenshot.

I have navigated to the `TodoApp-v2` from the menu as shown:

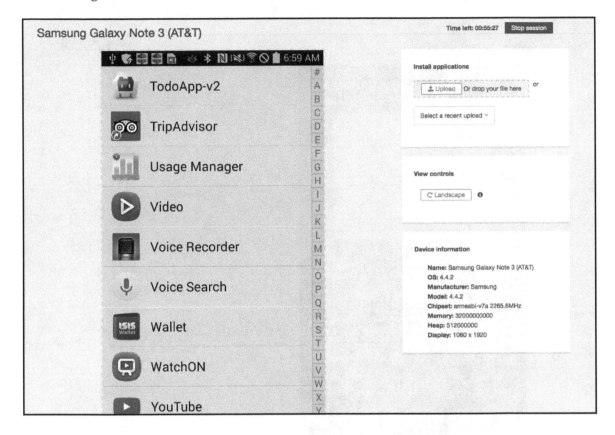

After launching the app, we can perform a login, manage todos, check out notifications, and so on:

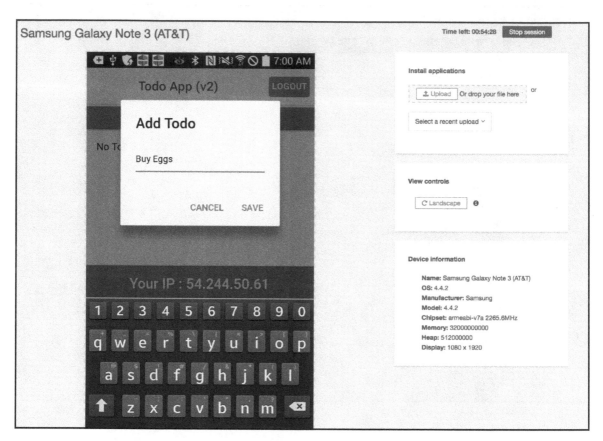

Once the testing is completed, we can stop the session. Once the session has been successfully terminated, we can get a copy of logs, videos, and network traffic in a downloadable format for further debugging:

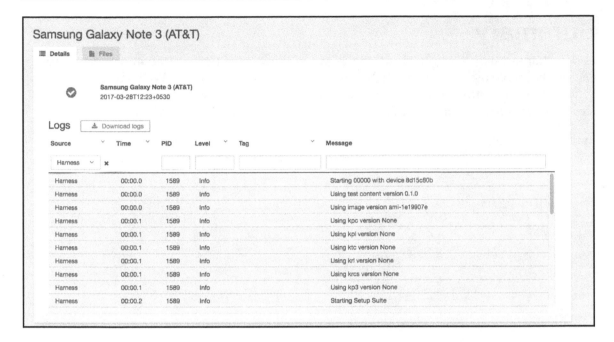

With this we have seen how to manually test an app on various devices.

Automation testing

Apart from the aforementioned ways of testing an app, we can build automated test cases using frameworks such as Appium (`http://appium.io/`). This way, using the Device Farm, we can upload the APK or IPA followed by the automation test suite. Then we pick a group of devices and execute the tests on them.

You can look up *Automating hybrid apps* (`http://appium.io/slate/en/master/?ruby#automating-hybrid-apps`) and *Verifying a Cordova or PhoneGap build with Smoke Tests and Appium* (`http://ezosaleh.com/verifying-a-cordovaphonegap-build-with-smoke-tests-appium`) to get an idea on writing automated tests for your hybrid app.

You can run these automated tests locally too in an emulator if you choose to.

Summary

In this chapter, we have gone through the two main ways of testing-unit and end-to-end testing. We have used Karma with Jasmine to unit test the Todo app. We have used Protractor with Jasmine for our end-to-end testing. We have also tested our app using AWS Device Farm's fuzz testing as well as by installing an app on a remote device of our choice.

In the next chapter, we will take a look at releasing and managing an Ionic app.

10
Releasing the Ionic App

In this chapter, we will take a look at three ways of generating the installer for your Ionic app. One uses the PhoneGap build service, the second uses the Cordova CLI, and, finally, the third uses the Ionic package service. We will generate installers for both Android and iOS operating systems. We will cover the following topics in this chapter:

- Generating Icons and Splash screens
- Validating config.xml
- Using the PhoneGap build service to generate installers
- Using the Cordova CLI to generate installers
- Using Ionic package to generate service

Preparing the app for distribution

Now that we have successfully built our Ionic app, we want to distribute it. The best way to reach a wider audience is with the help of the App stores. However, before we start distributing the app, we will need app-specific icons and splash screens. Splash screens are totally optional and depend on the product idea.

By default, when you run the following code:

```
ionic platform add android
```

or

```
ionic platform add ios
```

The CLI automatically adds a new folder named resources. You can check this out in Chapter 7, *Building Riderr App*. The resources folder consists of either Ionic or Android or both the subfolders, depending on how many platforms you have added, and in each of these folders, you will see two subfolders, named icon and splash.

You can keep the splash folder if your app uses splash screens, else delete the folder to save a few bytes of your final app installer.

To generate icons, you can get a copy of your icon greater than 1024 x 1024 and use any service, such as the following, to generate icons and splash screens for both Android and iOS:

- http://icon.angrymarmot.org/
- http://makeappicon.com/

 I have no association with any of the preceding services. You use these services at your own risk.

Alternatively, the best part is that you can place a file named `icon.png` and `splash.png` in the resources folder and run the following:

```
ionic resources
```

This will take care of uploading your images to the Ionic cloud, resizing them as needed, and saving them back to the resources folder.

 Be aware that you are uploading your content into a public/Ionic cloud.

If you want to convert only icons, you can use the following:

```
ionic resources --icon
```

For only splash screens, you can use this:

```
ionic resources --splash
```

 You can use `http://code.ionicframework.com/resources/icon.psd` to design your icon and `http://code.ionicframework.com/resources/splash.psd` to design your splash screens.
You can place an `icon.png` image, an `icon.psd` file, or an icon.ai file at the root of the resources folder and ionic resources will do the magic!

Updating the config.xml

- As we already know, `config.xml` is the single source of truth that the Cordova API trusts while generating the OS-specific installers. So, this file needs to be validated thoroughly before we start the deployment process. You can follow the checklist to ensure that all the things are in place:
- Widget ID is defined and valid
- Widget Version is defined and valid
- In the case of an app update, Widget Version is updated and valid
- Name tag is defined and valid
- Description is defined and valid
    - Author information is defined and valid
- Access tag is defined and is limited to the required domains (`https://github.com/apache/cordova-plugin-whitelist#network-request-whitelist`)
- Allow Navigation is defined and is limited to the required domains (`https://github.com/apache/cordova-plugin-whitelist#navigation-whitelist`)
- Allow Intent is defined and is limited to the required domains (`https://github.com/apache/cordova-plugin-whitelist#intent-whitelist`)
- Cross-check the preferences
- Cross-check the icons and splash image's path
- Cross-check the permissions if any
- Update `index.html` with the content security policy meta tag (`https://github.com/apache/cordova-plugin-whitelist#content-security-policy`)

Once the preceding points are verified, we will get started with the installer generation process.

The PhoneGap build service

The first approach we will take a look at is generating app installers using the PhoneGap build service. This is perhaps the simplest way to generate installers for Android and iOS.

The process is quite simple. We upload the entire project to the PhoneGap build service and it takes care of building the installer.

If you think uploading the complete project is not practical, you can upload only the www folder. However, you need make the following changes.

1. Move config.xml inside the www folder.
2. Move the resources folder inside the www folder.
3. Update the path of the resources folder in config.xml.

If you find yourself doing the preceding often, I would recommend using a build script to generate a PhoneGap build Deployable folder with the preceding changes made to the project.

If you are planning to release your app only for Android, you do not need to do anything more. However, if you are planning to generate iOS installers, you need to get an Apple Developer Account and follow the steps at http://docs.build.phonegap.com/en_US/signing_signing-ios.md.html to generate the required certificates.

You can also sign your Android app using the steps mentioned at http://docs.build.phonegap.com/en_US/signing_signing-android.md.html.

Once you have the required certificates and keys, we are good to start generating the installer. You can follow the given steps to make the process easy:

1. Create a PhonegGap account and log in (https://build.phonegap.com/plans)
2. Next, navigate to https://build.phonegap.com/people/edit and select the **Signing Keys** tab, and upload iOS and Android certificates.

3. Next, navigate to: `https://build.phonegap.com/apps` and click on **New App**. As part of the *Free plan*, you can have as many apps as you want as long as they are pulled from Public Git repos. Alternatively, you can create a private app from a Private repo or by uploading a ZIP file.

4. For testing the service, you can create a `.zip` file (not `.rar` or `.7z`) with the following folder structure:

   - `App` (root folder)
   - `config`.xml
   - `resources` (folder)
   - `www` (folder)

   This is all you need for the PhoneGap build to work.

5. Upload the ZIP file to `https://build.phonegap.com/apps` and create the app.

This process generally takes up to a minute to do its magic.

Sometimes, you may see unexpected errors from the build service. Wait for some time and try again. Depending on the traffic, sometimes the build process may take a bit longer than expected.

Generating Installers using Cordova CLI

We will look at creating installers using Cordova CLI.

Android installer

First, we will take a look at generating an installer for Android using the CLI. You can follow the given steps:

1. Open a new command prompt/terminal at the root of the project.
2. Remove unwanted plugins using the following:

```
ionic plugin rm cordova-plugin-console
```

3. Build the app in release mode with the following:

`cordova build --release android`

This will generate an unsigned installer in release mode and place it at `<<ionic project>>/platforms/android/build/outputs/apk/android-release-unsigned.apk`.

4. Next, we need to create a signing key. If you already have a signing key or you are updating an existing app, you can skip the next step.

5. The private key is generated using the keytool. We will create a folder named deploy-keys and save all these keys there. Once the folder is created, run the `cd` command and navigate into the folder and run this:

`keytool -genkey -v -keystore app-name-release-key.keystore -alias alias_name -keyalg RSA -keysize 2048 -validity 10000`

You will be asked the following questions, and you can answer them as shown:

```
→ deploy-keys keytool –genkey –v –keystore app-name-release-key.keystore –alias my-ionic-app –keyalg RSA –
keysize 2048 –validity 10000
Enter keystore password:
Re-enter new password:
What is your first and last name?
  [Unknown]:  Arvind Ravulavaru
What is the name of your organizational unit?
  [Unknown]:  Stack Engineering
What is the name of your organization?
  [Unknown]:  JackalStack Technologies Pvt. Ltd.
What is the name of your City or Locality?
  [Unknown]:  Hyderabad, India
What is the name of your State or Province?
  [Unknown]:  Andhra Pradesh
What is the two-letter country code for this unit?
  [Unknown]:  IN
Is CN=Arvind Ravulavaru, OU=Stack Engineering, O=JackalStack Technologies Pvt. Ltd., L="Hyderabad, India", S
T=Andhra Pradesh, C=IN correct?
  [no]:  YES

Generating 2,048 bit RSA key pair and self-signed certificate (SHA256withRSA) with a validity of 10,000 days
        for: CN=Arvind Ravulavaru, OU=Stack Engineering, O=JackalStack Technologies Pvt. Ltd., L="Hyderabad,
 India", ST=Andhra Pradesh, C=IN
Enter key password for <my-ionic-app>
        (RETURN if same as keystore password):
[Storing app-name-release-key.keystore]
```

If you lose this file, you cannot submit updates to the app store, ever. Note: To know more about the keytool and signing process, refer to `https://developer.android.com/studio/publish/app-signing.html`.

6. This is an optional step, you can copy the `android-release-unsigned.apk` to the `deploy-keys` folder and run the following commands from there too. I will leave the files where they are.

7. Next, we sign the unsigned APK using the jarsigner tool:

```
jarsigner -verbose -sigalg SHA1withRSA -digestalg SHA1 -keystore app-name-
release-key.keystore ../platforms/android/build/outputs/apk/android-
release-unsigned.apk my-ionic-app
```

You will be asked for the passphrase, which you have entered as the first step while creating the keystore. Once the signing process is completed, the existing `android-release-unsigned.apk` will be replaced with the signed version of the same name.

 We run the preceding command from inside the deploy-keys folder.

8. Finally, we run the `zipalign` tool to optimize the APK:

```
zipalign -v 4 ../platforms/android/build/outputs/apk/android-release-
unsigned.apk my-ionic-app.apk
```

The preceding command will create `my-ionic-app.apk` in the `deploy-keys` folder.

Now, you can submit this APK to the app store.

iOS installer

Next, we will generate an installer for iOS using XCode. You can follow the given steps:

1. Open a new command prompt/terminal at the root of the project.

2. Remove unwanted plugins:

```
ionic plugin rm cordova-plugin-console
```

3. Run:

```
ionic build -release ios
```

4. Navigate to platforms/iOS and launch the `projectname.xcodeproj` using XCode.

5. Once the project is inside XCode, select **Product** and then **Archive** from the navigation menu.

6. Next, select **Window** and select **Organizer** from the navigation menu. You will be shown a list of archives created.

7. Click on the archive snapshot we have created now, and click on **Submit**. The validation of your account is performed and then the app will be uploaded to iStore.

8. Finally, you need to log in to the iTunes store to set up screenshots, a description, and more.

This concludes the process of generating installers using the Cordova CLI.

Ionic package

In this section, we will look at Ionic package.

Uploading a project to Ionic cloud

Using Ionic cloud services to generate installers is quite simple. First, we upload our app to our Ionic account by running the following:

```
ionic upload
```

> Log in to your Ionic account before executing the preceding command. If your project has sensitive information, cross-check with Ionic license before uploading the app to the cloud.

Once the app is uploaded, an app ID will be generated for your app. You can find the app ID in the `ionic.config.json` file located at the root of the project.

Generating the required keys

You need to follow Step 5 in the **Generating Installers using Cordova CLI** section, the **Android Installer** subsection, to get the keystore file.

Next, we use the ionic package command to generate the installer:

```
ionic package <command> [options]
```

The options will consist of the following:

```
package <command> [options] ..................  Use Ionic Package to build your app
                                               <command> build android, build ios, list, info, or download
        [--release]  ..........................  (build <platform>) Mark this build as a release

        [--profile|-p <tag>]  ................  (build <platform>) Specify the Security Profile to use with this build

        [--noresources]  .....................  (build <platform>) Do not generate icon and splash screen resources during this build

        [--destination|-d <path>]  ...........  (download) Specify the destination directory to download your packaged app.
```

For instance, if you would like to generate an installer for Android in release mode, it will be as follows:

```
ionic package release android -k app-name-release-key.keystore -a my-ionic-
app -w 12345678 -r 12345678 -o ./ -e arvind.ravulavaru@gmail.com -p
12345678
```

 We are running the preceding command from inside the deploy-keys folder.

Similarly, the preceding command for iOS will be as follows:

```
ionic package release ios -c certificate-file -d password -f profilefile -o
./ -e arvind.ravulavaru@gmail.com -p 12345678
```

Summary

In this chapter, we saw how to release and manage an Ionic app. We saw how to generate installers using the PhoneGap build service, using Cordova CLI, and, finally, using Ionic Package.

In the next chapter, we will look at Ionic 3 and the key differences between Ionic 2 and Ionic 3.

Note that almost all the concepts we learned so far are still applicable in Ionic 3 as well.

11
Ionic 3

In the final chapter of Learning Ionic, Second Edition, we will look at the latest changes to the Ionic framework -- Ionic 3. We will also quickly touch upon Angular and its releases. In this chapter, we will look at the following topics:

- Angular 4
- Ionic 3
- Ionic 3 updates
- Ionic 2 versus Ionic 3

Angular 4

Since the launch of Angular 2, the Angular team has been working towards making Angular a stable and reliable framework for building applications. On 23 March, 2017, the Angular team released Angular 4.

What? Angular 4? What happened to Angular 3!!

Simply put, the Angular team adopted Semantic Versioning (`http://semver.org/`) to manage all the packages and dependences within the framework. In this process, one of the packages (`@angular/router`) has moved a complete major version ahead of the other packages, something like the following, due to the changes to the router package.:

Frameworks	Versions
`@angular/core`	v2.3.0
`@angular/compiler`	v2.3.0
`@angular/compiler-cli`	v2.3.0
`@angular/http`	v2.3.0
`@angular/router`	V3.3.0

Due to this misalignment and to avoid future confusion, the Angular team went ahead with Angular 4 instead of Angular 3.

Also, the **tentative release schedule** for future versions of Angular will be as shown:

Versions	Release dates
Angular 5	September/October 2017
Angular 6	March 2018
Angular 7	September/October 2018

You can read more about this at `http://angularjs.blogspot.in/2016/12/ok-let-me-explain-its-going-to-be.html`.

With Angular 4, there have been some significant under-the-hood changes. The following are the updates as part of Angular 4:

- Smaller and faster with a smaller generated code
- Updates to the `Animation` package
- Updates to `*ngIf` and `*ngFor`
- Upgrade to the latest TypeScript version

To know more about this release, refer to `http://angularjs.blogspot.in/2017/03/angular-400-now-available.html`.

Since Ionic follows Angular, they have upgraded the Ionic framework from version 2 to version 3 to move their base Angular version from 2 to 4.

Ionic 3

With the release of Angular 4, Ionic has upgraded itself and moved to Ionic 3.

Ionic version 3 (`https://blog.ionic.io/ionic-3-0-has-arrived/`) has added a couple of new features, such as IonicPage and LazyLoading. They have updated the base version of Angular to version 4 and pushed out some critical bug fixes as well. For more information, take a look at the change log for 3.0.0 at
`https://github.com/driftyco/ionic/compare/v2.3.0...v3.0.0`.

Ionic 2 to Ionic 3 changes are not breaking as we have seen from Ionic 1 to Ionic 2. Changes to Ionic 3 are more along the lines of enhancements and bug fixes, which are on top of Ionic 2.

Ionic 3 updates

Now, we will take a look at a few key updates to Ionic 3.

TypeScript update

For the Ionic 3 release, the Ionic team has updated the version of TypeScript to the latest version. The latest version of TypeScript has enhanced build times and type checking among other things. For a complete list of TypeScript updates, refer to the TypeScript 2.2 release notes
at: `https://www.typescriptlang.org/docs/handbook/release-notes/typescript-2-2.html`.

Ionic Page decorator

Ionic Page decorator helps implement deep linking better. If you remember our navigation example from `Chapter 4`, *Ionic Decorators and Services*, we have referred to actual class names while pushing and popping pages using the Nav Controller.

I am referring to `example9/src/pages/home/home.ts` here:

```
import { Component } from '@angular/core';
import { NavController } from 'ionic-angular';
import { AboutPage } from '../about/about';

@Component({
  selector: 'page-home',
  templateUrl: 'home.html'
})
export class HomePage {

  constructor(public navCtrl: NavController) {}

  openAbout(){
   this.navCtrl.push(AboutPage);
  }
}
```

We can implement the same using the `@IonicPage` decorator, as shown.

Let's update `example9/src/pages/about/about.ts`, as illustrated:

```
import { Component } from '@angular/core';
import { NavController, IonicPage } from 'ionic-angular';

@IonicPage({
   name : 'about'
})
@Component({
  selector: 'page-about',
  templateUrl: 'about.html'
})
export class AboutPage {

  constructor(public navCtrl: NavController) {}

  goBack(){
   this.navCtrl.pop();
  }
}
```

Note that the `@IonicPage` decorator has been added along with the `@Component` decorator. Now, we will update `example9/src/pages/home/home.ts`, as shown:

```
import { Component } from '@angular/core';
import { NavController } from 'ionic-angular';

@Component({
  selector: 'page-home',
  templateUrl: 'home.html'
})
export class HomePage {

  constructor(public navCtrl: NavController) {}

  openAbout(){
   this.navCtrl.push('about');
   }
}
```

Note the change to `this.navCtrl.push()`. Instead of passing the reference to the class, we are passing the name we have provided as a property on the `@IonicPage` decorator in `example9/src/pages/about/about.ts`. Also, now the pages will have the name added to the URL, that is, `http://localhost:8100/#/about`.

To know more about Ionic Page decorator, check out `http://ionicframework.com/docs/api/navigation/IonicPage`.

Also, check out IonicPage Module `http://ionicframework.com/docs/api/IonicPageModule/` for bundling multiple pages/components into one child module and referencing the same in `@NgModule` in `app.module.ts`.

Lazy Loading

Lazy loading is another new feature that has been added as part of the Ionic 3 release. Lazy loading lets us load a page only when needed. This will improve the start up time of the app and increase the overall experience.

You can take a look at the process by visiting `https://docs.google.com/document/d/1vGokwMXPQItZmTHZQbTO4qwj_SQymFhRS_nJmiH0K3w/edit` to start implementing Lazy Loading in your Ionic app.

At the time of writing this chapter, Ionic 3 is about a week old. There were a couple of issues/inconsistencies in the CLI as well as the scaffolded apps. Hopefully, these will be resolved by the time the book is out.

Ionic 2 versus Ionic 3

In this book, all the examples have been written with Ionic 2 in mind. Having said that, if you are using Ionic 3 to develop your Ionic apps, there should not be much of a change in the code. One key difference you will note in all the scaffolded apps is the introduction of IonicPage decorator and IonicPage Module.

You can always refer to the Ionic documentation to get more information on the latest version of these APIs.

Summary

With this, we conclude our Ionic journey.

To quickly summarize, we started with understanding why Angular, why Ionic, and why Cordova. Then, we saw how Mobile Hybrid apps work and where Cordova and Ionic fit in. Next, we looked at various templates of Ionic and went through Ionic components, decorators, and services. After that, we looked at theming Ionic apps.

Next, we went through Ionic Native and saw how to work with it. Using this knowledge, we built a Riderr app, which implements REST APIs, interfaces with device features using Ionic Native, and gives you the feel of a complete app that can be built using Ionic.

After that, we looked at Migrating Ionic 1 apps to Ionic 2 and how to test Ionic 2 apps. In Chapter 10, *Releasing the Ionic App*, we saw how to release and manage our app.

In this chapter, we saw the key changes in Ionic 3.

Check out the Appendix for more helpful information and a few Ionic services that are ready to be test driven/used in production apps.

Appendix

The main aim of this book is to get readers acquainted with as much of Ionic as possible. So, I have followed an incremental approach from Chapter 1 to Chapter 11, from the basics of Cordova to building an app with Angular Ionic and Cordova. We were pretty much focused on learning Ionic with the bare minimums.

In this appendix, I will show a few more options of the Ionic CLI and Ionic Cloud that you can explore.

Ionic CLI

Ionic CLI is growing more powerful day by day. Since we have been using Ionic CLI 2.1.14 throughout the book, I will be talking about the options from the same. Ionic CLI 2.2.2 or higher should also have almost the same options.

Ionic login

You can log in to your Ionic Cloud account in any one of three ways.

First, using prompt:

```
ionic login
```

Second, without prompt:

```
ionic login --email arvind.ravulavaru@gmail.com --password 12345678
```

And finally, using environment variables. You can set IONIC_EMAIL and IONIC_PASSWORD as environment variables and Ionic CLI will pick them up, without prompting. This could be somewhat an unsafe option, as the password would be stored in plain text.

 Note: You need to have an Ionic Cloud account for the authentication to succeed.

Ionic start

First we are going to take a look at the No Cordova flag option.

No Cordova

The start command is one of the simplest ways to scaffold a new Ionic application. In this book, we have used the start command to always create a new Cordova and Ionic project.

Also, Ionic can be used without Cordova as well.

To scaffold an Ionic project without Cordova, you need to run the start command with a -w flag or --no-cordova flag:

```
ionic start -a "My Mobile Web App" -i app.web.mymobile -w myMobileWebApp
sidemenu
```

The generated project should look like:

```
.
├── bower.json
├── gulpfile.js
├── ionic.config.json
├── package.json
├── scss
│   ├── ionic.app.scss
├── www
├── css
├── img
├── index.html
├── js
├── lib
├── manifest.json
├── service-worker.js
├── templates
```

Now, as usual, you can `cd` into the `myMobileWebApp` folder and run `ionic serve`.

Initializing a project with SCSS support

To initialize a project with SCSS enabled by default, you can run the start command with a `-s` or a `--sass` flag:

```
ionic start -a "My Sassy App" -i app.my.sassy --sass mySassyApp blank
```

Note: This command is not working as of the day of writing the code.

Listing all Ionic templates

To view the list of all templates available, run Ionic start with a -l or a --list flag:

```
ionic start -l
```

As of today, these are the available templates:

```
        blank ............... A blank starter project for Ionic
complex-list ........ A complex list starter template
maps ................ An Ionic starter project using Google Maps
    and a side menu
salesforce .......... A starter project for Ionic and Salesforce
sidemenu ............ A starting project for Ionic using a side
    menu with navigation in the content area
tabs ................ A starting project for Ionic using a simple
    tabbed interface
tests ............... A test of different kinds of page navigation
```

App ID

If you were using the Ionic Cloud services, you would be assigned an app ID for every project you created on the cloud (refer to the Ionic Cloud section in this chapter for more information). This app ID would reside in the `ionic.config.json` file, present at the root of the project.

When you scaffold a new project, the app ID is empty. And if you would like to associate the currently scaffolded project to an existing app in the cloud, you can run the start command with the `--io-app-id` flag and pass it the cloud generated app ID:

```
ionic start -a "My IonicIO App" -i app.io.ionic --io-app-id "b82348b5"
myIonicIOApp blank
```

Now the `ionic.config.json` should look like:

```
    {
  "name": "My IonicIO App",
  "app_id": "b82348b5"
}
```

Ionic link

The locally scaffolded project can be linked to a cloud project (refer to the Ionic Cloud apps section in this chapter for more information) at any time by running:

```
ionic link b82348b5
```

Or you can remove the existing app ID by running:

```
ionic link --reset
```

Ionic info

To view the installed libraries and their versions, run this:

```
ionic info
```

The information should look like:

```
Cordova CLI: 6.4.0
Ionic CLI Version: 2.1.14
Ionic App Lib Version: 2.1.7
ios-deploy version: 1.8.4
ios-sim version: 5.0.6
OS: macOS Sierra
Node Version: v6.10.1
Xcode version: Xcode 8.2.1 Build version 8C1002
```

Ionic state

Using the Ionic state command, you can manage the state of your Ionic project. Let us say that you are adding a couple of plugins and platforms to test something in your Ionic app. But you would not like to use these if they fail. In that case, you would use the save and restore command.

You can avoid saving the plugins or platforms to the `package.json` file by running them with a `--nosave` flag:

```
ionic plugin add cordova-plugin-console --nosave
```

Now, you have tested your app with a couple of new plugins (adding them using a `--nosave` flag) and things seem to work fine. Now you want to add them to your `package.json`, you can run:

```
ionic state save
```

This command looks up your installed plugins and platforms and then adds the required information to the `package.json` file. Optionally, you can save only plugins or platforms by running the preceding command with a `--plugins` or `--platforms` flag, respectively.

Once you have added a bunch of plugins and things are not working as expected, you can reset to the previous state by running:

```
ionic state reset
```

If you would like to restore your application to a list of Cordova plugins and platforms, you can update the same in `package.json` and run:

```
ionic state restore
```

Note: The `reset` command deletes the `platforms` and `plugins` folders and installs them again, whereas restore only restores the missing platforms and plugins in the `platforms` and `plugins` folders.

Ionic resources

When you add a new platform, by default the `resources` folder is created with icons and splash screens for the given platform. These icons and splash screens are default images. If you would like to use your logo or icon for the project, all you need to do is run the Ionic resources command.

This command will look for an image named `icon.png` inside the `resources` folder to create icons for all devices for that OS, and `splash.png` inside the `resources` folder to create splash screens for all the devices for that OS.

You can replace these two images with your brand images and run:

```
ionic resources
```

If you want to convert only icons, you can pass in an −i flag and only splash screens with a −s flag.

Note: You can also use .png and .psd (sample template: http://code.ionicframework.c om/resources/icon.psdand http://code.ionicframework.com/resources/splash.psd) or .ai files as well to generate icons. You can find more information here: http://blog.io nic.io/automating-icons-and-splash-screens/.

Ionic server, emulate, and run

Ionic provides an easy way to run your Ionic apps in browsers, emulators, and devices. Each of these three commands comes with a bunch of useful options.

If you want live reload to be running on an emulator as well as the actual device, while debugging, use the −l flag for live reload and −c to enable printing JavaScript console errors in the prompt. This is by far the best and most used utility in the Ionic CLI. This command saves at least 30% of your debugging time:

```
ionic serve -l -c
ionic emulate -l -c
ionic run -l -c
```

You can use the following flags while working with Ionic serve:

```
serve [options] ............................  Start a local development server for app dev/testing
     [--consolelogs|-c]  ....................  Print app console logs to Ionic CLI

     [--serverlogs|-s]  .....................  Print dev server logs to Ionic CLI

     [--port|-p]  ...........................  Dev server HTTP port (8100 default)

     [--livereload-port|-r]  ................  Live Reload port (35729 default)

     [--nobrowser|-b]  ......................  Disable launching a browser

     [--nolivereload|-d]  ...................  Do not start live reload

     [--noproxy|-x]  ........................  Do not add proxies

     [--address]  ...........................  Use specific address or return with failure

     [--all|-a]  ............................  Have the server listen on all addresses (0.0.0.0)

     [--browser|-w]  ........................  Specifies the browser to use (safari, firefox, chrome)

     [--browseroption|-o]  ..................  Specifies a path to open to (/#/tab/dash)

     [--lab|-l]  ............................  Test your apps on multiple screen sizes and platform types

     [--nogulp]  ............................  Disable running gulp during serve

     [--platform|-t]  .......................  Start serve with a specific platform (ios/android)
```

If your app has a different look and feel for Android and iOS, you can test both the apps at once by running:

```
ionic serve --lab
```

You can explore the other options listed previously as per your need.

While working with Ionic run and emulate, you can use the following options:

```
run <PLATFORM> [options] ..................... Run an Ionic project on a connected device
    [--livereload|-l] ....................... Live reload app dev files from the device (beta)

    [--address] ............................. Use specific address (livereload req.)

    [--port|-p] ............................. Dev server HTTP port (8100 default, livereload req.)

    [--livereload-port|-r] .................. Live Reload port (35729 default, livereload req.)

    [--consolelogs|-c] ...................... Print app console logs to Ionic CLI (livereload req.)

    [--serverlogs|-s] ....................... Print dev server logs to Ionic CLI (livereload req.)

    [--debug|--release] .....................

    [--device|--emulator|--target=F00]

emulate <PLATFORM> [options] ................. Emulate an Ionic project on a simulator or emulator
    [--livereload|-l] ....................... Live reload app dev files from the device (beta)

    [--address] ............................. Use specific address (livereload req.)

    [--port|-p] ............................. Dev server HTTP port (8100 default, livereload req.)

    [--livereload-port|-r] .................. Live Reload port (35729 default, livereload req.)

    [--consolelogs|-c] ...................... Print app console logs to Ionic CLI (livereload req.)

    [--serverlogs|-s] ....................... Print dev server logs to Ionic CLI (livereload req.)

    [--debug|--release] .....................

    [--device|--emulator|--target=F00]
```

This is quite self-explanatory.

Ionic upload and share

You can upload the current Ionic project to your Ionic Cloud account by running:

```
ionic upload
```

Note: You need to have an Ionic Cloud account to work with this feature.

Once the app is uploaded, you can head to `https://apps.ionic.io/apps` to view the newly updated app. You can share this app with anyone using the share command and pass in the e-mail address of the intended person:

```
ionic share arvind.ravulavaru@gmail.com
```

Ionic help and docs

At any point in time, you can view the list of all Ionic CLI commands by running:

```
ionic -h
```

You can open the docs page by running:

```
ionic docs
```

To view the list of available docs, you can run:

```
ionic docs ls
```

And to open a specific doc, you can run:

```
ionic docs ionicBody
```

Ionic Creator

The all-so amazing Ionic Creator is not yet available for Ionic 2. More information is available here: `http://docs.usecreator.com/docs/ionic-2-support-roadmap`.

Ionic Cloud

You can create and manage your Ionic apps at `https://apps.ionic.io/apps`. In the preceding commands, the app ID we were referring to is the app ID that gets generated when we create a new app using the `https://apps.ionic.io/apps`interface.

You can create a new app by clicking on the New App button inside the `https://apps.ionic.io/apps`page. Once the app is created, you can click on the app name and then you will be taken to the app details page.

You can update the app settings by clicking on the Settings link on the app details page.

Note: You can read more about setting up Ionic apps here: `http://docs.ionic.io/`.

Ionic Cloud also provides other services such as Auth, IonicDB, Deploy, Push, and Package.

To use any of these services, we need to first scaffold an Ionic app, and then add this app to Ionic Cloud by running:

```
ionic io init
```

Next, you can install the cloud client to interact with the cloud from the app:

```
npm install @ionic/cloud-angular --save
```

Once this is done, we set up the cloud setting in `src/app/app.module.ts`:

```
import { CloudSettings, CloudModule } from '@ionic/cloud-angular';

const cloudSettings: CloudSettings = {
  'core': {
    'app_id': 'APP_ID'
  }
};

@NgModule({
  declarations: [ ... ],
  imports: [
    IonicModule.forRoot(MyApp),
    CloudModule.forRoot(cloudSettings)
  ],
  bootstrap: [IonicApp],
  entryComponents: [ ... ],
  providers: [ ... ]
})
export class AppModule {}
```

Now we are all set to use the Ionic Cloud services.

Auth

Using the Auth service, we can easily authenticate a user against various social services. Not only social services such as Google, Twitter, and LinkedIn, we can also set up a simple e-mail and password authentication as well. You can view a list of authentication providers here: `http://docs.ionic.io/services/auth/#authentication-providers`.
And using the `Auth` service, this is how we manage authentication:

```
import { Auth, UserDetails, IDetailedError } from '@ionic/cloud-angular';

@Component({
    selector : 'auth-page'
})
export class AuthPage {
    private testUser: UserDetails = { 'email': 'user@domain.con',
'password': 'password' };
```

```
// construct
constructor(
    private auth: Auth,
    private user: User) {}

signup() {
    this.auth.signup(testUser).then(() => {
        // testUser is now registered
        console.log(this.user)
        this.updateLastLogin(); // update user data
    }, (err: IDetailedError < string[] > ) => {
        for (let e of err.details) {
            if (e === 'conflict_email') {
                alert('Email already exists.');
            } else {
                // handle other errors
            }
        }
    });
}

signin() {
    this.auth.login('basic', testUser).then(() => {
        // testUser is now loggedIn
    });
}

signout() {
    this.auth.logout();
}

updateLastLogin() {
    if (this.auth.isAuthenticated()) {
        this.user.set('lastLogin', new Date());
    }
}
}
```

The preceding code is a snippet on how to use the Auth service. To know more about how Auth service refer to: http://docs.ionic.io/services/auth/.

IonicDB

IonicDB is a cloud-hosted real-time database without the worry of scalability, data management, and security. If you have any exposure working with Firebase or Parse, IonicDB is quite similar to those.

A simple example of using IonicDB is as follows:

```
import {Database} from '@ionic/cloud-angular';

@Component({
    selector: 'todos-page'
})
export class TodosPage {
    public todos: Array < string > ;

    constructor(private db: Database) {
        db.connect();
        db.collection('todos').watch().subscribe((todos) => {
            this.todos = todos;
        }, (error) => {
            console.error(error);
        });
    }

    createTodo (todoText: string) {
        this.db.collection('todos').store({ text: todoText, isCompleted:
false });
    }
}
```

Refer to `http://docs.ionic.io/services/database/` for more options on IonicDB.

Deploy

Deploy is another powerful service, where an app installed on the user's device can be updated, without the user updating from the App Store. Any changes that do not involve changes in binary can be pushed using Deploy.

For more information on Deploy, refer to: `http://docs.ionic.io/services/deploy`

Push

The push service lets the app owners Send a push notification to their users. The Push service also lets app owners segment and target devices based on a type and send allows sending notifications to certain segments only.

Push notifications uses the Phonegap Push Plugin (`https://github.com/phonegap/phonegap-plugin-push`) with FCM (Firebase Cloud Messaging) for Android and iOS push for iOS devices.

For more information on Push, refer to: `http://docs.ionic.io/services/push/`.

Package

Using the Ionic package service, developers can generate APK and IPA for an Ionic project to share with other developers and testers. The same generated APK and IPA can be submitted to Play and App Stores as well.

For more information on Package, refer to: `http://docs.ionic.io/services/package/`.

Summary

In the last and final chapter of Learning Ionic, Second Edition, we have covered some key features of the Ionic CLI and looked at Ionic Cloud services.

Hopefully, this book has given you some idea on getting started with Ionic 2.

Thanks for reading through.

--Arvind Ravulavaru.

Index

CPSIA information can be obtained
at www.ICGtesting.com
Printed in the USA
FSHW021425011120
75339FS